Lecture Notes in Computer Science 8746

Commenced Publication in 1973
Founding and Former Series Editors:
Gerhard Goos, Juris Hartmanis, and Jan van Leeuwen

More information about this series at http://www.springer.com/series/7412

Bart Lamiroy · Jean-Marc Ogier (Eds.)

Graphics Recognition

Current Trends and Challenges

10th International Workshop, GREC 2013
Bethlehem, PA, USA, August 20–21, 2013
Revised Selected Papers

 Springer

Editors
Bart Lamiroy
Université de Lorraine
Vandoeuvre-lès-Nancy
France

Jean-Marc Ogier
Université de La Rochelle
La Rochelle
France

ISSN 0302-9743   ISSN 1611-3349   (electronic)
ISBN 978-3-662-44853-3   ISBN 978-3-662-44854-0   (eBook)
DOI 10.1007/978-3-662-44854-0

Library of Congress Control Number: 2014949558

LNCS Sublibrary: SL6 – Image Processing, Computer Vision, Pattern Recognition, and Graphics

Springer Heidelberg New York Dordrecht London

Printed on acid-free paper

Springer is part of Springer Science+Business Media (www.springer.com)

Preface

This volume contains a selection of refereed and extended versions of papers presented at the 10th IAPR Workshop on Graphics Recognition (GREC 2013), held in Bethlehem, PA, USA during August 20–21, 2013.[1]

The GREC workshops take place every two years, and aim at providing a unique atmosphere, fostering a very high level of interaction, discussion, and exchange of ideas (distinctly different from classical conference-like presentations) while providing high quality and good impact post-proceedings. It therefore forms an excellent opportunity for researchers and practitioners at all levels of experience to meet colleagues and to share new ideas and knowledge about graphics recognition methods. Graphics recognition is a subfield of document image analysis that deals with graphical entities in written documents, engineering drawings, maps, architectural plans, musical scores, mathematical notation, tables, diagrams, etc.

GREC 2013 has continued the tradition of past workshops held at Penn State University (USA, 1995), Nancy (France, 1997), Jaipur (India, 1999), Kingston (Canada, 2001), Barcelona (Spain, 2003), Hong Kong (China, 2005), Curitiba (Brazil, 2007), La Rochelle (France, 2009), and Seoul (South Korea, 2011), the post-proceedings of which have consistently been published as LNCS volumes by Springer Verlag. In this edition, once again, the GREC workshops have proven to live up to the expectations, and we are grateful to all attendees for contributing actively to the intense and rich level of interaction.

The program was, as usual, organized in a single-track two-day workshop. It comprised several sessions dedicated to specific topics related to graphics in document analysis and graphic recognition. Each session began with an introductory talk by the session chairs, describing the state of the art, putting the presented talks in a more global perspective, and stating the current open challenges of session topics. This introduction was then followed by a number of short talks presenting solutions to some of these questions or presenting results of the speaker's work. Each session was concluded by a panel discussion. This year, the session topics were: spotting, graphics recognition in context, perceptual-based approaches and grouping, low-level processing, content-based image retrieval, structure-based approaches and performance evaluation and ground truthing and, the presentation of the results from the ICDAR/GREC 2013 Competition on Music Scores and the GREC 2013 Arc and Line Segmentation Contest. In these contests, for each contestant, test images and ground truths were prepared in order to have objective performance evaluation conclusions on their methods.

In total, 32 papers were submitted and 29 participants registered for the workshop. After the event, and after extension of the submitted work by the authors based upon

---

[1] A similar version of this report was published in the January 2014 IAPR newsletter http://www.iapr.org/docs/newsletter-2014-01.pdf.

remarks and discussions during the workshop, all papers were reviewed again. As a final result, 18 of the presented papers plus both reports on the contests were selected for publication in this volume. Represented countries were Brazil, China, France, Germany, India, Japan, Luxembourg, Malaysia, Spain, Switzerland, and USA.

The opening talk was given by Prof. Jean-Marc Ogier from the Université de La Rochelle, France, GREC 2013 Program Chair and IAPR TC-10 Chair, and the closing talk and final panel discussion was chaired by the former IAPR TC-10 Chair Prof. Josep Lladós from the Universitat Autònoma de Barcelona, Spain.

We would particularly like to thank the authors for the quality of their submitted papers, the contest organizers for their time, great efforts, and availability, the Program Committee members for having contributed in a timely and professional manner to the reviewing process, and the session chairs for their insight and dedication. We also wish to gratefully acknowledge the group of organizers at Lehigh University for their great help in the local arrangements of the workshop.

The 11th IAPR Workshop on Graphics Recognition (GREC 2015) is planned to be held in Tunisia.

July 2014   Bart Lamiroy
                                                                              Jean-Marc Ogier

Organization

General Chair

Bart Lamiroy   Université de Lorraine – Loria UMR 7503, France

Program Chair

Jean-Marc Ogier   Université de la Rochelle – L3i, France

Local Arrangements Chair

Daniel Lopresti   Lehigh University, USA

Program Committee

Gady Agam   Illinois Institute of Technology, USA
Dorothea Blostein   Queen's University, Canada
Luc Brun   ENSICAEN, France
Jean-Christophe Burie   Université de la Rochelle – L3i, France
Bertrand Coüasnon   IRISA/INSA Rennes, France
Mickaël Coustaty   Université de la Rochelle – L3i, France
Mathieu Delalandre   Université François-Rabelais de Tours, France
Vincenzo Deufemia   Università di Salerno, Italy
David Doermann   University of Maryland, USA
Philippe Dosch   Université de Lorraine – Loria UMR 7503, France
Alicia Fornés   CVC, Universitat Autònoma de Barcelona, Spain
Pierre Héroux   Université de Rouen – LITIS EA 4108, France
Igor Filippov   SAIC-Frederick, Inc., USA
Tracy Anne Hammond   Texas A&M University, USA
Xiaoyi Jiang   Universität Münster, Germany
Joaquim Jorge   Technical University of Lisbon, Portugal
Walter Kropatsch   Vienna University of Technology, Austria
Rafael Dueire Lins   Universidade Federal de Pernambuco, Brazil
Wenyin Liu   City University, Hong Kong, China
Josep Lladós   CVC, Universitat Autònoma de Barcelona, Spain
Tong Lu   State Key Laboratory of Software Novel
                                                  Technology of China, China
Simone Marinai   University of Florence, Italy

Umapada Pal   Indian Statistical Institute, India
Jean-Yves Ramel   Université François-Rabelais de Tours, France
Romain Raveaux   Université François-Rabelais de Tours, France
Marçal Rusiñol   CVC, Universitat Autònoma de Barcelona, Spain
Gemma Sánchez   CVC, Universitat Autònoma de Barcelona, Spain
Angela Schwering   Universität Münster, Germany
Alan Sexton   University of Birmingham, UK
Salvatore Tabbone   Université de Lorraine – Loria UMR 7503, France
Chew Lim Tan   National University of Singapore, Singapore
Karl Tombre   Université de Lorraine – Loria UMR 7503, France
Ernest Valveny   CVC, Universitat Autònoma de Barcelona, Spain
Nicole Vincent   Université Paris Descartes (Paris 5), France
Muriel Visani   Université de la Rochelle – L3i, France
Toyohide Watanabe   Nagoya University, Japan
Su Yang   Fudan University, China
Richard Zanibbi   Rochester Institute of Technology, USA
Sun Zhengxing   Nanjing University, China

Contest Organizers

In alphabetical order...

Arc and Line Segmentation Contest

Hasan Al-Khaffaf   University of Duhok, Iraq
Thomas Breuel   Technical University of Kaiserslautern, Germany
Syed Saqib Bukhari   Technical University of Kaiserslautern, Germany
Mohd Azam Osman   University of Science, Malaysia
Faisal Shafait   University of Western Australia, Australia
Abdullah Talib   University of Science, Malaysia

Music Scores Competition on Staff Removal

Anjan Dutta   CVC, Universitat Autònoma de Barcelona, Spain
Alicia Fornés   CVC, Universitat Autònoma de Barcelona, Spain
Nicholas Journet   LaBRI, University of Bordeaux I, France
Van Cuong Kieu   Université de la Rochelle – L3i, France
Muriel Visani   Université de la Rochelle – L3i, France

Local Arrangements Committee

Jeanne Steinberg	Lehigh University, USA
Barri Bruno	Lehigh University, USA
Connor Tench	Lehigh University, USA

Contents

Low Level Processing

Performance Evaluation and Ground Truthing

Symbol Spotting and Retrieval

Spotting Graphical Symbols
in Camera-Acquired Documents in Real Time

Marçal Rusiñol[1,2]([✉]), Dimosthenis Karatzas[1], and Josep Lladós[1]

[1] Computer Vision Center, Dept. Ciències de la Computació, Edifici O, UAB,
08193 Bellaterra, Spain
{marcal,dimos,josep}@cvc.uab.cat
[2] L3i Laboratory, Université de La Rochelle, Avenue Michel Crépeau,
17042 La Rochelle Cédex 1, France

Abstract. In this paper we present a system devoted to spot graphical symbols in camera-acquired document images. The system is based on the extraction and further matching of ORB compact local features computed over interest key-points. Then, the FLANN indexing framework based on approximate nearest neighbor search allows to efficiently match local descriptors between the captured scene and the graphical models. Finally, the RANSAC algorithm is used in order to compute the homography between the spotted symbol and its appearance in the document image. The proposed approach is efficient and is able to work in real time.

1 Introduction

The problem of locating and recognizing specific graphical symbols within documents images has received the attention of the graphics recognition community for many years. Being a mature enough research topic [15], many different approaches can be found in the literature [14].

Usually, ad-hoc hand-crafted descriptor features [16] together with time consuming classifiers [7] or distances [5] are often proposed to solve the graphics recognition problem. However, most of the existing methods might not scale well to large scenarios mainly for their computational complexity [17] and their lack of generality. However, we strongly believe that recent proposals from other computer vision communities such as object recognition, scene classification or information retrieval at large can be easily adapted to the graphics recognition domain resulting in much generic and scalable methods. Although in the last years several works can be found that already used such techniques [10] in the graphics recognition context, we are surprised of seeing proposals that still completely disregard such progresses.

Following this idea, we present in this paper a graphics spotting application that work in real time with camera-acquired images of documents from various sources. For that purpose we have used a quite recent off-the-shelf lightweight

© Springer-Verlag Berlin Heidelberg 2014
B. Lamiroy and J.-M. Ogier (Eds.): GREC 2013, LNCS 8746, pp. 3–10, 2014.
DOI: 10.1007/978-3-662-44854-0_1

object matching framework combined with an also well-known approximate nearest-neighbor method that allows the detection and the classification to be performed in real time.

Specifically, the detection and classification of graphical symbols is performed by matching ORB features with FLANN indexing. A final RANSAC step is used in order to obtain the homography. In a first test scenario we printed several invoices from different providers, cropped their logotypes and tried to detect and classify those in a video feed from a standard webcam. The implemented method is able to work at real time with images at 1280×1024 resolution.

In the next sections we will briefly review the used key-point detector and descriptor together with the matching scheme we use. In the results section we will present several application scenarios in which such framework can be applied.

2   Feature Extraction

Graphical symbol recognition within images being a particular case of the object recognition problem, we used the well-known and popular framework of matching local descriptors extracted over interest key-points [6]. But not all of the available key-point matching strategies are efficient enough to be used in real time. We have thus used a set of selected methods that, although they might not present the better performances, they are fast to compute.

In order to extract interest key-points from a webcam feed, we have used the FAST key-point detector [12]. FAST is a high-speed corner detector that use machine learning techniques in order to speed-up the response of whether a candidate pixel is in fact a corner. We can see in Fig. 1 the obtained corner points that will be used to extract the local descriptors. In our experiments we appreciated that such corners are robust and stable despite their efficient extraction.

Once the key-points are extracted, local descriptors are computed over them. A large amount of local descriptors have been proposed in the recent object recognition literature [8], however, most of them are not efficient enough to be used in real-time applications. One of the most promising local descriptors is the efficient BRIEF descriptor [3]. BRIEF being a binary descriptor, aims at quickly comparing local features while requiring few amounts of memory.

The BRIEF descriptor outputs a set of bits obtained by comparing intensities of pairs of pixels within the local key-region. Such pairs of pixels in which the binary tests are performed are sampled from an isotropic Gaussian distribution since the pixels at the patch center ought to be more stable than in the patch perimeter. We can see an example of such binary test distribution in Fig. 2, extracted from [3].

However, the original FAST and BRIEF detector and descriptor presented some flaws. On the one hand FAST does not produce multi-scale features so we might have some problems when trying to find graphical symbols in a scene at a different scale from their model. On the other hand, in BRIEF, since the binary

Fig. 1. Example of the extracted keypoints.

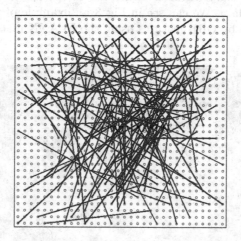

Fig. 2. Example of the binary test distribution from the BRIEF descriptor, extracted from [3].

tests were performed over a static point distribution, the method is not rotation invariant. Although a recent contribution by the authors propose how to achieve such invariances [2], in our work we used a slight modification of the BRIEF descriptor known as ORB (Oriented FAST and Rotated BRIEF) presented by Rublee et al. in [13].

The ORB framework propose to compute corners by applying the FAST method over a scale pyramid of the image. By using such pyramid, the obtained key-points are extracted at different scales. In addition, a measure of the corner orientation is extracted by means of the intensity centroid [11]. Then, a rotation-aware version of the BRIEF descriptor is applied to the oriented and scaled key-regions. The ORB framework is then able to match key-points from objects under scale and orientation changes while performing much faster than well-known local detectors and descriptors such as SIFT or SURF.

3   Symbol Matching

In order to perform object recognition by matching local key-points at real time, we need some nearest neighbor matching algorithm efficient enough. Although the BRIEF framework outputs a binary descriptor that can be compared with Hamming distances, there is a number of approximate nearest neighbor methods that allow an important speedup of the matching step. In this paper we used the FLANN library [9] which provide an interface to several approximate nearest neighbor algorithms such as randomized kd-trees, hierarchical k-means trees, local sensitive hashing (LSH), etc. and which automatically tunes the parameters of such methods in order to obtain the desired precision degree. In our scenario, since we deal with binary features we decided to use the LSH algorithm [1] in order to index our data. We can see in Fig. 3 an example of the matched local key-points described by ORB features using the FLANN matcher.

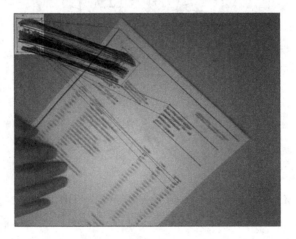

Fig. 3. Example of the local key-point matching.

Having several model graphical symbols in our dataset that we want to find in the video feed, the matching step is applied separately to each model. The model which receives more votes is the one that is considered as being present in the scene.

In a final step, we used the well-known RANSAC [4] algorithm in order to filter out the outliers matches and to find the homography between the recognized model symbol and its instance appearing in the scene.

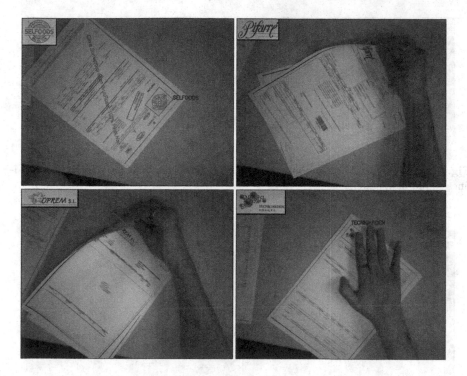

Fig. 4. Screen-shots of the logo spotting in invoice images.

4   Experimental Results

Since in this paper we have used off-the-shelf methods that have already been thoroughly evaluated in their respective original papers, rather than providing an exhaustive evaluation of their behavior we preferred to qualitatively assess their performances in the context of graphics-rich documents.

Our main test scenario was to acquire administrative documents, such as invoices, with a webcam and on-the-fly spot the graphical logos that appeared in them. We can see in Fig. 4 some screen-shots of this spotting procedure. We refer the reader to our website[1] where the complete video demos are available. We can appreciate that the used framework is able to tolerate well rotation and scale changes, perspective changes, occlusions and illumination changes.

We also tested other application scenarios such as spotting logos in color catalogs or graphical advertisements published in old newspapers. We also tested to spot non-graphical information such as the headlines of those old newspapers also appreciating good performances. We can find some screen-shots of such applications in Fig. 6.

Finally, we tested to spot graphical symbols appearing in line-drawing images. In those experiments we found out that really simple symbols represented by

---

[1] http://www.cvc.uab.es/~marcal/demos/spotting.html

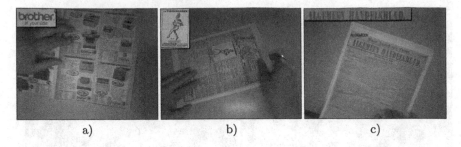

Fig. 5. Screen-shots of the symbol spotting in (a) color catalogs, (b) ads and (c) headlines in old newspapers.

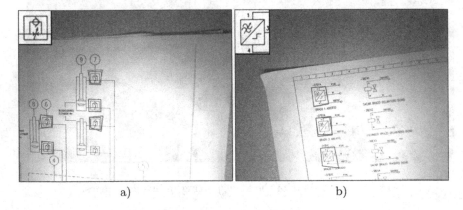

Fig. 6. Screen-shots of the symbol spotting in line-drawing images.

low-textured graphics were quite difficult to spot by matching local descriptors, since the BRIEF descriptor proved not to be very discriminant in such scenario. However, for a little bit more complex symbols, such as the ones presented in Fig. 5, the method performs well as well.

It is worth to mention that by using the RANSAC method we are assuming that we only look for a single instance of a model symbol in the scene under analysis. In order to be able to spot several symbols in the same image, we divided the image by a multi-resolution overlapping grid. Then the RANSAC method was applied locally and independently at each image cell, allowing to spot several symbols as shown in Fig. 6(a) and Fig. 5.

Both ORB features and FLANN indexing library are integrated within the OpenCV library. A Python + Opencv 2.4 version of the source code of the presented method is available through our website.

5   Conclusions

In this paper we have presented how state-of-the-art techniques from the object recognition field can be successfully applied to the problem of symbol spotting.

Not only the proposed techniques are performant, but they are also quite efficient, making them very suitable for either real-time applications or applications embedded in smartphones.

We strongly believe that the graphics recognition community should not only focus on ad-hoc recognition processes specifically designed to work in our domain, but rather take advantage of the latest progresses in other computer vision areas.

Acknowledgment. This work has been partially supported by the People Programme (Marie Curie Actions) of the Seventh Framework Programme of the European Union (FP7/2007-2013) under REA grant agreement no. 600388, and by the Agency of Competitiveness for Companies of the Government of Catalonia, ACCIÓ; and by the Spanish Ministry of Education and Science under projects TIN2009-14633-C03-03, TIN2011-25606 and TIN2012-37475-C02-02.

References

1. Andoni, A., Indyk, P.: Near-optimal hashing algorithms for approximate nearest neighbor in high dimensions. Commun. ACM - 50th Anniversary Issue: 1958–2008 **51**(1), 117–122 (2008)
2. Calonder, M., Lepetit, V., Ozuysal, M., Trzcinski, T., Strecha, C., Fua, P.: BRIEF: computing a local binary descriptor very fast. IEEE Trans. Pattern Anal. Mach. Intell. **34**(7), 1281–1298 (2012)
3. Calonder, M., Lepetit, V., Strecha, C., Fua, P.: BRIEF: binary robust independent elementary features. In: Daniilidis, K., Maragos, P., Paragios, N. (eds.) ECCV 2010, Part IV. LNCS, vol. 6314, pp. 778–792. Springer, Heidelberg (2010)
4. Fischler, M.A., Bolles, R.C.: Random sample consensus: a paradigm for model fitting with applications to image analysis and automated cartography. Commun. ACM **24**(6), 381–395 (1981)
5. Lladós, J., Martí, E., Villanueva, J.J.: Symbol recognition by error-tolerant subgraph matching between region adjacency graphs. IEEE Trans. Pattern Anal. Mach. Intell. **23**(10), 1137–1143 (2001)
6. Lowe, D.G.: Distinctive image features from scale-invariant keypoints. Int. J. Comput. Vision **60**(2), 91–110 (2004)
7. Luqman, M.M., Brouard, T., Ramel, J.Y.: Graphic symbol recognition using graph based signature and bayesian network classifier. In: Proceedings of the International Conference on Document Analysis and Recognition, pp. 1325–1329 (2009)
8. Mikolajczyk, K., Schmid, C.: A performance evaluation of local descriptors. IEEE Trans. Pattern Anal. Mach. Intell. **27**(10), 1615–1630 (2005)
9. Muja, M., Lowe, D.G.: Fast approximate nearest neighbors with automatic algorithm configuration. In: Proceedings of the International Conference on Computer Vision Theory and Applications, pp. 331–340 (2009)
10. Nguyen, T.O., Tabbone, S., Boucher, A.: A symbol spotting approach based on the vector model and a visual vocabulary. In: Proceedings of the International Conference on Document Analysis and Recognition, pp. 708–712 (2009)
11. Rosin, P.L.: Measuring corner properties. Comput. Vis. Image Underst. **73**(2), 291–307 (1999)

12. Rosten, E., Drummond, T.W.: Machine learning for high-speed corner detection. In: Leonardis, A., Bischof, H., Pinz, A. (eds.) ECCV 2006, Part I. LNCS, vol. 3951, pp. 430–443. Springer, Heidelberg (2006)
13. Rublee, E., Rabaud, V., Konolige, K., Bradski, G.: ORB: an efficient alternative to SIFT or SURF. In: Proceedings of the International Conference on Computer Vision, pp. 2564–2571 (2011)
14. Rusiñol, M., Lladós, J.: Symbol Spotting in Digital Libraries: Focused Retrieval over Graphic-rich Document Collections. Springer, London (2010)
15. Syeda-Mahmood, T.: Indexing of technical line drawing databases. IEEE Trans. Pattern Anal. Mach. Intell. 21(8), 737–751 (1999)
16. Wenyin, L., Zhang, W., Yan, L.: An interactive example-driven approach to graphics recognition in engineering drawings. Int. J. Doc. Anal. Recogn. 9(1), 13–29 (2007)
17. Yang, S.: Symbol recognition via statistical integration of pixel-level constraint histograms: a new descriptor. IEEE Trans. Pattern Anal. Mach. Intell. 27(2), 278–281 (2005)

A Product Graph Based Method for Dual Subgraph Matching Applied to Symbol Spotting

Anjan Dutta[1]([✉]), Josep Lladós[1], Horst Bunke[2], and Umapada Pal[3]

[1] Computer Vision Center, Universitat Autònoma de Barcelona, Barcelona, Spain
{adutta,josep}@cvc.uab.es
[2] Institute of Computer Science and Applied Mathematics,
Universität Bern, Bern, Switzerland
bunke@iam.unibe.ch
[3] CVPR Unit, Indian Statistical Institute, Kolkata, India
umapada@isical.ac.in

Abstract. Product graph has been shown as a way for matching subgraphs. This paper reports the extension of the product graph methodology for subgraph matching applied to symbol spotting in graphical documents. Here we focus on the two major limitations of the previous version of the algorithm: (1) spurious nodes and edges in the graph representation and (2) inefficient node and edge attributes. To deal with noisy information of vectorized graphical documents, we consider a *dual edge graph* representation on the original graph representing the graphical information and the product graph is computed between the dual edge graphs of the *pattern graph* and the *target graph*. The dual edge graph with redundant edges is helpful for efficient and tolerating encoding of the structural information of the graphical documents. The adjacency matrix of the product graph locates the pair of similar edges of two operand graphs and exponentiating the adjacency matrix finds similar random walks of greater lengths. Nodes joining similar random walks between two graphs are found by combining different weighted exponentials of adjacency matrices. An experimental investigation reveals that the recall obtained by this approach is quite encouraging.

Keywords: Product graph · Dual edge graph · Subgraph matching · Random walks · Graph kernel

1 Introduction

Product graph was introduced for computing the random walk graph kernel for measuring the similarity between two graphs. Recently it has been used for subgraph matching and applied for spotting symbols on graphical documents [3]. In this paper we propose an extension and improvement of the product graph methodology that was proposed in [3]. Particularly, this work mainly focuses on the two major limitations of the previous version of the method: (1) spurious nodes and edges that are generated during low level image processing and

© Springer-Verlag Berlin Heidelberg 2014
B. Lamiroy and J.-M. Ogier (Eds.): GREC 2013, LNCS 8746, pp. 11–24, 2014.
DOI: 10.1007/978-3-662-44854-0_2

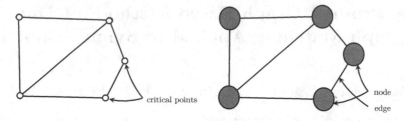

Fig. 1. Each critical point detected by the vectorization technique is considered as a node and the straight lines joining them are considered as the edges.

(2) inefficient node and edge attributes. Of course, these problems are application and representation dependent, but there is no doubt that the proposed solution is more robust to distortion and noise, which will be further useful for other applications and representations.

Graph representation of graphical documents involves some low level image processing such as binarization, skeletonization, vectorization etc. For example, we use Qgar[1] for vectorizing the given binary images. This particular vectorization generates critical points and connectivity information between them. For representing a document with a graph, we consider the critical points as the nodes and the lines joining them as the edges (Fig. 1). The main problem in this kind of low level image processing is the addition of noisy information. As an example, Fig. 2(b) shows the graph representation of the symbol in Fig. 2(a) under the previously mentioned representation scheme, whereas Fig. 2(c) shows an ideal graph representation of the symbol (considering the junctions as the nodes and their connections as the edges). Here we can see an example of the introduction of numerous spurious nodes near the junctions and corners. Note that such a vectorization can also generate spurious and discontinuous edges. This kind of structural noise always creates problems for matching or comparing (sub)graphs. It is true that with a different kind of graph representation it may be possible to solve the problem more efficiently, but dealing with this kind of distortions or noise at the graph level is interesting for other domain also as it gives more robustness in the matching method.

Product graph has been introduced for computing random walk graph kernels [6]. In our previous work, we introduced product graph for subgraph matching and applied it for spotting symbols in graphical documents [3]. Formally, a symbol spotting method can naturally be formulated as a subgraph matching problem where a *query symbol* can be represented as a *pattern graph* and the big *target document* can be represented as a *target graph*. For more information on symbol spotting methods based on graph representation we refer to [4,8], where a literature review is given. Product graph provides an efficient comparison technique between a subgraph and a graph in terms of different substructures (in this case random walks) which allows the entire subgraph matching process to

---

[1] http://www.qgar.org

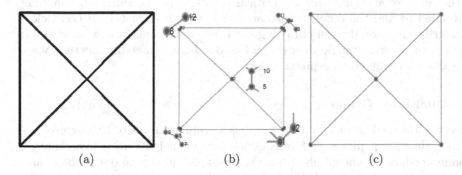

Fig. 2. Difference between a real graph representation and an ideal graph representation: (a) an architectural symbol, (b) the graph representation of the symbol in (a) after doing the vectorization (note the spurious nodes near the corners and junctions), (c) an ideal graph representation of the symbol in (a).

be computed online. The product graph finds the similar pair of edges in the operand graphs. This information can be obtained from the adjacency matrix of the product graph. Exponentiating the adjacency matrix provides the information about similar pair of nodes which are connected with random walks of greater lengths. This was the main motivation of the work in [3] but one of the problems was selecting efficient node and edge attributes, especially when the graphs contain noise or distortions like spurious nodes and edges, and the possibility of discontinuous edges. To solve this problem in this paper we introduce the *dual edge graph DG* with redundant edges of the original graph G and consider the product graph of the dual edge graphs. Here the dual edge graph DG of the original graph G is a graph that has a vertex corresponding to each edge of G and an edge joining two neighbouring edges in G. In this work we use a dual edge graph with redundant edges to cope with the distortions and noise as explained in Sect. 2. The variation of dual graph provides us robust node and edge labels and with this information the product graph is better suited for subgraph matching applied to symbol spotting.

The rest of the paper is organized into three sections. In Sect. 2, we present the methodology to represent the graphical documents with dual graph with redundant edges, computing the node and edge labels and computing the product graphs to spot the symbol on documents. Section 3 contains a description of our current experimental results. After that, in Sect. 4, we conclude the paper and discuss future directions of work.

2   Methodology

Let $G_M = (V_M, E_M)$ be the basic graph representing the model or query symbol and $G_I = (V_I, E_I)$ be the same representing the input or target document, where V_M and V_I are the set of vertices, in this case the critical points, and E_M and E_I

are the set of edges connecting the critical points. Now the subgraph matching is intended to find the different instances or occurrences of G_M in G_I. Below we describe the procedure of obtaining the dual edge graph from a basic graph and then we describe the product graph based subgraph matching methodology using the dual edge graph representation.

2.1 Dual Edge Graph

In general, the dual graph of a plane graph is a graph that has vertex corresponding to each face (or plane) and an edge joining two neighbouring faces sharing a common edge in plane graph. We bring the same analogy to our problem and assign a node to each edge of the original graph and an edge joining two neighbouring nodes. We can call this graph as dual edge graph. In this article, as we are not dealing with any other type of dual graph, we can alternatively call it dual graph. Furthermore, we will call the nodes, edges of the dual edge graph respectively as dual nodes, dual edges. We denote $DG = (DV, DE)$ as the dual edge graph of the edge graph $G = (V, E)$.

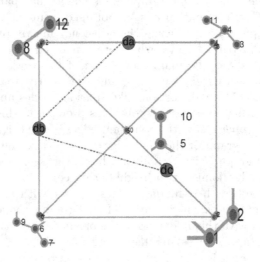

Fig. 3. Details of adding redundant edges in the dual graph considering only three nodes da, db and dc and $n = 3$: The gdist$(da, db) = 2$ and gdist$(db, dc) = 3$, that is why there exist edges (da, db) and (db, dc) but since gdist$(da, dc) = 4$, there is no edge (da, dc) (Note the spurious nodes, edges near the corners and junctions in the original graph that are plotted in green continuous line) (Color figure online).

Let $G_M = (V_M, E_M)$ be an unattributed edge graph representing a model or query symbol and $G_I = (V_I, E_I)$ be an unattributed edge graph representing an input or target document. Then we can get the dual edge graphs $DG_M = (DV_M, DE_M)$ and $DG_I = (DV_I, DE_I)$ of G_M and G_I respectively, where $DV_M = E_M$ and $DV_I = E_I$. Here it should be mentioned that we will denote a dual node which joins two nodes, say, v_i, v_j in the edge graph as dv_{ij} (see Fig. 3). Now the dual edge sets of DG_M and DG_I are respectively defined as follows:

$$DE_M = \{(du_{ij}, du_{kl}) : \text{gdist}(du_{ij}, du_{kl}) \leq dn \in \mathbb{N} \text{ and } du_{ij}, du_{kl} \in DV_M\} \quad (1)$$

$$DE_I = \{(dv_{ij}, dv_{kl}) : \text{gdist}(dv_{ij}, dv_{kl}) \leq dn \in \mathbb{N} \text{ and } dv_{ij}, dv_{kl} \in DV_I\} \quad (2)$$

Here gdist(du, dv) stands for the minimum number of edges (in the edge graph) one has to traverse for going to dv from du (or to du from dv for undirected graph, which is our case). dn is connectivity parameter regulating the connections between any two dual nodes. The dual graphs with dual edge sets (in magenta) can be seen in Fig. 4 which shows some stability in the representation as visually we can observe the existence of common graph structures.

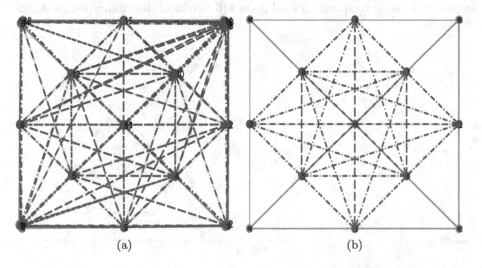

(a)   (b)

Fig. 4. Original graph and redundant dual graph representation (with $dn = 3$) of (a) a real symbol and (b) an ideal symbol. The original graph is plotted with green continuous line and its corresponding dual graph with redundant edges is plotted with magenta discontinuous line. (Best viewed in colour.) (Color figure online)

Given this dual edge graph representation we assign node and edge labels to capture the local structural information and create attributed dual graphs $DG_M = (DV_M, DE_M, \alpha_M, \beta_M^1, \beta_M^2)$ and $DG_I = (DV_I, DE_I, \alpha_I, \beta_I^1, \beta_I^2)$. Here $\alpha_I : DV_I \rightarrow \mathbb{R}^7$ is a node labelling function and is defined as $\alpha_I(dv_{ij}) = $ Hu moments invariants [7] of the acyclic graph paths between v_i and v_j of length less than or equal to $m \in \mathbb{N}$, $dv_{ij} \in DV_I$. Similarly, $\alpha_M(du_{ij})$ is the same node labelling function but defined in DG_M. It is to be mentioned that for each path, we get a vector of dimension seven and hence for a node dv in a dual graph DG, we get a set of Hu moments invariants, let us denote the set as $Hu(dv)$. The distance between two dual nodes du, dv is computed as the minimum cost of assigning each path of $Hu(du)$ to a path in $Hu(dv)$.

$\beta_I^1 : DE_I \to \mathbb{R}$ is an edge labelling function and is defined as:

$$\beta_I^1(dv_{ij}, dv_{kl}) = \min \angle(dv_{ij}, dv_{kl}), (dv_{ij}, dv_{kl}) \in DE_I.$$

$\beta_I^2 : DE_I \to \mathbb{R}$ is another edge labelling function and is defined as:

$$\beta_I^2(dv_{ij}, dv_{kl}) = \frac{\mathrm{mdist}(dv_{ij}, dv_{kl})}{\max(\mathrm{length}(dv_{ij}), \mathrm{length}(dv_{kl}))}, (dv_{ij}, dv_{kl}) \in DE_I.$$

here $\mathrm{mdist}(dv_{ij}, dv_{kl})$ is the length of the line joining the midpoint of the edges dv_{ij} and dv_{kl}. β_M^1 and β_M^2 are defined respectively as β_I^1 and β_I^2 but in DE_M.

The main limitation of this representation that one could face is when the extremities of a certain edge of the edge graph do not have any other connection. In that case the corresponding dual node will lose local discrimination as shown in Fig. 5a.

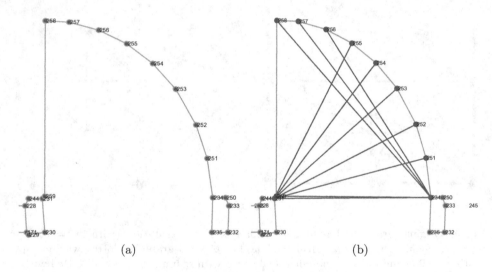

Fig. 5. An example of transitive closure edges: (a) original graph representation of *door1*, (b) edges (shown in blue) connect the pair of nodes that were not connected by more than one graph paths in the original graph representation (Color figure online).

We resolve this difficulty by relating those nodes in the edge graph by a relation inspired by the *transitive closure* of a graph. For that we select the pair of nodes u, v such that $(u, v) \in E$ but there is no other graph path between u and v. Let V^* be the set of all such nodes. V^* may contain two different kind of nodes. Ones having an adjacent node from $V - V^*$ i.e. $u \in V^*$ and $v \in V - V^*$ such that $\exists (u, v) \in E$, let us call all such nodes as V_1^* (for example nodes like 251 and 254 in Fig. 5). And others having adjacent nodes only from V^* i.e. $u, v \in V^*$ so that $(u, v) \in E$, let us call such nodes as V_2^* (for example nodes like 271, 272, 273 and so on in Fig. 5). We update the edge set E by adding edge (u, v) where $u \in V_1^*$ and $v \in V_2^*$ and there exist at least one graph path between them. We can call this new kind of edge as *transitive closure edge*. We update both the edge graphs G_I, G_M and assign a dual node to each transitive closure edge and connect them with dual edges accordingly. The Hu moments of the set of paths joining the extremities of the transitive closure edges serve as the attributes of the new nodes. The attributes of the new dual edges are computed as explained previously. In this way we update DG_I and DG_M, respectively.

This dual graph gives us the attributed graphs and because of having redundant edges the representation is stable to distortions such as spurious edges, nodes. Moreover, the idea of transitive closure gives us the possibility to group several similar patterns.

So given the dual graph representation of the graphical documents, the symbol spotting problem can be formulated as a subgraph matching problem. Let $DG_M = (DV_M, DE_M, \alpha_M, \beta_M^1, \beta_M^2)$ and $DG_I = (DV_I, DE_I, \alpha_I, \beta_I^1, \beta_I^2)$ be the dual graphs of the edge graphs G_M and G_I respectively.

2.2   Product Graph

Product graph $G_P = (V_P, E_P)$ of DG_I and DG_M relates the target graph DG_I and the pattern graph DG_M with the node and edge sets. The properties or the conditions are included in the set definitions as follows:

$$V_P = \{(du_{ij}, dv_{ij}) : du_{ij} \in DV_M, dv_{ij} \in DV_I, \alpha_M(du_{ij}) \simeq \alpha_I(dv_{ij}),$$
$$\beta_M^1(du_{ij}, du_{kl}) \simeq \beta_I^1(dv_{ij}, dv_{kl}) \text{ and } \beta_M^2(du_{ij}, du_{kl}) \simeq \beta_I^2(dv_{ij}, dv_{kl})\}$$

and given the above set of nodes, the edge set E_P will be:

$$E_P = \{((du_{ij}, dv_{ij}), (du_{kl}, dv_{kl})) : (du_{ij}, du_{kl}) \in DE_M, (dv_{ij}, dv_{kl}) \in DE_I\}$$

We use the parameters t_α, t_{β_1} and t_{β_2} for measuring the node and edge similarities as follows:

$$\alpha_M(du_{ij}) \simeq \alpha_I(dv_{ij}) \Leftrightarrow |\alpha_M(du_{ij}) - \alpha_I(dv_{ij})| \leq t_\alpha$$

Here

$$|\alpha_M(du_{ij}) - \alpha_I(dv_{ij})| = \sum_{p_1 \in Hu(du_{ij})} \min_{p_2 \in Hu(dv_{ij})} d(p_1, p_2) + \sum_{p_2 \in Hu(dv_{ij})} \min_{p_1 \in Hu(du_{ij})} d(p_1, p_2)$$

is a modified Hausdorff distance as investigated in [5] and $d(., .)$ denotes the Euclidean distance.

$$\beta_M^1(du_{ij}, du_{kl}) \simeq \beta_I^1(dv_{ij}, dv_{kl}) \Leftrightarrow |\beta_M^1(du_{ij}, du_{kl}) - \beta_I^1(dv_{ij}, dv_{kl})| \leq t_{\beta_1}$$

$$\beta_M^2(du_{ij}, du_{kl}) \simeq \beta_I^2(dv_{ij}, dv_{kl}) \Leftrightarrow |\beta_M^2(du_{ij}, du_{kl}) - \beta_I^2(dv_{ij}, dv_{kl})| \leq t_{\beta_2}$$

From the above definition of product graph it is clear that an edge in the product graph G_P corresponds to a pair of similar edges in DG_M and DG_I. A simple synthetic example is given in Fig. 6, where we have two different graphs with discrete node labels, one having labels $\{a, b, c, d, e\}$ and the other with labels $\{x, y, z\}$. For simplicity, let us ignore the edge labels. Now, if we define the node label similarities as $a = x$, $b = y$ and $c = z$, we get the product graph in Fig. 6. Here, each edge in the product graph locates a pair of edges in the operand graphs.

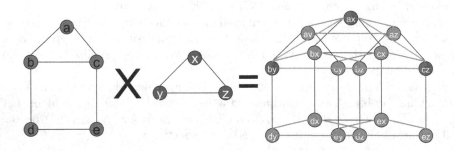

Fig. 6. Demonstration of product graph computation with a synthetic example.

2.3   Powers of Adjacency Matrix

It is a well known fact that the (i, j)th element of the adjacency matrix of a graph denotes the number of edges from the ith node to the jth node and vice versa for undirected graphs. If we exponentiate the adjacency matrix to the power of n, then the (i, j)th element of the exponentiated adjacency matrix denotes the number of random walks of length n from the node i to the node j. So, if we multiply the adjacency matrix E_P of the product graph G_P with itself, we get the E_P^2. The (i, j)th element of E_P^2 denotes the number of walks of length two between nodes i and j. Since matrix multiplication is associative we can exponentiate E_P as follows to get E_P^n:

$$E_P^n = E_P.(E_P)^{n-1} = (E_P)^{n-1}.E_P$$

Then from the known fact it follows that the (i, j)th element of E_P^n always denotes the number of walks of length n between i and j [6]. Since an edge in E_P denotes the similarity between respective connected node pairs, walks of longer length denote series of similar nodes between DG_M and DG_I. This information is helpful for getting nodes in DG_I that are similar to nodes in DG_M and it can be utilized by integrating different weighted exponentiations of E_P into a new matrix A as follows:

$$A = \sum_{i=1}^{nl} \lambda^i \times E_P^i \qquad (3)$$

where nl is the maximum number of times the matrix E_P is being exponentiated and λ is sufficiently small to converge the above summation.

These weights to different walk lengths are inspired by the traditional random walk graph kernel [6]. This way of weightings reduces the influence of walks of greater lengths because they often contains redundant or repeated information. We have observed that for sufficiently smaller value of λ such as $\lambda \in [0.1, 0.2]$ the above sum converges rapidly. However, this fact was also observed by Gärtner *et al.* [6].

Now let us take an example of the matrix A as follows:

$$
A = \begin{array}{c} \\ (du_1,dv_1) \\ \vdots \\ (du_{l-1},dv_{k-1}) \\ (du_l,dv_k) \\ (du_{l+1},dv_{k+1}) \\ \vdots \\ (du_m,dv_n) \end{array}
\begin{array}{cccccc}
(du_1,dv_1) & \cdots & (du_k,dv_l) & (du_{k+1},dv_{l+1}) & \cdots & (du_m,dv_n) \\
0 & \cdots & 0 & 0 & \cdots & 0 \\
\vdots & \ddots & \vdots & \vdots & \ddots & \vdots \\
0 & \cdots & 0 & x_1 & \cdots & 0 \\
0 & \cdots & x_2 & 0 & \cdots & 0 \\
0 & \cdots & 0 & x_3 & \cdots & 0 \\
\vdots & \ddots & \vdots & \vdots & \ddots & \vdots \\
0 & \cdots & 0 & 0 & \cdots & 0
\end{array}
$$

where $m < n$ and $1 < k, l \leq m, n$.

Let us further assume for simplicity that only x_1, x_2 and x_3s are the real numbers greater than zero and all the other values in A are zero. As, for example, $x_1 \neq 0$, this particularly signifies that $du_{l-1} \simeq dv_{k-1}$ and $du_{l+1} \simeq dv_{k+1}$ and also $(du_{l-1}, du_{l+1}) \simeq (dv_{k-1}, dv_{k+1})$ according to the node and edge similarity defined before. Now it can be noted that if two nodes u, v in a graph $G = (V, E)$ are connected with more than one walks, they supposed to have more and more random walks of different lengths which should be reflected in the matrix A. Following this explanation it is to be mentioned that similar nodes in DG_M and DG_I should be connected with different walks in the product graph G_P. So the non zero entry in the combined weighted matrix A identifies the similar nodes in DG_I with DG_M and with this the occurrences of the graph DG_M can be found in DG_I. The similar pair of nodes in the redundant dual graphs should be connected in the matrix A as above and the dissimilar pair of nodes should get the zero entries, as in the exponentiation of the adjacency matrix E_P, the existence of solitary graph edge must be diminished. The connected sub-component in the matrix A (in this case component with non zero entries viz. x_1, x_2 and x_3) can be found by searching maximal subgroup of entries that are mutually reachable (`graphconncomp` function in the `matlab`). Each component is then regarded as a single instance of the pattern graph in the target graph and can be found according to the position of the second nodes of the vertices of A.

3   Experimental Results

Our experiments were conducted on the SESYD dataset[2] [2]. This dataset contains 10 different subsets and 16 query symbols (Fig. 8). Each of the subsets

---

[2] http://mathieu.delalandre.free.fr/projects/sesyd/symbols/floorplans.html

contains 100 synthetically generated floorplans. All the floorplans in a subset are created from the same floorplan template by putting different model symbols in different places in random orientation and scale. In this experiment we have only considered a subset of 300 images (floorplans16-01, floorplans16-05 and floorplans16-06) and all the query symbols. For each retrieved instance of a given symbol if there exist an overlapping with the ground truth of the same symbol, we compute the overlapping ratio as follows:

$$\text{overlapping ratio} = \frac{area(A) \cap area(B)}{area(A) \cup area(B)}$$

where A is the area of the retrieved symbol and B is the area of the corresponding symbol in the ground truth. A retrieval is classified as true positive if the overlapping ratio is greater than 0.5.

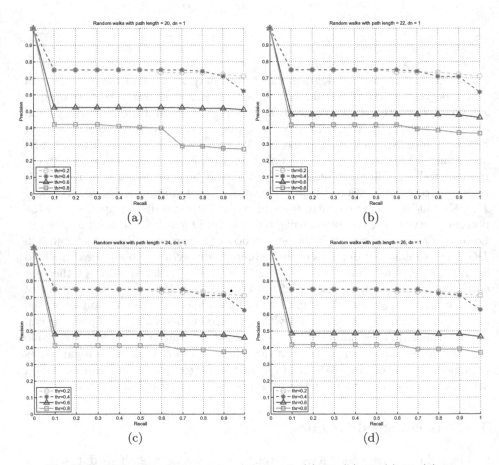

Fig. 7. Precision Recall curves for path length (a) 20, (b) 22, (c) 24, (d) 26.

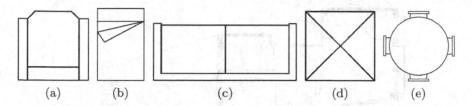

(a)	(b)	(c)	(d)	(e)

Fig. 8. Examples of model symbols: (a) *armchair*, (b) *bed*, (c) *sofa2*, (d) *table1*, (e) *table3*.

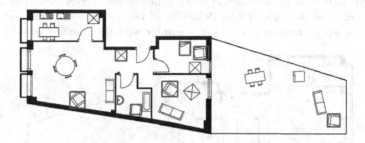

Fig. 9. Qualitative results of spotting *armchair* which shows correct detection of all the occurrences of *armchair*, at the same time it includes two false detection of *bed* and *table1* respectively.

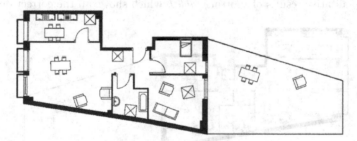

Fig. 10. Qualitative results of spotting *bed* which shows correct detection of the only one occurrence of *bed*, note there is no false detection.

All the experiments are done with the parameter values set as: $t_{\beta_1} = 6$, $t_{\beta_2} = 0.2$, we have observed that these two parameters are quite stable through all the images. However the other parameter t_α plays an important role selecting the compatible nodes while computing the product graph. For that reason we have performed a detailed experiments varying the parameter t_α from 0.2 to 0.8 with the step 0.2. Also we consider the length of the paths used as node labels as another parameter and for that we have performed experiments varying the path length from 20 to 26 with the step 2. All the experiments are performed by setting the connectivity parameter $dn = 2$.

For each of the pattern graphs we perform our product graph based subgraph matching method for spotting symbols on the documents and as an output we

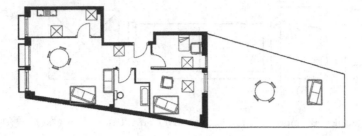

Fig. 11. Qualitative results of spotting *sofa2* which shows correct detection of all the occurrences of *sofa2* and also it false detection of two instances of *armchair*. This is because of the square regions in *armchair* resemble with the square region in *sofa2*.

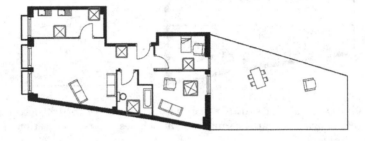

Fig. 12. Qualitative results of spotting *table1* which shows all the correct detection.

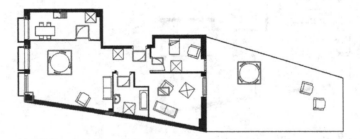

Fig. 13. Qualitative results of spotting *table3* which shows all the correct detection but a lot of false positives most of them resemble with the smaller subpart of the symbol *table3*.

obtain a ranked list of retrieved zones supposed to contain the queried graph. To evaluate the ranked list of retrievals we have drawn the precision recall curves for each set of parameters for each path length and they are shown in Fig. 7, where Fig. 7a shows the precision recall curves for path length 20, Fig. 7b for path length 22 and so on. From the plots, it is clear that the length of the paths used for node labels do not effect so much the overall performance of the system. It sometime can affect the bigger symbols where small paths can not connect the extremities of a dual node but in our case (or dataset) the range of path lengths considered were enough to handle all category of symbols. The parameter t_α has a good influence on the performance of the system. It is clear from the plots that the performance of the system drops while increasing t_α, this is because larger values of t_α create lot of nodes in the product graph and hence increase the number of false positives. Moreover, increasing this parameter increase the computation time, this is also due to the increment of the number of nodes in the product graph.

For an overall performance evaluation we have computed the precision (**P**), recall (**R**) and F-measure (**F**). The present system with the best set of parameters has obtained **P** = 78.20 %, **R** = 81.43 %, **F** = 76.49 %, which is quite better than the method in [3]. Some qualitative results are shown in Figs. 9, 10, 11, 12 and 13[3].

4   Conclusions

In this paper we have extended the product graph methodology by using the dual graph rather than the original representation as a basis. It turns out that this dual graph representation with redundant edges provides a robust way to deal with noise and distortions in the structural information. The product graph exhibits similar walks and exponentiation of the product graph's adjacency matrix allows one to extract simultaneous similar walks of any desired length. So these walks similarities help to get similar set of nodes in the pattern and target graph. The precision recall values obtained by the method are very encouraging albeit we experienced false positives with larger values of t_α. A closer analysis reveals that this kind of false positives are generated due to the tottering between the nodes in the product graph [9]. So one direction of our future work will address the removal of totterings from exponentiated adjacency matrices [1,10]. Another possible improvement can address the exact nature of matching the nodes while computing the product graph, which needs a threshold. Finding such a threshold is often difficult and heuristic. A possible improvement can come from working with similarities on the full product graph, which needs further research activities. One more direction of future work will concern detailed experimental study on various datasets to show the efficiency of the graph matching algorithm.

Acknowledgements. This work has been partially supported by the Spanish projects TIN2009-14633-C03-03, TIN2011-24631, TIN2012-37475-C02-02, 2010-CONE3-00029 and the PhD scholarship 2013FI_B2 00074.

References

1. Aziz, F., Wilson, R.C., Hancock, E.R.: Backtrackless walks on a graph. IEEE Trans. Neural Networks Learn. Syst. (TNNLS) **24**(6), 977–989 (2013)

---

[3] For all the qualitative results the interested readers are referred to http://www.cvc.uab.es/~adutta/Research/ProductGraph/res_rw.php.

2. Delalandre, M., Pridmore, T.P., Valveny, E., Locteau, H., Trupin, É.: Building synthetic graphical documents for performance evaluation. In: Liu, W., Lladós, J., Ogier, J.-M. (eds.) GREC 2007. LNCS, vol. 5046, pp. 288–298. Springer, Heidelberg (2008)
3. Dutta, A., Gibert, J., Lladós, J., Bunke, H., Pal, U.: Combination of product graph and random walk kernel for symbol spotting in graphical documents. In: Proceedings of the International Conference of Pattern Recognition (ICPR), pp. 1663–1666 (2012)
4. Dutta, A., Lladós, J., Pal, U.: A symbol spotting approach in graphical documents by hashing serialized graphs. Pattern Recogn. (PR) **46**(3), 752–768 (2013)
5. Fischer, A., Suen, C.Y., Frinken, V., Riesen, K., Bunke, H.: A fast matching algorithm for graph-based handwriting recognition. In: Kropatsch, W.G., Artner, N.M., Haxhimusa, Y., Jiang, X. (eds.) GbRPR 2013. LNCS, vol. 7877, pp. 194–203. Springer, Heidelberg (2013)
6. Gärtner, T., Flach, P.A., Wrobel, S.: On graph kernels: hardness results and efficient alternatives. In: Schölkopf, B., Warmuth, M.K. (eds.) COLT/Kernel 2003. LNCS (LNAI), vol. 2777, pp. 129–143. Springer, Heidelberg (2003)
7. Ming-Kuei, H.: Visual pattern recognition by moment invariants. IRE Trans. Inf. Theor. **8**(2), 179–187 (1962)
8. Lladós, J., Valveny, E., Sánchez, G., Martí, E.: Symbol recognition: current advances and perspectives. In: Blostein, D., Kwon, Y.-B. (eds.) GREC 2001. LNCS, vol. 2390, pp. 104–128. Springer, Heidelberg (2002)
9. Mahé, P., Ueda, N., Akutsu, T., Perret, J.-L., Vert, J.-P.: Graph kernels for molecular structure-activity relationship analysis with support vector machines. J. Chem. Inf. Model. (JCIM) **45**(4), 939–951 (2005)
10. Stark, H.M., Terras, A.A.: Zeta functions of finite graphs and coverings. J. Adv. Math. (JAM) **121**(1), 124–165 (1996)

Hierarchical Plausibility-Graphs for Symbol Spotting in Graphical Documents

Klaus Broelemann[1](✉), Anjan Dutta[2], Xiaoyi Jiang[1], and Josep Lladós[2]

[1] Department of Mathematics and Computer Science,
University of Münster, Münster, Germany
{broele,jiang}@uni-muenster.de

[2] Computer Vision Center, Universitat Autònoma de Barcelona, Barcelona, Spain
{adutta,josep}@cvc.uab.es

Abstract. Graph representation of graphical documents often suffers from noise such as spurious nodes and edges, and their discontinuity. In general these errors occur during the low-level image processing viz. binarization, skeletonization, vectorization etc. Hierarchical graph representation is a nice and efficient way to solve this kind of problem by hierarchically merging node-node and node-edge depending on the distance. But the creation of hierarchical graph representing the graphical information often uses hard thresholds on the distance to create the hierarchical nodes (next state) of the lower nodes (or states) of a graph. As a result, the representation often loses useful information. This paper introduces plausibilities to the nodes of hierarchical graph as a function of distance and proposes a modified algorithm for matching subgraphs of the hierarchical graphs. The plausibility-annotated nodes help to improve the performance of the matching algorithm on two hierarchical structures. To show the potential of this approach, we conduct an experiment with the SESYD dataset.

1 Introduction

Graphs are an efficient way of representing graphical documents specially for line drawings. Since documents often suffer from noise, the representation with graphs also results in distorted graphs. The distortions can include spurious nodes and edges, and discontinuity in them (see Fig. 1). Hierarchical graph representation is a way of solving this kind of structural errors hierarchically where the node-node and node-edge are merged hierarchically depending on the node-node or node-edge distance [3].

The main motivation of the work comes from [1], where the authors used the hierarchical representation of the segmented image regions and later used an approximated maximal clique finding algorithm on the association graph of the two hierarchical graphs to match the two hierarchical representations [2,8]. In particular, the aforementioned work was applied to match two different natural images for classification.

© Springer-Verlag Berlin Heidelberg 2014
B. Lamiroy and J.-M. Ogier (Eds.): GREC 2013, LNCS 8746, pp. 25–37, 2014.
DOI: 10.1007/978-3-662-44854-0_3

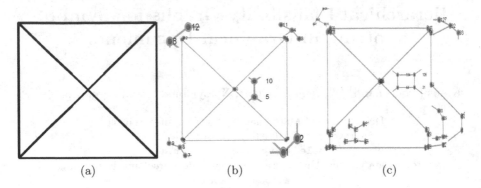

Fig. 1. Examples of the structural distortions (spurious nodes, edges, discontinuous edges) for a graphical symbol: (a) A graphical symbol called *table1*, (b), (c) Graph representations of two different instances of the symbol *table1* when appeared in floorplans, these instances are cropped from bigger graphs representing floorplans. Graph representation of documents involves low level image processing viz. binarization, skeletonization, vectorization etc. which further add structural noise such as spurious nodes, edges etc. The example shows how even a undistorted symbol can become distorted after represented with graph (note the spurious nodes and edges near the junction and corners.).

The construction of graph representation of graphical documents follows some inter-dependent pre-processing steps such as binarization, skeletonization, polygonal approximation. These low level preprocessing steps result in the vectorized documents which often contain some structural errors. In this work our graph representation considers the critical points as the nodes and the lines joining them as the edges. So often the graph representation contains spurious nodes, edges, disconnection between nodes etc. (see Fig. 1). Our present work is an extension of the work in [3] where we dealt with this kind of distortions in the graph level, to do that we proposed hierarchical representation of graphs because the hierarchical representation of graphs allows to incorporate the various segmentation errors hierarchically. But the node-node or node-edge merging was performed depending on a hard threshold which resulted in some loss of information. In this work we are assigning plausibilities to the nodes as a function of the distance and use them for matching. The work is still in progress and the results show some methodological improvement.

The rest of the paper is organized into four sections. In Sect. 2 we present the methodology of sub graph matching. Section 3 contains the detailed experimental results. After that, in Sect. 4, we conclude the paper and discuss future work.

2   Methodology

An essential part for graph based symbol spotting methods is the representation of graphical objects. This representation often contains low-level vectorization errors that basically affect subsequent graph matching methods. In this section we present a hierarchical representation that overcomes these problems by covering different possible vectorizations and estimating their plausibilities.

First we will give a brief overview of the initial vectorization and some errors that can occur due to it. Afterwards, we will describe our hierarchical representation and how this representation overcomes the vectorization errors.

2.1 Vectorization

Graph representation of documents follows some preprocessing steps, vectorization is one of them. Here vectorization can be defined as approximating the binary images to a polygonal representation. In our method we have used the Rosin-West algorithm [9] which is implemented in the Qgar package[1]. This algorithm works without any parameter except one to prune the isolated components. The algorithm produces a set of critical points and the information whether they are connected. Our graph representation considers the critical point as the nodes and the lines joining them as the edges.

Vectorization Errors. The resulting graph can contain vectorization errors. Reasons for that can be inaccurate drawings, artifacts in the binarization or errors in the vectorization algorithm. There are different kinds of vectorization errors that can occur. Among these, we concentrated on the following ones:

Gaps. In the drawing there can be small gaps between lines that ought to be connected. Reasons for that can be inaccurate drawings as well as mistakes in the binarization. The result can either be two unconnected nodes at the border of the gap or a node on one and an edge on the other side of the gap. Beside caused by errors, gaps can also be drawn intentionally to separate nearby symbols.

Split nodes. On the other hand, one original node can be split into two or more nodes. This can happen, if lines in the drawing do not intersect exactly at one point. Another reason are artifacts from the skeletonization step. Nearby nodes that seem to be a split node can be the result of fine details instead of vectorization errors.

Dispensable nodes. The vectorization can create nodes of order two that divide a straight edge into two or more parts. One reason for these nodes are small inaccuracies in the drawing that cause a local change in direction. For a later symbol spotting, these nodes are often undesired and should be removed. Nevertheless, in some cases such structures reflect details of the symbol. Examples of these errors can be seen in Fig. 1.

Though all these errors can be corrected in a post-processing step, a simple post-processing causes other problems: often it is not clear for the system whether a situation is an error or intentional. To deal with this uncertainty, we introduce a hierarchical representation that will be described in the next part.

---

[1] http://www.qgar.org/

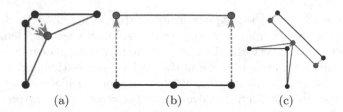

Fig. 2. Three cases for simplification. Displayed are the original nodes and edges (black) and the simplified nodes and their edges (gray): (a) Merge nodes (b) Remove dispensable node (c) Merge node and edge.

2.2   Hierarchical Graph Construction

This section describes the construction of hierarchical graph that is able to cover different possible vectorizations. This enables a later graph matching algorithm to deal with the uncertainties whether a part of the graph is intentional drawn or caused by a vectorization error.

The basic idea of our approach is to extend a given graph G so that it contains the different possibilities of interpretation. These possibilities are connected hierarchically and assigned with a plausibility measure. The hierarchy allows us to embed the constraint just to match one interpretation into the graph matching. In Sect. 2.3 we will give further details for the graph matching, the hierarchical constraint and how to use plausibilities for the matching.

In order to create different possible vectorizations, we take the initial vectorization represented in G and simplify it step by step. For this purpose, we identify three cases that allow a simplification. These three cases will be motivated in the following. Afterwards the plausibilities are introduced and based on this a formal definition of our simplification steps is given.

Nearby nodes. Both gaps in drawing as well as split nodes result in nodes near to each other and can be solved by merging these nodes. Since nearby nodes can also be the result of correct vectorization, e.g. due to two nearby symbols, we store both versions and hierarchically connect the merged node with the basic nodes. The merged node inherits all connection of its basic nodes. Figure 2(a) shows an example for such a merging step.

Dispensable nodes. In case of dispensable nodes, the vectorization error can be solved be removing the node. Again, a hierarchical structure can store both versions. As described before we only consider dispensable nodes that have two neighbors. The simplified versions of these neighbors are directly connected. This is shown in Fig. 2(b). Applying this rule multiple times allows us to remove chains of dispensable nodes.

Nodes near to edges. The third simplification is the merging of nodes with nearby edges. In this way the second kind of gaps can be corrected. To merge a node with an edge, the edge has to be divided into two edges by a copy of the node. This can be seen for an example in Fig. 2(c).

Plausibility. The major novelty of this paper is the use of plausibilities. The aim of these plausibilities is to measure the likelihood of a certain simplification to be correct. By doing so, we can prioritize matching of likely structures and still keep the ability of matching unlikely ones. To compute the plausibility for a certain simplification we identify basic features and describe the plausibility as function of these features. The features are described in the following:

Merging nodes. The plausibility for merging very near nodes is high and it decreases with increasing distance between the nodes. Thus, the distance between the nodes is taken as feature to measure the plausibility.

Removing nodes. Removing a node means to merge two edges. We consider the removal as plausible if the resulting edge is similar to the two original edges. There different features that can be used to measure this similarity. One possibility is the angle between bot edges. If the angle is near to 180°, the resulting edge will be near to the original edges. Another measurement is the distance of the node to the resulting edge, either absolute or relative to the length of the edge. For our experiments we used the angle feature.

Merging nodes with edges. Similar to merging nodes, we take the distance of the edge to the node as feature for the plausibility.

To measure the plausibility for the three previously mentioned cases, we define three functions:

1. function $\delta_1 : V \times V \to \mathbb{R}$ to measure the plausibility for merging two nodes.
2. function $\delta_2 : V \to \mathbb{R}$ to measure the plausibility for removing a node.
3. function $\delta_3 : V \times E \to \mathbb{R}$ to measure the plausibility for merging a node with an edge.

For the concrete implementation we used exponential functions applied to the features, e.g.

$$\delta_1(u, v) = \alpha_1 \exp(-\beta_1 \cdot d(u, v))$$

The functions δ_2 and δ_3 are defined analogously, replacing $d(u, v)$ by the respective features.

Our approach also allows other plausibility measurements. Note that our previous work [3] without plausibilities can be seen as a special case of this work by choosing binary measurements, i.e.

$$\delta_1(u, v) = \begin{cases} 1 \text{ if } d(u, v) < T_1 \\ 0 \text{ otherwise} \end{cases}$$

The plausibilities are used to identify possible simplifications. For this purpose we define a threshold T_0 and only perform hierarchical simplifications for constellations that have a plausibility greater than a T_0.

Recursive Definition. Based on the previous motivation we will give a recursive definition of our hierarchical graphs that reflects the construction algorithm based on the vectorization outcome.

The result of the vectorization is an undirected graph $G = (V_G, E_G, \sigma_G)$ where V_G it the set of nodes, $E_G \subseteq V_G \times V_G$ is the set of edges and $\sigma_G : V_G \to \mathbb{R}^2$ is a labeling function that maps the nodes to their coordinates in the plane.

A hierarchical graph has two kinds of edges: undirected neighborhood edges and directed hierarchical edges. Hierarchical edges represent simplification operations, i.e. they link nodes from the original graph arising from the vectorization to successor nodes representing simplified vectorizations. In addition, each node is assigned with a plausibility value. Formally, we define a hierarchical graph H as a tuple $H = (V, E_N, E_H, \sigma, p)$ with the neighborhood edges $E_N \subseteq V \times V$, the hierarchical edges $E_H \subseteq V \times V$ and plausibility values $p : V \to \mathbb{R}$.

Note that there is a difference between the plausibility of a node (given by the function p) and the plausibility of a simplification (given by δ_i, $i = 1, 2, 3$). The reason for this difference is, that a plausible simplification with implausible nodes results in implausible nodes.

Furthermore, given two nodes $u, v \in V$ let $u \rightsquigarrow v$ denote that v is a hierarchical successor of u and $L(u)$ denote the set of all predecessors of u that belong to G: $L(u) = \{v \in V_G | v \rightsquigarrow u\}$. Based on these functions and formulations we can define the hierarchical simplification $H = \mathcal{H}(G) = (V, E_N, E_H, \sigma, p)$ of G by the following rules:

Initial. As initialization for the recursion, G is a subgraph of H. We define a base plausibility $p(v) = 1$ for all initial nodes $v \in V_G$.

Merging. For $u, v \in V$ with $\delta_1(u, v) > T_0$ there is a merged node $w \in V$ with

- w is a hierarchically successor of u and v:
  $\forall s \in V : s \rightsquigarrow w \Leftrightarrow s \rightsquigarrow u \vee s \rightsquigarrow v \vee s \in \{u, v\}$
- w has all neighbors of u and v except u and v:
  $\forall s \in V : (s, w) \in E_N \Leftrightarrow ((s, u) \in E_N \vee (s, v) \in E_N) \wedge s \notin \{u, v\}$
- w lies in the center of its leaf nodes:
  $\sigma(w) = \frac{1}{|L(w)|} \sum_{s \in L(w)} \sigma(s)$
- The plausibility of w is defined by δ_1 and the plausibilities of u and v:
  $p(w) = \delta_1(u, v)p(u)p(v)$
  If there are different ways to create w, we assign the maximal plausibility to w.

Removing. For a dispensable node $u \in V$ with $\delta_2(u) > T_0$ there exist two neighbor nodes $v, w \in V_G$, i.e. $(u, v), (u, w) \in E_N$. Since v and w can have hierarchical successors from other simplifications, these have to be included in the definition: for all $v_i : (v_i, u) \in E_N \wedge v \in L(v_i)$ there exists a $\bar{v}_i$. In the same way a set of $\bar{w}_j$ is defined.

- $\bar{v}_i$ hierarchical successor of v_i: $(v_i, \bar{v}_i), (w_j, \bar{w}_j) \in E_H$
- to cover all possibilities, there is neighborhood connection between all of $\bar{v}_i$ and all $\bar{w}_j$. Furthermore, the $\bar{v}_i$ has the same connections as v_i with exception of the removed node u:
  $(s, \bar{v}_i) \in E_N \Leftrightarrow ((s, v_i) \in E_N \wedge s \neq u) \vee \exists j : s = w_j.$ (analogous for w_j)
- The coordinates do not change: $\sigma(v_i) = \sigma(\bar{v}_i)$, $\sigma(w_j) = \sigma(\bar{w}_j)$
- $p(\bar{v}_i) = \delta_2(u)p(v_i)$

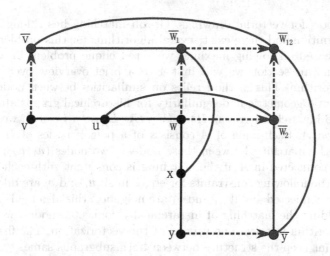

Fig. 3. An example for removing nodes. Note that the possibility of removing two adjacent nodes of w creates four different possible interpretations of w, e.g. $\bar{w}_1$ stands for removing u but keeping x

In this definition the successors of u and w have to be included. The reason for this can be seen in the example in Fig. 3: if the removing is done iteratively, removing u will lead to $\bar{v}$ and $\bar{w}_1$. A subsequent removal of x has to create $\bar{w}_2$ and $\bar{w}_{12}$ in order to cover both possibilities: just remove x and remove u and x. This will give a plausibility of:

$$p(\bar{w}_{12}) = \delta_2(x)p(\bar{w}_1) = \delta_2(x)\delta_2(u)p(w)$$

Node/Edge merging. For $u \in V, e = (v, w) \in E$ with $\delta_3(u, e) > T_0$ there exist simplifications $\bar{u}, \bar{v}, \bar{w}$ with

- $\bar{u}, \bar{v}, \bar{w}$ are hierarchically above u, v, w:
  $\forall s \in V : s \rightsquigarrow \bar{u} \Leftrightarrow s \rightsquigarrow u \vee s = u$ (analogue for v, w)
- $\bar{u}$ intersects the edge between $\bar{v}$ and $\bar{w}$:
  $\forall s \in V : (s, \bar{u}) \in E_N \Leftrightarrow ((s, u) \in E_N \vee s \in \{\bar{v}, \bar{w}\}$
- The coordinates do not change: $\sigma(u) = \sigma(\bar{u})$, $\sigma(v) = \sigma(\bar{v})$ and $\sigma(w) = \sigma(\bar{w})$
- $p(\bar{u}) = \delta_3(u, e)p(u)$ (analog for v, w)

Based on these recursive rules, we construct the smallest hierarchical graph that satisfies these rules, i.e. no additional nodes are added. Here it is to be noted that the hierarchical simplification $\mathcal{H}(G)$ of the graph G always contains the graph G.

2.3 Graph Matching

In this section we will describe how to make use of the hierarchical graph representation described in the previous section for subgraph matching in order to spot symbols for vectorial drawings. Graph matching has a long history in pattern recognition and there exist several algorithms for this problem [4]. Our approach is based on solving maximal weighted clique problem in association graphs [2]. In this section we will first give a brief overview over the graph matching algorithm. This method relies on similarities between nodes. Hence, we will present a geometric node similarity for hierarchical graphs afterwards.

Given two hierarchical graphs $H^i = (V^i, E_N^i, E_H^i, \sigma^i)$, $i = 1, 2$, we construct the association A. Each node of A consists of a pair of nodes of H^1 and H^2, representing the matching between these nodes. Two nodes (u_1, u_2), $(v_1, v_2) \in H_1 \times H_2$ are connected in A, if the matching is consistent with each other, i.e. they respect the following constraints for edges in A: u_i and v_i are different, not hierarchically connected and if u_1 and v_1 are neighbor, this also holds for u_2 and v_2. By forbidding the matching of hierarchically connected nodes, we force the matching algorithm to select one version of the vectorization. The first and the third constraint keep the structure between both subgraphs same.

We use replicator dynamics [2] to find the maximal weighted clique of the association graph and, hence, the best matching subgraphs of H^1 and H^2. Based on the results of this, we perform the following steps to spot symbols. Let us consider H^1 be the query graph or the model graph and H^2 be the input graph where we want to spot the instances of H^1. First of all we perform n iterations and in each iteration we perform the replicator dynamics to find the correspondences of the H^1 to H^2. Since the replicator dynamics only provide a one-to-one matching, in each iteration we obtain the correspondences from the nodes of H^1 to the nodes of H^2. So for m nodes in H^1 we get m nodes in H^2. But it is not constrained that these m nodes in H^2 will belong to the same instance of H^1. So to obtain the different instances of the H^1 we consider each of the m nodes in the H^2 and all the neighborhood nodes of a node which can be reached within a k graph path distance. The graph path distance between two nodes is calculated as the minimum total number of nodes between the two nodes. Let us denote this set of nodes as V_s^1 and consider all the hierarchical and normal edges connecting the nodes in V_s^1 as in H^1, this forms a subgraph which we can denote as $H_s^1 = (V_s^1, E_{s_N}^1, E_{s_H}^1, \sigma_s^1)$. We again apply the replicator dynamics to get the best matching subgraph and compute the bounding box around the nodes of best correspondences. The bounding box gives the best matching region of interest expected to contain instance of a query symbol.

The complexity of replicator dynamics is $\mathcal{O}(|A|^2)$ (see [1]). Since we perform n iterations, we get a complexity of $\mathcal{O}(n \cdot |A|^2)$. In order to reduce the computation time we use the fact that the symbols are much smaller than floorplans. We create overlapping parts of the floorplan and perform the matching between the symbol and the parts. These parts have to be big enough to ensure that the symbols are completely included in at least one part. The construction of the hierarchical graph takes about 2 or 3 s for an average floorplan, the matching takes several minutes.

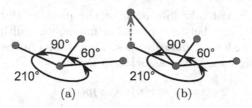

Fig. 4. Example for node labels for graphs based on angles between edges: (a) for planar graphs and (b) for hierarchical graphs. Both will be labeled with (90, 210, 60).

Node Attributes. The graph matching algorithm operates on the association graph with similarity labels for the nodes. To use this algorithm, we have to define the similarity between two nodes of the hierarchical graph. Since the matching reflects geometric structures, we use geometric attributes for the similarity.

In a non-hierarchical planar graph, a single node can be labeled by the sequence of adjacent angles which sum up to 360°. Figure 4(a) gives an example for such a labeling. This naive approach will cause some problems for hierarchical graph since nodes can have several hierarchically connected neighbors. Thus, the number of possible vectorizations has a strong influence on the node description. Because the number of possibilities is also affected by the level of distortion of the original image, such an approach is not robust to distortion.

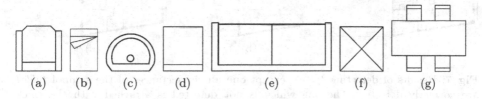

Fig. 5. Model symbols in the SESYD dataset: (a) *armchair*, (b) *bed*, (c) *sink1*, (d) *sofa1*, (e) *sofa2*, (f) *table1*, (g) *table2*.

To reduce the influence of the hierarchical structure and the distortion on the node labeling, we use only edges to nodes that have no predecessor connected with the central node. An example for that can be seen in Fig. 4(b): though the central node is connected to four nodes, only three edges are used to compute the node label.

To compute the similarity between two node labels, we define an editing distance on these labels. The editing operations are rotating one edge, i.e. lowering one angle and rising another one, removing one edge, i.e. merging two angles, and rotating the whole description. The last operation is cost-free and makes the similarity rotation-invariant. The cost for rotating an edge is set to the angle of rotation. The cost for removing an edge is set to a fixed value.

Using this editing distance, we can define the similarity $s(u, v)$ between nodes $u \in H^1$ and $v \in H^2$. This similarity is based on the nodes and their direct neighborhood, but do not take into account the plausibilities of the nodes. In order to prefer matchings between plausible nodes, we multiply the similarity between two nodes with their plausibilities. This results in the final weight $\omega_{u,v}$ for the corresponding node in the association graph:

$$\omega_{u,v} = p(u)s(u,v)p(v)$$

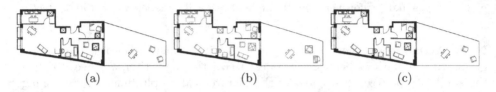

(a)   (b)   (c)

Fig. 6. Results of detecting *table1*, note that all the instances of the symbol *table1* are correctly detected even the ones attached with the walls. In reality these walls are thin and hence less distorted during the vectorization, (b) Results of spotting *table1* by the previous version of the method [3], (c) Results of spotting *table1* by Dutta *et al.* [7].

(a)   (b)   (c)

Fig. 7. Results of detecting *table1*, except one all the instances of the symbol *table1* are correctly detected. The one which is not detected is attached with the thick black pixels, (b) Results of spotting *table1* by the previous version of the method [3], (c) Results of spotting *table1* by Dutta *et al.* [7].

3   Experimental Results

Since the work still is in progress, we have conducted a short experiment to check the performance of the algorithm. Our experiments were conducted on the images taken from the SESYD dataset [5][2]. Originally, this dataset contains 10 different subsets and 16 query symbols (Fig. 5). These query symbols are available to evaluate our method with the ground truth. Each of the subsets contains 100 synthetically generated floorplans. All the floorplans in a subset are created from the same floorplan template by putting different model symbols in different places in random orientation and scale.

---

[2] http://mathieu.delalandre.free.fr/projects/sesyd/symbols/floorplans.html

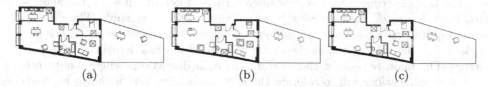

(a)   (b)   (c)

Fig. 8. Results of detecting *table1*, note that all the instances of the symbol *table1* are correctly detected even the one which is connected with thick black pixels, (b) Results of spotting *table1* by the previous version of the method [3], (c) Results of spotting *table1* by Dutta *et al.* [7].

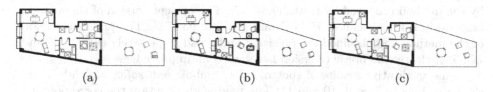

(a)   (b)   (c)

Fig. 9. Results of detecting *table1*, here two of the symbols are not detected and one of them are isolated but heavily distorted by the vectorization algorithm, (b) Results of spotting *table1* by the previous version of the method [3], (c) Results of spotting *table1* by Dutta *et al.* [7].

(a)   (b)   (c)

Fig. 10. Results of detecting *bed*, here the single instance of *bed* is correctly detected, note that in this case the instance is also attached with thin black pixel, (b) Results of spotting *bed* by the previous version of the method [3], (c) Results of spotting *bed* by Dutta *et al.* [7].

(a)   a   (c)

Fig. 11. (a) Results of detecting *sofa2*, here both the instances are correctly detected among which one of them was partially attached with thick wall, (b) Results of spotting *sofa2* by the previous version of the method [3], (c) Results of spotting *sofa2* by Dutta *et al.* [7].

For this experiment we have considered three different subsets (*floorplan16-01*, *floorplan16-05*, *floorplan16-06*) and all the 16 model symbols. The method works quite well for six of the symbols: *armchair, bed, door2, sofa1, sofa2* and *table1*. For the other symbols the method resulted in miss detection, false positives. The main reason for these errors are high distortions where our hierarchical simplifications fail to tolerate the errors. Usually, Vectorization methods perform worse with black thick pixels and create lot of distortions in the vectorized information. The average quantitative results for the successful symbols (as mentioned above) are listed in the Table 1 where the first row shows that for current version of the method, the second row shows that for previous version of the method [3], the third row shows graph-matching with a planar graph (with the preprocessing of this paper) and the last row shows the quantitative results by the method proposed by Dutta *et al.* [7]. The present version of the method has obtained a precision of 75.17 % and recall of 93.17 %. The previous version of the method had obtained the precision and recall respectively as 32.99 % and 77.55 %, clearly the present version has gained an improvement.

Some qualitative results of spotting the symbols *bed, sofa2* and *table1* are shown in Figs. 6, 7, 8, 9, 10 and 11. The figures also contain the corresponding results obtained by the method proposed in [3,7]. For more qualitative results the interested reader can visit www.cvc.uab.es/~adutta/results_phgr.php.

Table 1. Results obtained by the proposed method and the comparison with the previous version [3] and a previously proposed symbol spotting method [7].

Method	P	R	F
Current version	75.17	93.17	83.21
Previous version [3]	32.99	77.55	46.29
Without Hierarchy	54.55	90.00	67.92
Dutta et al. [7]	69.19	67.28	68.22

Another method proposed by some of the authors uses a product graph for symbol spotting [6]. This method performs similar for the given dataset. The reason to develop this additional method is the potential of the hierarchical graph to deal with more inaccurate drawings, like hand-drawn sketches. This ability comes with the disadvantage of longer computational times due to the higher complexity of a hierarchical graph and the use of node labels.

4   Conclusion and Future Works

In this paper we have proposed an extension of the previously proposed hierarchical graph representation. We have introduced plausibilities to the nodes of the hierarchical graph, these plausibilities help to better match the hierarchical substructures through the computation of the association graph. The present method still has some scope of improvement, as we have shown in the experimental results that all kind distortions particularly heavy distortions viz. connected to thick black walls and etc. still can not be solved. So the future work will address the further improvement of the method regarding noise. With the improvement, the construction of the hierarchical graph for this kind of graph representation is becoming complex and time taking. So another direction of future work will also concern about constructing hierarchical graph for different kind of graph representation. We have investigated that the hierarchical matching algorithm used by us sometime fails to find local optima and hence the solution is erroneous. We further investigated that a little modification of the matching algorithm provides much better results. Therefore improvement of the hierarchical matching will also be considered as a future work.

Acknowledgement. This work has been partially supported by the Spanish projects TIN2009-14633-C03-03, TIN2011-24631, TIN2012-37475-C02-02, the PhD scholarship 2013FI_B2 00074, the International Research Training Group 1498 "Semantic Integration of Geospatial Information" funded by DFG (German Research Foundation), and the Doctoral Scholarship of the University of Münster.

References

1. Ahuja, N., Todorovic, S.: From region based image representation to object discovery and recognition. In: Hancock, E.R., Wilson, R.C., Windeatt, T., Ulusoy, I., Escolano, F. (eds.) SSPR & SPR 2010. LNCS, vol. 6218, pp. 1–19. Springer, Heidelberg (2010)
2. Bomze, I., Pelillo, M., Stix, V.: Approximating the maximum weight clique using replicator dynamics. IEEE TNN **11**(6), 1228–1241 (2000)
3. Broelemann, K., Dutta, A., Jiang, X., Lladós, J.: Hierarchical graph representation for symbol spotting in graphical document images. In: Gimel'farb, G., Hancock, E., Imiya, A., Kuijper, A., Kudo, M., Omachi, S., Windeatt, T., Yamada, K. (eds.) SSPR & SPR 2012. LNCS, vol. 7626, pp. 529–538. Springer, Heidelberg (2012)
4. Conte, D., Foggia, P., Sansone, C., Vento, M.: Thirty years of graph matching in pattern recognition. IJPRAI **18**(3), 265–298 (2004)
5. Delalandre, M., Pridmore, T.P., Valveny, E., Locteau, H., Trupin, É.: Building synthetic graphical documents for performance evaluation. In: Liu, W., Lladós, J., Ogier, J.-M. (eds.) GREC 2007. LNCS, vol. 5046, pp. 288–298. Springer, Heidelberg (2008)
6. Dutta, A., Lladós, J., Bunke, H., Pal, U.: A product graph based method for dual subgraph matching applied to symbol spotting. In: Proceedings of the International Workshop on Graphics Recognition (GREC), pp. 7–11 (2013)
7. Dutta, A., Lladós, J., Pal, U.: A symbol spotting approach in graphical documents by hashing serialized graphs. Pattern Recogn. **46**(3), 752–768 (2013)
8. Pelillo, M., Siddiqi, K., Zucker, S.: Matching hierarchical structures using association graphs. IEEE TPAMI **21**(11), 1105–1120 (1999)
9. Rosin, P.L., West, G.A.W.: Segmentation of edges into lines and arcs. Image Vis. Comput. **7**(2), 109–114 (1989)

Towards Searchable Line Drawings, a Content-Based Symbol Retrieval Approach with Variable Query Complexity

Nibal Nayef$^{(\boxtimes)}$, Wonmin Byeon, and Thomas M. Breuel

Technical University Kaiserslautern, Kaiserslautern, Germany
{nnayef,tmb}@iupr.com,
byeon@rhrk.uni-kl.de

Abstract. Current symbol spotting and retrieval methods are not yet able to achieve the goal of both high accuracy and efficiency on large databases of line drawings. This paper presents an approach for focused symbol retrieval as step towards achieving such a goal by using concepts from image retrieval. During the off-line learning phase of the proposed approach, regions of interest are extracted from the drawings based on feature grouping. The regions are then described using an off-the-shelf descriptor. The similar descriptors are clustered, and finally a visual symbol vocabulary is learned by an SVM classifier. The vocabulary is constructed assuming no knowledge of the contents of the drawings. During on-line retrieval, the classifier recognizes the descriptors of query regions. A query can be a partial or a complete symbol, can contain contextual noise around a symbol or more than one symbol. Experimental results are presented for a database of architectural floor plans.

Keywords: Symbol retrieval · Multi-part graphical query · Visual symbol vocabulary · Technical line drawings

1 Introduction

Symbol recognition and retrieval in technical line drawings is one of the main challenges in document analysis and graphics recognition communities. State-of-the-art methods work well on small databases of isolated symbols, but their performance significantly decreases on large databases of complicated drawings containing many symbols connected to each other and to connection lines. To achieve realistic large scale symbol retrieval, we could use ideas from the field of content-based retrieval in natural image databases. The famous bag-of-visual-words (BoVW) approach [2], with its many variants, have been successfully used in large scale object retrieval and image analysis tasks. The main idea there is not to search images one by one looking for a queried object, but rather to perform off-line content analysis of an image database, and create a compact and quickly accessible representation of the whole database. Such representation

© Springer-Verlag Berlin Heidelberg 2014
B. Lamiroy and J.-M. Ogier (Eds.): GREC 2013, LNCS 8746, pp. 38–49, 2014.
DOI: 10.1007/978-3-662-44854-0_4

can be searched quickly for a query. The symbol retrieval approach presented in this paper, loosely follows some of the concepts of the BoVW approach. Our approach consists of an off-line and an on-line stage. Within the off-line stage, local regions of interest (ROIs) are extracted from the line drawings, and then described by a shape descriptor. The descriptors are clustered, and then prepared to be quickly accessible based on queries. The idea behind this stage is to create a compact and quickly accessible representation of the contents of the line drawings database. Within the on-line stage, contents similar to images of query symbols are retrieved. Our approach is for focused retrieval, which means retrieval with localization of the queried symbol inside the retrieved line drawings.

The rest of this paper is organized as follows. Section 2 reviews the related work in comparison to the proposed approach. Section 3 explains the overall proposed approach with a detailed description of each step. In the section after that, we present the performance evaluation of the proposed retrieval system. Finally, we present conclusions and directions for future work.

2 Related Work

Some state-of-the-art methods/systems that perform symbol spotting or retrieval, follow the BoVW approach as well. Nguyen et al. [18] proposed a symbol spotting method that is very similar to the BoVW model. In their work, DOG-SIFT [13] is used to detect ROIs. The ROIs are described using shape context descriptor, and then clustered by k-means to build a visual vocabulary. An inverted file index is built from the clusters (similar to the inverted index of text retrieval systems). The location information of the ROIs are also kept in the index, since the spotting system should locate regions in the drawing rather than returning the complete drawings. It is not clear how their method would scale using a larger number of symbols and line drawings.

Kong et al. [10] presented a symbol spotting/retrieval method where the ROIs are found using overlapping sliding windows. The ROIs are then described by a shape descriptor called the deformed blurred shape model. The descriptions are computed at different scales and orientations. Then the vectors describing the ROIs are clustered using k-means. In their method (as well as in the method of Nguyen et al. [18]), k-means is used as a clustering method. The use of such a simple clustering method means relying more on the goodness of the output of the preceding ROI detection and description steps. In [10], those steps use overlapping sliding windows, which are not invariant to scale and rotation. This results in different ROIs that should correspond to the same symbol part. Moreover, the used ROI-descriptor is not invariant to rotation and scale, so, the ROIs have to be stored many times at different scales and orientations. The increased number of ROIs makes it harder for a clustering algorithm to output the correct partitioning of the data. For indexing, hash tables are built from the clusters for each image, where the labels of the clusters are the keys to a hash table. In their system, such a table is used for every image. This requires processing each image of the database sequentially during spotting/retrieval. Moreover, scalability is an issue when using a hash table.

Luqman et al. [14] extracted ROIs from graph-based representations. The ROIs are converted to fuzzy structural signatures. This descriptor is also introduced by them where a structural graph representation is converted to a numerical vector representation. The similar signatures are then clustered together using agglomerative (or hierarchical) clustering method. The city distance is used as a similarity measure of clustering. Labels are assigned to clusters. An inverted file index is used for indexing the contents of the drawings. The keys of this index are learned by a Bayesian network, and the index naturally contains the ROIs locations and the labels of the clusters to which they belong. During the on-line querying, the ROIs of a query are extracted and described, and then classified as a member of some cluster. The corresponding ROIs in the drawings are retrieved by looking up the index.

The retrieval approach presented in this paper, includes detection of regions of interest (ROIs) using feature grouping proposed by the authors [16]. This ROI detection method has been shown to be highly accurate in finding regions that correspond to similar parts of symbols despite transformations. In the description step, we use a pixel-based compact symbol descriptor proposed by Yang [21], that is invariant to transformations and robust to noise. As for creating the compact and quickly accessible representation of the line drawings, we use the concept of the visual symbol vocabulary from the BoVW approach. We create a visual vocabulary of the database by k-means clustering and SVM learning. The presented approach has the ability to deal with different query complexity thanks to the region detection step. A query could contain contextual noise (additional line segments), or could have multiple parts. Retrieval of a query is performed on the each of the query regions.

The authors have also recently presented another symbol retrieval system [17] that has the same structure as the one proposed here. The system in [17] outperforms state-of-the-art methods including the one presented in this paper. However, our work in [17] requires big memory and time resources for the off-line stage, as the clustering step is based on accurate geometric matching of shapes. Additionally, the time required for on-line query retrieval depends on the size of the visual vocabulary, and it also uses geometric matching for comparing a query with the elements of the visual vocabulary. So, in this paper, we investigate techniques for faster query symbol look up time, and we will seek to improve higher localization and retrieval accuracy. The performance of the approach presented here compares favorably to other state-of-the-art methods.

3   Description of the Retrieval Approach

The retrieval approach proposed in this paper has two stages. The steps of the first stage – the off-line stage – are as follows. First, ROIs of line drawings are identified (Subsect. 3.1). The identified ROIs correspond to symbols' parts up to complete symbols. This step is accomplished via grouping line segment features of the line drawings. The method used for feature grouping was introduced by the authors in [16]. Second, an off-the-shelf symbol descriptor is applied on the extracted ROIs to represent them in vector format. We use the symbol descriptor introduced by Yang [21]. The descriptors are the visual words of the line drawings database. The next step is applying k-means clustering to group the similar descriptors together. Finally, an SVM classifier is trained on clusters to learn the class labels of the clusters, where each cluster should contain similar visual words corresponding to similar symbol parts.

In the on-line stage, a query symbol is given as input. The ROIs of the query are detected and described using the same methods used in the off-line stage. The trained SVM classifier quickly classifies the descriptors of the query regions as belonging to which clusters. All the similar regions from the drawings database are then retrieved from the clusters. The following subsections describe each step of the retrieval approach in more detail.

3.1 Detection of Regions of Interest

We argue that the ROI-finding step is the most important step within a content-based retrieval system. The ROIs should be detected consistently and accurately such that a region that corresponds to a symbol is always found in different drawings regardless of the position and the transformation of that symbol. If a method is capable of finding ROIs in such a consistent way, then the later steps of describing, clustering and retrieving those regions become easier to develop and would yield better performance.

We will use a region detection method from our previous works in [15, 16], which is based on feature grouping. We have illustrated the accuracy of this method and its invariance to transformed regions in [15, 16]. In the following we describe how the method works.

Images of line drawings are given as input to the region detection method. First, to vectorize the line drawings, simple preprocessing is applied: edge detection followed by sampling line segments along the edges. The edges may be straight or curved, the process of sampling line segments along the edges converts all the edges to straight line segments. For example, a curved edge will be converted into a set of small straight segments. The line segments are the features of the line drawings. A set of line segments are grouped together if they form a convex shape. Grouping line segments based on convexity was introduced by Jacobs [7, 8] to find meaningful shapes or parts of objects. Such feature grouping method is invariant to scaling and rotation. After finding initial groups of line segments that satisfy convexity property, the following cleaning up steps are carried out: removing all groups that have less than 3 segments, and groups that are cyclic repetitions of each other. As a last step, a group whose bounding box falls completely within a bounding box of another group, is discarded.

After these steps, we get a list of groups of line segments. Each group consists of line segment features that were grouped based on the method described above. The goal is to identify ROIs in a line drawing, hence, we define an *ROI* as the **region (bounding box) that contains a group of line segment features**.

Figure 1 shows the output of the grouping method applied on a line drawing. The shaded parts are the ROIs found by the method. In the figure, red

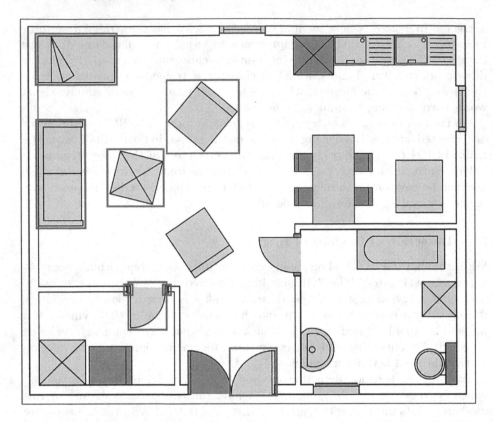

Fig. 1. Output of the region detection method shown on a complete line drawing. The found **ROIs (symbols' parts)** of a line drawing are shown shaded (adjacent different ROIs have different shading). Red bounding boxes are drawn around **only some** of the found ROIs for clarity of illustration (Color figure online).

bounding boxes are drawn around some of the found ROIs, we also use different shading for adjacent ROIs. It can be seen that the found ROIs correspond mostly to meaningful parts of the symbols up to complete symbols. Note that those symbols appear in different sizes and rotations within a line drawing. For each region, we need to keep information about where this region can be found in a line drawing, i.e. which image it comes from and its location in that image.

3.2   Description of Regions of Interest

The extracted interest regions contain symbol parts up to complete symbols. A shape descriptor is needed to represent a region in a vector form. The vector representation can then be used for the following steps of clustering and learning. Ideally, a symbol descriptor should be used to compute such a vector representation. In this step of our proposed approach, any off-the-shelf symbol descriptor can be used to represent the extracted regions. We have chosen the one proposed by [21], as it has high accuracy in recognizing symbols. This descriptor is invariant to similarity transformation and is robust to noise as shown in Yang's experiments. In the following we present a brief review of the used descriptor, the complete details can be found in [21].

Yang's symbol descriptor is represented by two histograms. Each histogram contains both statistical and structural information of a shape. Each pixel with its surrounding pixels describes the shape by certain constrains (length-ratio and angle) which provide the detailed structure of the symbol with rotation-scale invariance. In addition, it is robust to noise or distortion by quantization and integration to the fixed dimensions.

The procedure of the descriptor is as follows: (1) shape skeletonization (2) computing pixel-level constraints (3) generating length-ratio (LRH) and angle (AH) based histograms for each pixel (4) statistical integration of all pixels based on LRH and AH. From this integration, we finally obtain two fixed dimensional vectors.

The skeleton of the input shape is sampled into N pixels. Those are N reference points $(P_k, k \in \{0, ..N - 1\})$. Each reference point describes the relationship with all other pixels by length-ratio and angle:
$\{(L_{ij}, \Theta_{ij}) \mid i \in [1, N - 2]; j \in [i + 1, N - 1]\}$ (except P_k), where:

$$L_{ij} = min\{\mid P_k P_i \mid / \mid P_k P_j \mid, \mid P_k P_j \mid / \mid P_k P_i \mid\} \tag{1}$$

$$\Theta_{ij} = \angle P_i P_k P_j \tag{2}$$

$\mid P_k P_i \mid$ and $\mid P_k P_j \mid$ are the length of the two vector $P_k P_i$ and $P_k P_j$. The advantage of this representation is that it is not affected by scaling and rotation.

These constraints between every pair of pixels are in a range $[0, 1]$ for length-ratio and $[0, 180]$ for angle. We then construct the matrix to show the distribution of the constraints as well as to generalize the form:

$$LRH = \begin{bmatrix} n_1(P_0) & n_2(P_0) & \cdots & n_M(P_0) \\ \vdots & \vdots & & \vdots \\ n_1(P_k) & n_2(P_k) & \cdots & n_M(P_k) \\ \vdots & \vdots & & \vdots \\ n_1(P_{N-1}) & n_2(P_{N-1}) & \cdots & n_M(P_{N-1}) \end{bmatrix} \tag{3}$$

where

$$n_{\{1..M\}}(P_k) = \frac{2}{(N-1)(N-2)} Hist_{\{1..M\}}(L_k) \tag{4}$$

$Hist_{\{1..M\}}(L_k)$ is the histogram for the reference point P_k divided by the number of bins M.

Finally, statistical integration of points $P_{k \in \{0..N-1\}}$ is performed from the previous matrix LRH (SIHA-LRH) and we obtain:

$$SIHA - LRH = \begin{bmatrix} m_1(1) & m_2(1) & \cdots & m_M(1) \\ m_1(2) & m_2(2) & \cdots & m_M(2) \\ \vdots & \vdots & & \vdots \\ m_1(Q) & m_2(Q) & \cdots & m_M(Q) \end{bmatrix} \tag{5}$$

where

$$m_i\,(1..Q) = \frac{1}{N}\,Hist_{\{1..Q\}}(n_i(P_{\{0..N-1\}})) \tag{6}$$

$Hist_{\{1..Q\}}(n_i(P_{\{0..N-1\}}))$ is the histogram divided as Q number of bins for each column i $\in$ {1..M} of LRH. Note that this is applied on the matrix of dimensions $Q \times M$. So, from Eq. 6, we obtain a vector for length-ratios, which is the first part of the descriptor. The vector of angles is constructed in the same manner (SIHA-AH), but the dimension is not necessarily same as SIHA-LRH.

In order to get the final vector form, the two vectors of length-ratio and angle are concatenated into one vector. The same symbol descriptor is applied on all the regions extracted in the previous step. In his work, Yang [21] proposed the sum of absolute differences (SAD) to compare the similarity/difference between descriptors. As will be seen in the next subsection, we use the Euclidean distance (square root of the sum of squared differences) to compare descriptors in the next clustering step. Either distance can be used.

3.3   Clustering and Learning the Classes of the Clusters

At this step of off-line content analysis of line drawings, we have thousands of descriptors of regions of interest. Analogous to the BoVW approach, those descriptors are the visual words of the line drawings. Performing the search in a large space of visual words is computationally expensive, and does not allow for interactive browsing and searching the contents of line drawings. That's why a more compact representation is required in order to provide acceptable search response time. The numerous methods that follow the BoVW approach use techniques such as k-means clustering [12], self-organizing maps [6] and vector quantization [5,11] for creating compact representations from high dimensional feature spaces [9,19].

Similarly, we use standard k-means clustering for grouping the similar descriptors together. The input to the clustering method is the list of descriptors – in vector form – computed in the previous step. Recall that each descriptor represents a region of interest, that in turn represents a symbol part up to a complete symbol. Figure 2 shows examples of the constructed clusters.

Clustering parameters – mainly the number of clusters – should be chosen to be proportional to the expected number of regions that could be extracted from the symbol alphabet that is used to draw technical line drawings of some domain. The number of clusters is one of the factors affecting the relation between recall and precision values in the retrieval process. Other enhanced clustering techniques can be used to improve this step. Our goal here is just to develop a framework for retrieval, and show that invariant region detection and description are more critical to the performance of the overall retrieval system.

Once the clusters are created, the only remaining step is to prepare them for query retrieval, such that, when a query descriptor is given, the retrieval system can decide quickly, to which cluster the query belongs. For this purpose, an SVM classifier is used. The classifier is trained on the clusters, where the members of a cluster are the training samples of a class. The class is assigned the same label

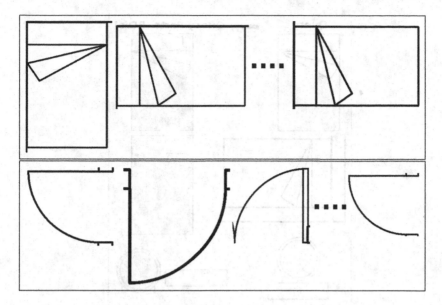

Fig. 2. Examples of the resulting clusters of ROIs (symbols parts). K-means clustering is applied on the descriptors of the ROIs to get such clusters.

of the cluster. The used SVM classifier is from the python MLPY package that implements libSVM [1], with a "linear" kernel type.

Alternatively, the means of the clusters can be used for comparisons with a query. However, it would be slower in case of a large number of classes. Moreover, a learning step in the retrieval framework could be useful in other datasets that might have labeled training data.

3.4 On-line Query Retrieval

A query symbol can be a segmented symbol from the symbol alphabet of the technical drawings, or can be a cropped region from a line drawing. A query that is cropped from a drawing may contain contextual noise around the symbol, such as connection lines or parts from neighboring symbols. The first step to deal with a query, is to extract its regions of interest using the same method discussed in Subsect. 3.1. The contextual noise around a query will not be parts of the interest regions. After that, a descriptor is computed from each region of a query as explained in Subsect. 3.2. Figure 3 shows the extracted regions of interest for different queries. Extracting the regions and computing the descriptors of the query do not consume much time as a query is usually very small compared to a complete line drawing.

Finally, the regions are classified by the trained SVM classifier. The similar regions from all the drawings are retrieved from the cluster that has the same label. If a query symbol consists only of one region, then no further steps are required. For multi-region queries, a voting procedure or a spatial verification

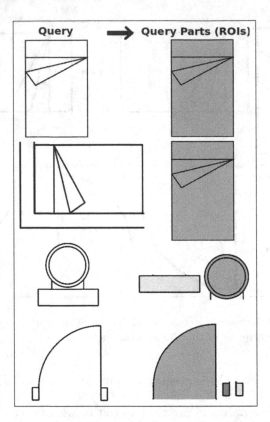

Fig. 3. The left column shows examples of the used query symbols. The second symbol in that column is a cropped symbol from a line drawing, the rest are segmented symbols from the alphabet. The right column shows the extracted regions of interest (ROIs) from the queries on the left.

step can be applied to retrieved regions from different clusters. We have presented a spatial verification step in our recent work in [17] within a geometric-based symbol retrieval system. Such steps can be added to the approach presented in this paper to improve the precision.

4 Performance Evaluation

The database we use for evaluation has 300 images of architectural floor plans. The images are a subset of the graphics recognition database called "Sesyd". The database is publicly available[1], and it contains different types of technical line drawings. The ground truth is also provided with the database. The ground truth contains information (label and bounding box location) of each symbol in all the drawings.

---

[1] http://mathieu.delalandre.free.fr/projects/sesyd/index.html

The generation of the database is described in [3,4]. The images of the database are synthetic clean images of line drawings that imitate real complete floor plans with sizes between 2M to 7M pixels. Different subsets of this database have been used for evaluation of symbol spotting systems in [14,18]. The GREC-2011 symbol spotting contest[2] [20] used a set of images very similar to the images of the Sesyd database, as the images of the contest were generated using the same system of [3,4].

The recall and precision measures are used to evaluate the retrieval results of the proposed approach as follows. If the bounding box of a retrieved region contains at least 75 % of an instance of the query symbol (or a query region), this is counted as a true positive, otherwise, it is a false positive. Figure 4 shows the recall-precision curve of the retrieval results. Each value on the curve is the average of the recall-precision values obtained for different queries that have a total of 2249 instances in the database of the 300 line drawings.

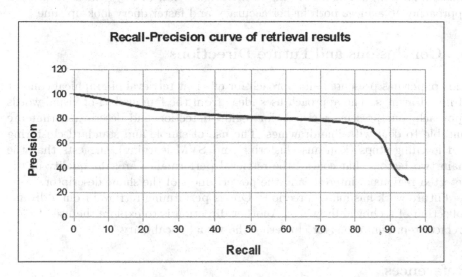

Fig. 4. Retrieval results of the proposed approach. A number of queries of different complexity levels are used, the queries have a total of 2249 instances in 300 line drawings. The shown curve is the average achieved performance of the queries.

The results in Fig. 4 show a range of good performance in terms of both recall and precision. We argue that this is due to the accuracy and invariance of the used region detection method, and also the shape descriptor. We have used simple standard clustering and learning steps (k-means clustering and SVM learning) that were used by other systems for the same purpose, this suggests that the main factors that control the retrieval performance are: the quality of the detected regions of interest, and the powerfulness of the shape descriptor.

---

[2] http://iapr-tc10.univ-lr.fr/index.php/symbolrecognitionhome

We would like to briefly report the performance of state-of-the-art approaches that follow the BoVW approach for symbol spotting and retrieval. Luqman et al. [14] used a number of query symbols and 200 line drawings from the same database used here. On this set of images, according to the recall-precision curve obtained from the authors of [14], at recall values between 60.0 % and 70.0 %, the precision was 60.0 %. For recall values above 85.0 %, the precision was below 50.0 %. Kong et al. [10] used a number of query symbols on 42 line drawings from a different database. According to the recall-precision curve in [10], at recall values between 50 % and 70 %, the precision was between 62 % and 42 % respectively.

The approach presented in this paper – although unimproved by spatial verification or post-processing – performs better than those state-of-the-art approaches. As we mentioned in Sect. 2, although our recent work in [17] outperforms the approach presented in this paper, it is rather time and memory consuming. It would be interesting to investigate how to merge ideas from both approaches to achieve both higher accuracy and faster query look-up time.

5   Conclusions and Future Directions

This paper has presented an approach for efficient retrieval of graphical content of line drawings. The approach uses ideas from the famous bag-of-visual-words approach, but presents methods for region detection and description that are suitable to deal with line drawings. The use of simple and standard clustering and learning steps (k-means clustering and SVM learning), suggests that the main two factors that control the retrieval performance are: the quality of the detected regions of interest, and the powerfulness of the shape descriptor.

Future work has many directions. One is performing retrieval from a diverse collection of technical drawings. Another direction is to explore the use of hierarchical representations for clustering the visual vocabulary.

References

1. Chang, C.C., Lin, C.J.: LIBSVM: a library for support vector machines. ACM Trans. Intell. Syst. Technol. **2**(3), 27:1–27:27 (2011)
2. Csurka, G., Dance, C.R., Fan, L., Willamowski, J., Bray, C.: Visual categorization with bags of keypoints. In: Workshop on Statistical Learning in Computer Vision (ECCV), pp. 1–22 (2004)
3. Delalandre, M., Pridmore, T.P., Valveny, E., Locteau, H., Trupin, É.: Building synthetic graphical documents for performance evaluation. In: Liu, W., Lladós, J., Ogier, J.-M. (eds.) GREC 2007. LNCS, vol. 5046, pp. 288–298. Springer, Heidelberg (2008)
4. Delalandre, M., Valveny, E., Pridmore, T., Karatzas, D.: Generation of synthetic documents for performance evaluation of symbol recognition and spotting systems. Int. J. Doc. Anal. Recogn. (IJDAR) **13**(3), 187–207 (2010)
5. Gersho, A., Gray, R.M.: Vector Quantization Signal Compression. Kluwer, Norwell (1991)

6. Honkela, T., Kohonen, T.: Kohonen network. Scholarpedia **2**(1), 1568 (2007)
7. Jacobs, D.W.: Robust and efficient detection of salient convex groups. Pattern Anal. Mach. Intell. (PAMI) **18**(1), 23–37 (1996)
8. Jacobs, D.W.: Grouping for recognition. Technical report, Cambridge, MA, USA (1989)
9. Jurie, F., Triggs, B.: Creating efficient codebooks for visual recognition. In: Proceedings of the Tenth IEEE International Conference on Computer Vision (ICCV'05), pp. 604–610 (2005)
10. Kong, X., Valveny, E., Snchez, G., Wenyin, L.: Symbol spotting using deformed blurred shape modeling with component indexing and voting scheme. In: Graphics Recognition Workshop (GREC), online proceedings (2011)
11. Linde, Y., Buzo, A., Gray, R.: An algorithm for vector quantizer design. IEEE Trans. Commun. **28**(1), 84–95 (1980)
12. Lloyd, S.P.: Least squares quantization in PCM. IEEE Trans. Inf. Theor. **28**, 129–137 (1982)
13. Lowe, D.G.: Object recognition from local scale-invariant features. In: Proceedings of the International Conference on Computer Vision, pp. 1150–1157 (1999)
14. Luqman, M.M., Brouard, T., Ramel, J., Llodos, J.: A content spotting system for line drawing graphic document images. In: International Conference on Pattern Recognition (ICPR), pp. 3420–3423 (2010)
15. Nayef, N., Breuel, T.M.: Building a symbol library from technical drawings by identifying repeating patterns. In: Kwon, Y.-B., Ogier, J.-M. (eds.) GREC 2011. LNCS, vol. 7423, pp. 69–78. Springer, Heidelberg (2013)
16. Nayef, N., Breuel, T.M.: Statistical grouping for segmenting symbols parts from line drawings, with application to symbol spotting. In: Proceedings of the 2011 International Conference on Document Analysis and Recognition (ICDAR), pp. 364–368 (2011)
17. Nayef, N., Breuel, T.M.: Efficient symbol retrieval by building a symbol index from a collection of line drawings. In: Document Recognition and Retrieval XX (DRR), vol. 8658. SPIE (2013)
18. Nguyen, T., Tabbone, S., Boucher, A.: A symbol spotting approach based on the vector model and a visual vocabulary. In: International Conference on Document Analysis and Recognition (ICDAR), pp. 708–712 (2009)
19. Sivic, J., Zisserman, A.: Video google: efficient visual search of videos. In: Ponce, J., Hebert, M., Schmid, C., Zisserman, A. (eds.) Toward Category-Level Object Recognition. LNCS, vol. 4170, pp. 127–144. Springer, Heidelberg (2006)
20. Valveny, E., Delalandre, M., Raveaux, R., Lamiroy, B.: Report on the symbol recognition and spotting contest. In: Kwon, Y.-B., Ogier, J.-M. (eds.) GREC 2011. LNCS, vol. 7423, pp. 198–207. Springer, Heidelberg (2013)
21. Yang, S.: Symbol recognition via statistical integration of pixel-level constraint histograms: a new descriptor. Pattern Anal. Mach. Intell. (PAMI) **27**(2), 278–281 (2005)

Graphics Recognition in Context

Adaptive Contour Classification of Comics Speech Balloons

Christophe Rigaud[1,2]($\boxtimes$), Dimosthenis Karatzas[2], Jean-Christophe Burie[1],
and Jean-Marc Ogier[1]

[1] Laboratory L3i, University of La Rochelle,
Avenue Michel Crépeau, 17042 La Rochelle, France
{christophe.rigaud,jcburie,jmogier}@univ-lr.fr
[2] Computer Vision Center, Universitat Autònoma de Barcelona,
08193 Bellaterra (Barcelona), Spain
dimos@cvc.uab.es

Abstract. Comic books digitization combined with subsequent comic book understanding give rise to a variety of new applications, including content reflowing, mobile reading and multi-modal search. Document understanding in this domain is challenging as comics are semi-structured documents, with semantic information shared between the graphical and textual parts. Speech balloon contour analysis reveals the speech tone which is an essential step towards a fully automatic comics understanding. In this paper we present the first approach for classifying speech balloon in scanned comic books where we separate and analyze their contour variations to classify them as "smooth" (normal speech), "wavy" (thought) or "zigzag" (exclamation). The experiments show a global accuracy classification of 85.2 % on a wide variety of balloons from the eBDtheque dataset.

Keywords: Image processing · Contour/shape separation · Contour classification

1 Introduction

Comic books are a widespread cultural expression and are commonly accepted as the "ninth art". Comics are a hybrid medium, combining textual and visual information in order to convey their narrative. Digitization combined with subsequent document understanding of comic books is therefore of interest, both in order to add value to existing paper-based comic heritage, but also to bridge the gap between the paper and electronic comic media.

In comics content understanding, speech balloons (or speech bubbles) present a lot of interest since they are the link between the textual content and the person providing two major pieces of information, the location of the speaker (balloon tail), and the speech tone according to the different patterns which are along the contour of the balloon. If we are able to automatically determine

© Springer-Verlag Berlin Heidelberg 2014
B. Lamiroy and J.-M. Ogier (Eds.): GREC 2013, LNCS 8746, pp. 53–62, 2014.
DOI: 10.1007/978-3-662-44854-0_5

which balloons are for normal speech, though and exclamation then we will make progress in comics content understanding. From our knowledge, speech balloon classification has not been studied before and is related to the fields of shape and contour classification in planar images.

Shape classification is a well developed field, especially in a template matching context. Three well know methods are Curvature Scale Space (CSS) [1], Fourier Descriptor [23] and Invariant Moments [9]. A recent work [14] explains that CSS is more appropriate for shapes containing a high number of inflections as marine animals [1]. Apart for document understanding, shape classification was also studied for image retrieval such as marine creature [16], leaves [22], illicit tablet [14], anthropology [10] and visual shape descriptor [4]. A good shape representation overviews are given by [21, 24]. Nevertheless, they are not discriminant enough for our purpose because speech balloon are most of the time compact and symmetric and hand drawn.

In the literature, contour classification is strongly related to shape classification purposes [13, 20]. It has been applied for video [3, 11, 18], trademark retrieval [12], speech recognition [6]. Also, wavelet decomposition [5] and invariant moment [17].

Regarding the speech balloons, shape and contour contain different type of information. Depending on the style of the comics and the structure of the panel, the author makes the shape similar to rectangle, square, circle, oval or non geometric which provide very few information about the story. The shape does not provide a lot of information about how the text is spoken contrary to the contour. In fact, there are features throughout the contour edge that qualify the contained text (see Fig. 1). We propose to analyse the contour to classify speech balloons.

Speech balloon classification is a real challenge if we consider a lot of different comics styles. First, each author has his own representation of the speech sounds. Second, the reader interpretation is subjective (each balloon style is interpreted in comparison to the already read balloon styles). For those reasons, it is really hard to directly define the purpose (e.g. dialog, thought, exclamation) of a speech balloon without knowing its context in the story. In fact, the context is defined by both graphic (e.g. other strokes, protagonists personality) and textual (e.g. vocabulary, punctuation) elements. For instance, Fig. 1 shows six different speech balloon comics styles from the eBDtheque dataset [7] where we can see the difficulty to assign one class for each balloon without knowing others balloon shapes and the contained text.

Note, speech balloon classification is complementary to speech balloon detection that has already been studied using white connected component extraction and filtering [2, 8] or active contour model [19].

The next section details the balloon shape/contour information separation, description and classification. Section 3 evaluates the proposed method by showing the results of speech balloon classification. Finally, Sects. 4 and 5 discuss and conclude this work.

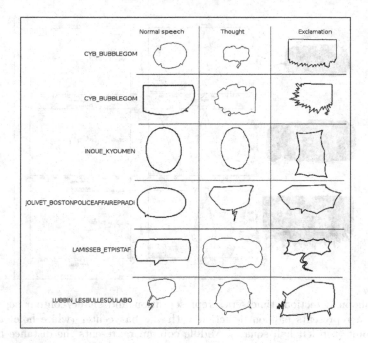

Fig. 1. Examples of speech balloons from 6 comics albums (rows) that represent 3 different expressions (columns) from the eBDtheque dataset [7].

2   Proposed Method

The input of the proposed method is a pixel-level balloon contour detection that can comes from any of the reviewed methods in the literature (e.g. [2,8,19]). In this section we detail how we perform the shape and contour separation, the contour description and finally the classification using a Bayesian classifier.

2.1   Shape/Contour Separation

As introduced in Sect. 1, the discriminant information for speech balloon classi-fication is not in the global shape but in the contour variations.

First, we propose to represent the speech balloon as a time series (one dimen-sional signal over 360°) which corresponds to the distance in number of pixels between the balloon barycentre and the contour points.

Second, we perform a shape/contour separation to be able to analyse only the contour variation (including the balloon tail). We approximate the global shape s by smoothing the original signal o using a sliding window of size M and substracting the result from the original signal to preserve only the contour information c independently from the shape: $c = o - s$. The smoothed contour s is a centered local average of o, see Eq. 1. Examples are given in Fig. 2.

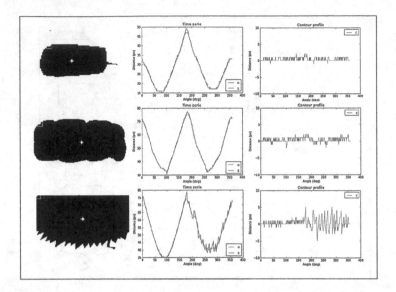

Fig. 2. Balloon detection, time series representation and shape/contour separation. Left column represents balloon detection with the barycenter (white hole) and the starting point (top left half square). Middle column represents the distance between the barycenter and the balloon boundary over 360° (clockwise) where the original signal o is in blue and the smoothed signal s in red. Right column is the difference between s and o.

$$s(o) = \frac{1}{M} * \sum_{-M/2}^{+M/2} o \tag{1}$$

where M is the window size.

2.2   Contour Description

Contour description encodes the contour variations relatively to the balloons size to be invariant to page format and definition. The level of variation can be computed from different features, the main difficulty is to be invariant to the comics drawing diversity. In this study, we describe the contour signal c by using a variance-based two dimensional descriptor, more precisely the standard deviation σ. The variance or the standard deviation have the advantage to be simple and generic at describing any data distribution by measuring the data dispersion which is what we need if we aim at measuring the difference of dispersion between the original and the smoothed contours. In order to be invariant to the image definition and scale, we normalize each feature of the descriptor by the original signal average $\bar{o}$ (average radius).

The first dimension aims to differentiates contours which have a high variations ("zigzag" type) from the others ("wavy" and "smooth" types). The second dimension aims to discriminate "wavy" and "smooth" types according to the standard deviation of the superior and inferior signal part from the average $\bar{c}$. For instance, if a contour has a higher standard deviation in the bellow signal part than the above signal part (according to the average $\bar{c}$) then the contour has more peaks in the direction of its barycenter than the opposite, which is not a characteristic of the "smooth" type but "wavy".

The first feature f_1 consists in measuring the standard deviation σ_c of the contour signal c normalized by the original signal average $\bar{o}$, see Eq. 2.

In order to measure the second feature f_2, we split the contour signal c in two signals c_{pos} and c_{neg} which correspond to the signal parts that are strictly above and bellow the average $\bar{c}$ (see Fig. 3) and then we measure the standard deviation differences, see Eq. 3.

$$f_1 = \frac{\sigma_c}{\bar{o}} \qquad (2)$$

where f_1 is the feature one, σ_c the contour standard deviation normalized by $\bar{o}$ the average of the signal o.

$$f_2 = \frac{\sigma_{neg} - \sigma_{pos}}{\bar{o}} \qquad (3)$$

where f_2 is the feature two, σ_{pos} and σ_{neg} are the standard deviations of the signals c_{pos} and c_{neg} respectively. The difference is normalized by $\bar{o}$.

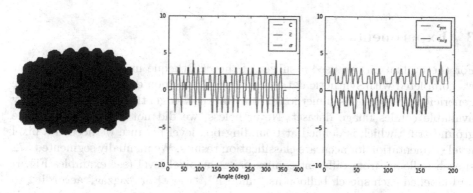

Fig. 3. Contour signal decomposition. Left part is the concerned speech balloon, middle part is its contour profile and right part is the positive and negative decomposition according to the contour average $\bar{c}$. Both signal have not the same length because we ignore values that are equal to the average value $\bar{c}$ in order to not bias the standard deviation.

2.3   Contour Classification

Contour classification is performed according to the selected contour descriptor (see Sect. 2.2) by using a naive Bayesian Classifier [15]. The reason why we chose this classifier is because it requires a small amount of training data. Let a label set $L = (l_1, l_2, l_3)$ represent the three contour classes "smooth", "wavy" and "zigzag". Given a new unlabelled contour c described by its descriptor $D = (f_1, f_2)$, the naive Bayes approach assigns D to a class l_{MAP} as follow:

$$l_{MAP} = \text{argmax}_l P(l|D) = \text{argmax}_l \frac{P(l)P(D|l)}{P(D)} = \text{argmax}_l P(l)P(D|l) \quad (4)$$

where $P(l)$ is the *a priori* probability of class l and $P(D|l)$ is the conditional probability of a given descriptor D to be in the class l. This conditional probability follows a Gaussian distribution for which we learn the parameters during the training step. An example of the Gaussian distribution parameters is given Table 1. Those parameters can be used for other dataset containing similar images without the need to re-train the classifier.

Table 1. Example of Gaussian distribution parameters of feature f_1 and f_2.

	Smooth		Wavy		Zigzag	
	μ	σ	μ	σ	μ	σ
Feature f_1	0.019	0.012	0.042	0.020	0.148	0.118
Feature f_2	−0.004	0.006	0.007	0.010	−0.017	0.023

3   Experiments

For the evaluation, we used a subset of the eBDtheque image dataset [7] that we completed with synthetic data to enlarge the balloon diversity and show the genericity of the proposed method. From our knowledge, this is the only publicly available comics image dataset. Nevertheless, we did not use the eBDtheque ground truth which is defined at bounding box level because we needed a pixel level segmentation for accurate classification results. We manually segmented 372 speech balloons from different comics pages at pixel level (see examples Fig. 4) and labelled each speech balloon as "smooth", "wavy" or "zigzag" according to the features that compose their contour edge (see Sect. 2.2). The ground truth is composed by 68 %, 18.3 % and 13.7 % speech balloons of type "smooth", "wavy" and "zigzag" respectively. This unbalanced repartition reflects the usual speech balloon repartition in comics. The data will be included in the next version of the eBDtheque dataset ground truth.

For the shape/contour separation part (Sect. 2.1) we first cast the original signal o into 360 values and then we use a window of size $M = 20$ according to the parameter validation Table 2 (maximum average and global accuracy).

We evaluated our method based on a one-versus-all scenario, classification results are presented in Table 3 for different descriptors. First we show the effect

Fig. 4. Examples of speech balloons pixel level segmentation.

Table 2. Validation of parameter M for $D = (f_1, f_2)$ scenario.

	Accuracy per class (%)				
	Smooth	Wavy	Zigzag	Average	Global
$M = 10$	80.63	**70.58**	58.80	70.00	75.8
$M = 20$	**89.30**	69.1	86.20	**81.53**	**85.2**
$M = 30$	88.53	67.64	**86.25**	80.81	84.4
$M = 40$	87.35	61.76	82.35	77.15	81.99
$M = 50$	79.05	63.23	80.39	74.22	76.34

of the two features f_1 and f_2 separately with without a priori information $P(l_1) = P(l_2) = P(l_3)$ and then using the prior probabilities about the classes repartition in the testing set $P(l_1) = 0.68, P(l_2) = 0.183$ and $P(l_3) = 0.137$. We detailed our best results in the confusion matrix Table 4. All the material for reproducing and comparing the results presented in this paper are publicly available upon request and online at http://ebdtheque.univ-lr.fr/references/.

Table 3. Classification result accuracy for different descriptor configuration.

	Accuracy per class (%)				
	Smooth	Wavy	Zigzag	Average	Global
$D = (f_1)$	86.5	48.5	70.6	68.5	77.4
$D = (f_2)$	89.3	69.1	86.2	81.5	85.2
$D = (f_1, f_2)$	89.3	**69.1**	**86.2**	**81.5**	**85.2**
$D = (f_1, f_2) + priors$	**93.3**	55.9	82.4	77.2	84.9

The different accuracy results Table 3 show that the second feature f_2 is more discriminant than the first one f_1 and their combination does not exceed the second itself. Adding the prior knowledge about the testing classes repartition improves the "smooth" class only and decrease the two others. The global accuracy represents the number of good classification divided by the number of

Table 4. Classification confusion matrix.

		Classification		
		Smooth	Wavy	Zigzag
Ground truth	**Smooth**	227	21	5
	Wavy	17	47	4
	Zigzag	4	3	44

element to classify independently from the class. The confusion matrix Table 4 shows good classification results for the "zigzag" class even for cases that are quite different in terms of drawing styles (see Fig. 5) and sources (real and synthetic). Concerning the "smooth" and "wavy" classes, some speech balloons are very hard to classify out of context causing confusion (see Fig. 6). Also, the tail of the balloon creates some noise and the radius average ($\bar{o}$) we use to normalize the descriptor features may not be appropriate for elongated balloons.

Fig. 5. Correct classification examples for "zigzag" (top) and "smooth" classes (bottom).

Fig. 6. Wrong classification examples which have been classified as "smooth" instead of "wavy" in the first row and "wavy" instead of "smooth" in the second row.

4   Discussion

The proposed method covers the comics balloon classification in general accept for open balloons. However, in this particular case, we can probably use extra features (e.g. tail type recognition, language analysis) to get more information about the text tone. Also, other distortion measures have to be investigated, especially for "wavy" contours that are the most difficult contour to classify using the proposed method. Concerning the tail region, we believe that it creates noise that confuse the classification. Its removal would improve the accuracy of the classification. Speech balloon classification can be improved by analysing the nature of the contained text using natural language analysis. In a future work, this contour classification will be completed by a semantic analysis to give a meaning to each class given a particular album.

5   Conclusion

In this paper we propose a contour classification method for comics speech balloons based on balloon shape approximation, contour time series extraction and description. The evaluation section shows a global accuracy of 85.2 % for which the defined "smooth" and "zigzag" speech balloons are well classified (more than 85 %) but there is room for improvement concerning the "wavy" balloons. From our knowledge, this is the first work about speech balloon classification in the literature that will be continued to handle more comics specificities until having a complete comics understanding framework able to make the link between texts, balloons and speakers.

Acknowledgment. This work was supported by the European Doctorate founds of the University of La Rochelle, the European Regional Development Funds, the region Poitou-Charentes (France), the General Council of Charente Maritime (France), the town of La Rochelle (France) and the Spanish research projects TIN2011-24631, RYC-2009-05031. The authors would like to thanks Audrey Adam for her tedious work on the construction of the pixel level ground truth.

References

1. Abbasi, S., Mokhtarian, F., Kittler, J.: Curvature scale space image in shape similarity retrieval. Multimedia Syst. **7**(6), 467–476 (1999)
2. Arai, K., Tolle, H.: Method for real time text extraction of digital manga comic. Int. J. Image Process. (IJIP) **4**(6), 669–676 (2011)
3. Bader, T., Räpple, R., Beyerer, J.: Fast invariant contour-based classification of hand symbols for HCI. In: Jiang, X., Petkov, N. (eds.) CAIP 2009. LNCS, vol. 5702, pp. 689–696. Springer, Heidelberg (2009)
4. Bober, M.: Mpeg-7 visual shape descriptors. IEEE Trans. Circ. Syst. **11**(6), 716–719 (2001)
5. Cenkery, C.: Wavelet contour classification. In: Proceedings of the 20th Workshop of the Austrian Association for Pattern Recognition (OAGM/AAPR) on Pattern Recognition, 1996, Leibnitz, Austria, pp. 263–271. R. Oldenbourg Verlag GmbH, Munich, Germany (1996)

6. Grigoriu, A., Vonwiller, J., King, R.: An automatic intonation tone contour labelling and classification algorithm. In: 1994 IEEE International Conference on Acoustics, Speech, and Signal Processing, ICASSP-94, vol. 2, pp. II-181. IEEE (1994)
7. Guérin, C., Rigaud, C., Mercier, A., et al.: eBDtheque: a representative database of comics. In: Proceedings of International Conference on Document Analysis and Recognition (ICDAR), Washington DC (2013)
8. Ho, A.K.N., Burie, J.C., Ogier, J.M.: Panel and Speech Balloon Extraction from Comic Books. In: 2012 10th IAPR International Workshop on Document Analysis Systems, pp. 424–428, Mar 2012
9. Hu, M.K.: Visual pattern recognition by moment invariants. IRE Trans. Inf. Theory **8**(2), 179–187 (1962)
10. Keogh, E., Wei, L., Xi, X., Hee Lee, S., Vlachos, M.: Lb keogh supports exact indexing of shapes under rotation invariance with arbitrary representations and distance measures. In: VLDB, pp. 882–893 (2006)
11. Kühne, G., Richter, S., Beier, M.: Motion-based segmentation and contour-based classification of video objects. In: Proceedings of the Ninth ACM International Conference on Multimedia, pp. 41–50. ACM (2001)
12. Leung, W.H., Chen, T.: Trademark retrieval using contour-skeleton stroke classification. In: Proceedings of the 2002 IEEE International Conference on Multimedia and Expo, ICME'02, vol. 2, pp. 517–520. IEEE (2002)
13. Liu, H.C., Srinath, M.D.: Partial shape classification using contour matching in distance transformation. IEEE Trans. Pattern Anal. Mach. Intell. **12**(11), 1072–1079 (1990)
14. Lopatka, M., Houten, W.V.: Science and justice automated shape annotation for illicit tablet preparations: a contour angle based classification from digital images. Sci. Justice **53**(1), 60–66 (2013)
15. Mitchell, T.M.: Mach. Learn., 1st edn. McGraw-Hill Inc., New York (1997)
16. Mokhtarian, F., Abbasi, S.: Shape similarity retrieval under affine transforms. Pattern Recogn. **35**(1), 31–41 (2002). doi:10.1016/S0031-3203(01)00040-1
17. Mukundan, R., Ramakrishnan, K.: Moment Functions in Image Analysis: Theory and Applications, vol. 100. World Scientific, Singapore (1998)
18. Richter, S., Kühne, G., Schuster, O.: Contour-based classification of video objects. In: Proceedings of SPIE, vol. 4315, p. 608 (2001)
19. Rigaud, C., Karatzas, D., Van de Weijer, J., Burie, J.C., Ogier, J.M.: An active contour model for speech balloon detection in comics. In: Proceedings of the 12th International Conference on Document Analysis and Recognition (ICDAR). IEEE (2013)
20. Sun, K.B., Super, B.J.: Classification of contour shapes using class segment sets. In: IEEE Computer Society Conference on Computer Vision and Pattern Recognition, CVPR 2005, vol. 2, pp. 727–733. IEEE (2005)
21. Veltkamp, R.C., Tanase, M.: Content-based image retrieval systems: A survey. Technical report (2000)
22. Wang, Z., Chi, Z., Feng, D.: Shape based leaf image retrieval. IEEE Proc. Vis. Image Signal Process. **150**(1), 34–43 (2003)
23. Zahn, C.T., Roskies, R.Z.: Fourier descriptors for plane closed curves. IEEE Trans. Comput. **c–21**(3), 269–281 (1972)
24. Zhang, D., Lu, G.: Review of shape representation and description techniques. PR **37**(1), 1–19 (2004)

Modified Weighted Direction Index Histogram Method for Schema Recognition

Hiroshi Kajiwara[1], Hiroharu Kawanaka[1(✉)], Koji Yamamoto[2],
Haruhiko Takase[1], and Shinji Tsuruoka[1]

[1] Mie University, 1577 Kurima-machiya, Tsu, Mie 514-8507, Japan
kawanaka@elec.mie-u.ac.jp
http://www.ip.elec.mie-u.ac.jp/~kawanaka/
[2] Suzuka University of Medical Science, 1001-1 Kishioka,
Suzuka, Mie 510-0293, Japan

Abstract. Recently, many clinical documents have been computerized because of diffusion of Hospital Information Systems (HIS). On the other hand, a large amount of paper-based documents are not used effectively, and these are now still archived as paper documents in hospitals. The authors proposed document image recognition methods for medical/clinical document retrieval. We also discussed the recognition method for schema (medical line drawing) images in the document, because these had key information for document retrieval. However, annotations added to the schema made the feature vector change drastically, as a result the recognition accuracy was reduced. This paper discussed a schema recognition method considering annotations. Actual schema images used in the hospital were employed as experimental materials. We confirmed that the recognition accuracy of the proposed method was improved to 98.52 %.

Keywords: Schema recognition · Medical/clinical document retrieval · Weighted direction index histogram · Modified bayesian discriminant function

1 Introduction

Recently, many information systems for medical/clinical use have been developed and employed in hospitals [1,2]. For example, literature [1] shows the system called Health Evaluation through Logical Processing, and it provides clinical/hospital administration and financial services. Kapoor *et al.* built a patient information system for healthcare networks. By spreading of such systems, many researches on medical informatics are also reported [3,4]. Savova *et al.* discuss the text analysis and knowledge extraction system in literature [3]. Some researchers propose the roadmap to develop a future medical/clinical information systems and discuss future research directions on medical informatics [5–7]. By developing of medical/clinical information systems and research outcomes, computerization

© Springer-Verlag Berlin Heidelberg 2014
B. Lamiroy and J.-M. Ogier (Eds.): GREC 2013, LNCS 8746, pp. 63–73, 2014.
DOI: 10.1007/978-3-662-44854-0_6

of medical/clinical procedures has progressed greatly in recent years. On the other hand, a large amount of paper-based clinical documents generated before computerization are still archived. These documents are good sources for clinical researches and educations because they have long histories of medical/clinical examinations of each patient.

The authors have been discussing document analysis methods for clinical documents and their applications [8–10]. For example, we developed a system to convert them to XML data with search tags considering their contents [8,9]. In literature [10], we also discussed the "schema" recognition method. A schema is a kind of line drawings to show affected parts of the body and their conditions, thus it also has key information for clinical document retrieval. The literature proposed the recognition method using Weighted Direction Index Histogram Method (WDIHM) and Modified Bayesian Discrimination Function (MBDF) [11–13]. By using the method, more than 90 % of the schemas could be recognized correctly and it was shown that they would be effective keys for clinical document retrieval. However, the method could not recognize them correctly when many or large annotations were added to the schema. Actually, there are a lot of such schemas in the archived documents, and if the problem is solved, they would be also key information.

In this paper, we discuss a schema recognition method considering annotations to improve recognition accuracy of the conventional method. In the proposed method, annotations in the schema image are automatically detected and a feature vector is generated considering them. Evaluation experiments using actual schemas are conducted to discuss the effectiveness of the proposed method. We also show future plans as well as the advantages and problems of the proposed method.

2   Materials

2.1   Schemas

Figure 1 shows an example of clinical documents with a schema. Generally, schema models body sites such as skeletons, internal organs and so on. Medical doctors often use them instead of sketches to make medical documents such as medical records, discharge summaries and clinical reports. For example, Fig. 1 shows a patient's progress note and a physical examination report, respectively [14,15]. In Fig. 1(a), there is a chest schema in the document and the mark and comment, which are usually called "annotations", are usually added by medical doctors for explanation. In this case, the lower lobe of the left lung is blacked out and a simple Japanese comment, which means "shadow" in English, is added besides the mark. This annotation means that there is an X-Ray shadow on the lower lobe of left lung. Generally, the employed schemas and medical terms for annotations heavily depend on disease types and conditions, thus they would be key information for document retrieval. Our goal is to recognize schemas and annotations correctly and generate search tags shown in Fig. 2.

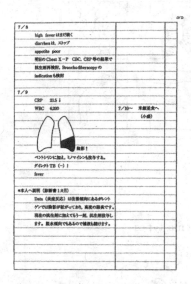
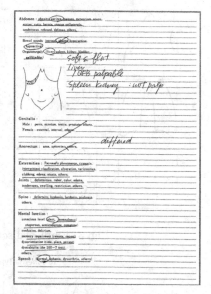

(a) Progress Report (Printed)   (b) Physical Examination (Handwritten)

Fig. 1. Examples of clinical documents with schema

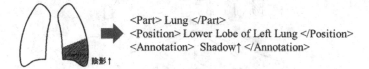

<Part> Lung </Part>
<Position> Lower Lobe of Left Lung </Position>
<Annotation> Shadow↑ </Annotation>

Fig. 2. Schema with annotation and generated XML

2.2 Employed Schemas

In this paper, we employed actual schema images as experimental materials. In many hospitals, Hospital Information Systems are now running and more than 100 kinds of schemas are available on the system. Of course, these schemas were also used for old medical/clinical documents before the introduction of the HIS. These documents are not still scanned and computerized even if they are typed documents. In addition, we have many handwritten medical/clinical documents with schemas as well as printed ones. These documents should also be scanned and archived as electrical data for document retrieval.

We used 10 kinds of schemas shown in Fig. 3, which were typical and frequently used in hospitals. Fifty annotations were added to each schema by 10 students. In this process, we showed examples of schema images with annotations added by medical doctors to them first, and then various annotations were added based on the examples by them. Of course, all of them do not know the detail of recognition algorithm and not attend this project. Next, to discuss robustness of

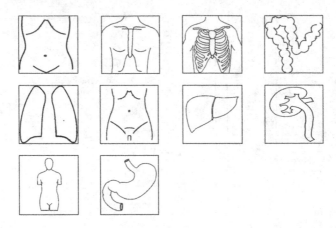

Fig. 3. Employed schema types

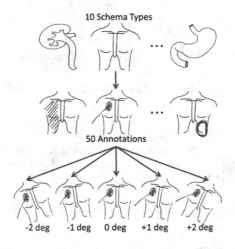

Fig. 4. Preparation of experimental materials

the proposed method, the obtained images were rotated $-2, -1, 1$ and 2 degrees, respectively (Fig. 4). The number of schema images for experiments is 2500.

3   Problems of WDIHM in Schema Recognition

As feature extraction method, this paper employs Weighted Direction Index Histogram Method (WDIHM) in the conventional method [10]. Figure 5 illustrates the rough image of WDIHM. In the method, the input schema image is divided into 7×7 sub-regions first. After this, the contour of the image is traced and a direction index histogram in each sub-region is then generated using chain codes. The histogram reflects contour shape of the schema in each sub-region.

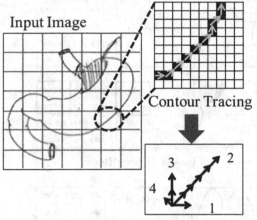

Fig. 5. Rough image of weighted direction index histogram method

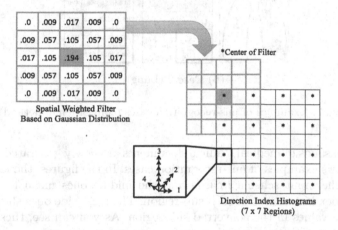

Fig. 6. Spatial weighted filter based on Gaussian distribution

After this, the spatial weighted filter based on Gaussian distribution is applied to the histograms to reduce the dimension of feature vectors. Figure 6 shows the outline of the Gaussian filter and its application. In this process, the center of the filter is put on the marked regions and then the weighted direction index histograms are calculated by convolution operation. The parameters of the filter are determined based on literature [12]. By this processing, these sub-regions are converted to 16 (4×4) sub-regions. Finally, a feature vector for recognition is generated by using the values of the histograms.

By using Weighted Direction Index Histogram Method and Modified Bayes Discriminant Function, we could obtain more than 90 % recognition accuracy. However, the obtained recognition accuracy is not enough for practical use,

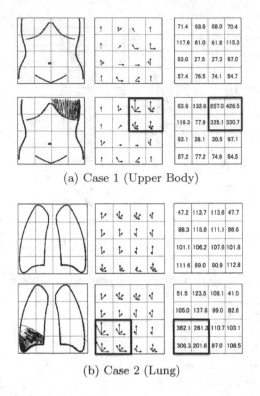

(a) Case 1 (Upper Body)

(b) Case 2 (Lung)

Fig. 7. Examples of mis-recognition cases (conventional method)

because thousands of medical/clinical documents are newly generated every day. Figure 7 shows examples of mis-recognition cases. In the figures, the left side figures show the input schema images and the middle ones mean the obtained direction index histograms in each sub-region. The right side ones show the sum of histogram values in the converted sub-region. As you can see, these schemas have large annotations and the contour shapes of them have been drastically changed due to the annotations. This also makes the histogram values change drastically, as a result, the coefficients of the feature vector are changed compared with those of the other vectors in the same category. This is the reason for the mis-recognition. Of course, the conventional method cannot also recognize schemas with many annotations correctly because of the same reason. To solve the problem, the conventional schema recognition method should be improved.

4   Revised Weighted Direction Index Histogram Method for Schema Recognition Considering Annotations

4.1   Pre-processing

Basically, the flow of the proposed method is the same as that of the conventional method. The proposed method mainly consists of two phases, the first one is

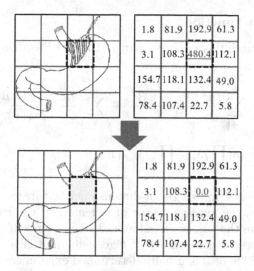

Fig. 8. Outline of the revised WDIH method

generation of recognition dictionary, and the second one is schema recognition. First, we apply pre-processing, *e.g.* binarization, noise reduction and normalization, to all scanned schema images. In this method, we employ the Otsu's method as the binarization [16]. To reduce salt and pepper noises, median filters are applied to them. After the processing, the sizes of the images are changed to 350×350 pixels to generate normalized images.

4.2 Feature Extraction Considering Annotations

As stated in Sect. 3, annotations make the feature vector change drastically because the feature vector is generated based on information of contours. To prevent the problem and improve recognition accuracy, this paper revises the conventional feature extraction method using WDIH.

Figure 8 shows the outline of the revised feature extraction method. As you can see, the sum value in the region with the annotation is quite larger than those of others. On the other hand, there is no annotation in the other regions and the coefficients of the feature vector corresponding to such regions are not changed drastically. In the proposed method, N_z regions are selected based on the sum of the histogram values in each region, and then all histogram values in the selected regions are set to zero. In this paper, the above procedure is applied to all schema images to make feature vectors, and the generated vectors are used to make a recognition dictionary. In this method, a co-variance matrix among each category is calculated using the feature vectors, and it is also used for recognition. By using this method, it is expected that the annotation does not change the coefficients of feature vector drastically. Consequently, the recognition accuracy would be improved.

4.3 Discriminant Function

For schema recognition, this paper employs Modified Bays Discriminant Function (MBDF) [11,12].

$$d^l(x) = \sum_{i=1}^{k} \frac{\{_l\varphi_i{}^t (x -_l \mu)\}^2}{_l\lambda_i} + \sum_{i=k+1}^{n} \frac{\{_l\varphi_i{}^t (x -_l \mu)\}^2}{_l\lambda_{k+1}}$$
$$+ ln(\prod_{i=1}^{k} {}_l\lambda_i \cdot \prod_{i=k+1}^{n} {}_l\lambda_{k+1}) \tag{1}$$

In the above formula, x means the n-dimensional feature vector of the input schema, and $_l\mu$ does the average vector of schema l in the recognition dictionary. $_l\lambda_i$, and $_l\varphi_i$ are the i-th eigen value and eigen vector of schema l, respectively. k is the highest order number of eigenvalue and engen vectors used in the function. The value of k is usually determined experimentally ($1 \leq k \leq n$). Modified Bayesian Discrimination Function calculates dissimilarity between the input image and an original schema image in the dictionary. As a recognition result, this method outputs the schema type with the smallest dissimilarity. In this paper, the parameters of the discriminant function were decided preliminary based on literature [11,12].

5 Experimental Results and Discussions

In the evaluation experiments, 5 schema images were picked up from them as testing images, and others, *i.e.* 2495 images, were used to make a recognition dictionary. This procedure was repeatedly applied to them until all input images are recognized. To discuss the relationship between recognition accuracy and the number of eliminating regions (N_z), we conducted experiments by changing N_z from 0 to 10. We also discussed the number of sub-regions for generating feature vector (N_r). The value of N_r was set to 25 (5×5), 36 (6×6) and 49 (7×7) in the experiments.

Table 1 shows the obtained results. The bold and underlined values mean the highest recognition accuracy in each N_r. In the case N_z is 0 and N_r is 16, the obtained recognition accuracy is equivalent to that of the conventional method because a feature vector is generated by using all histograms. As you can see, this table shows that the proposed method improved recognition accuracy. This table also indicates that recognition accuracy was improved by segmenting the input image into smaller sub-regions. As a result of the experiments, we obtained the highest recognition accuracy (98.52 %) when N_r was 36 and 49. The obtained accuracy was enough for practical use in hospitals.

Figure 9 shows the highest recognition accuracy of the proposed method and the conventional method in each N_r. This graph means that the recognition accuracy of the proposed method was significantly higher than that of the conventional method (*p value* < 0.01). When the recognition rate was the highest, the proposed method recognized the schemas shown in Fig. 7 correctly. However, the proposed method could not recognize any schemas correctly.

Figure 10 shows examples of mis-recognition cases. In the case of Fig. 10(a), the proposed method could not eliminated the annotation completely, and then some coefficients of the feature vector were drastically changed. In the case of (b), the size of the annotation was not so large, but it had a large lead line in the schema area. As a result, the shape of the schema was drastically changed compared with those of schemas in the recognition dictionary due to the lead line. The proposed method employs only the histogram values to detect annotations in the schema. This strategy is so simple, but does not work well in such cases. As other approaches, methods considering density and/or texture information might be effective. However, these methods are almost equivalent to the proposed

Table 1. Experimental results (recognition rate)

N_z	# of Sub-Regions (N_r)			
	16 (4×4)	25 (5×5)	36 (6×6)	49 (7×7)
0	93.04%	96.36%	95.84%	96.72%
1	96.20%	97.04%	97.20%	97.48%
2	96.52%	97.40%	98.08%	98.48%
3	**96.72%**	97.28%	98.24%	**98.52%**
4	96.20%	**97.48%**	98.36%	**98.52%**
5	96.20%	98%	98.26%	**98.52%**
6	96.20%	96.76%	**98.52%**	98.12%
7	96.20%	96.44%	97.68%	97.76%
8	96.20%	96.04%	97.48%	97.68%
9	96.20%	94.88%	97.28%	97.52%
10	96.20%	94.32%	96.44%	97.16%

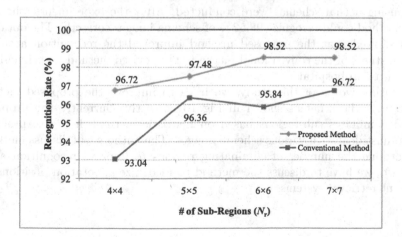

Fig. 9. Recognition accuracies of proposed method and conventional method

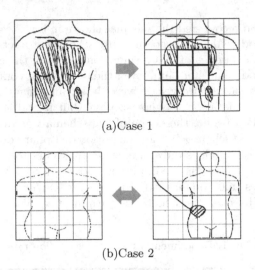

(a)Case 1

(b)Case 2

Fig. 10. Examples of mis-recognition cases (proposed method)

method essentially, because direction index histogram is obtained by using the information of contours and it also reflects the texture complexity in each region. More investigations would be required to solve the problems and improve the performance of the proposed method.

6   Conclusion

In this paper, we proposed the schema recognition method considering annotations for medical/clinical document retrieval systems. We revised the conventional feature extraction method using WDIH. This paper also discussed the number of sub-regions for generating feature vector. Some evaluation experiments using actual schemas were conducted. After the experiments, the proposed method could recognize 98.52 % of schema images correctly. The obtained results showed that the proposed method improved the recognition accuracy and robustness of the conventional method. The revised method was enough for practical use in hospitals.

As future works of this study, we have to improve the proposed method to recognize the schemas shown in Fig. 10 correctly. Currently the proposed method eliminates sub-regions based on heuristic method, however, practical system must deal with various schema images. The authors will discuss methods to determine the number of eliminating regions to improve recognition accuracy. Also, we have to discuss the method to recognize annotation positions for document retrieval systems.

References

1. Kuperman, G.J., Gardner, R.M., Pryor, T.A.: HELP: A Dynamic Hospital Information System. Springer, New York (2012)
2. Kapoor, B., Kleinbart, M.: Building an integrated patient information system for a healthcare network. J. Cases Inf. Technol. **14**(2), 27–41 (2014)
3. Savova, G.K., Masanz, J.J., Ogren, P.V., et al.: Mayo clinical Text Analysis and Knowledge Extraction System (cTAKES): architecture, component evaluation and applications. J. Am. Med. Inform. Assoc. **17**(5), 507–513 (2010)
4. Venot, A., Burgun, A., Quantin, C.: Medical Informatics, e-Health: Fundamentals and Applications. Springer, Paris (2014)
5. Haux, R.: Medical informatics: past, present, future. Int. J. Med. Inform. **79**(9), 599–610 (2010)
6. Bates, D.W., Bitton, A.: The future of health information technology in the patient-centered medical home. Health Aff. **29**(4), 614–621 (2010)
7. Blumenthal, D.: The "Meaningful Use" regulation for electronic health records. N. Engl. J. Med. **363**(6), 501–504 (2010)
8. Kawanaka, H., Sumida, T., Yamamoto, K., Shinogi, T., Tsuruoka, S.: Document recognition and XML generation of tabular form discharge summaries for analogous case search system. Meth. Inf. Med. **46**(6), 700–708 (2007)
9. Hayashi, H., Kawanaka, H., Nakamura, S., Yamamoto, K., Takase, H., Tsuruoka, S.: Document type and structure recognition and its evaluation for scanning system. In: The 30th Joint Conference on Medical Informatics, pp. 895–898 (2010)
10. Kawanaka, H., Yamamoto, K., Takase, H., Tsuruoka, S.: Document image processing for hospital information systems. In: Kalloniatis, C. (ed.) Modern Information Systems. InTech, Rijeka (2012)
11. Kimura, F., Wakabayashi, T., Tsuruoka, S., Miyake, Y.: Improvement of handwritten Japanese character recognition using weighted direction code histogram. Pattern Recogn. **30**(8), 1329–1337 (1997)
12. Tsuruoka, S., Kurita, M., Harada, T., Kimura, F., Miyake, Y.: Handwritten KANJI and HIRAGANA character recognition using weighted direction index histogram method. Trans. Inst. Electron. Inf. Commun. Eng. **J70–D**(7), 1390–1397 (1987)
13. Tsuruoka, S., Morita, H., Kimura, F., Miyake, Y.: Handwritten character recognition adaptable to the writer. In: Proceedings of IAPR Workshop on CT - Special Hardware and Industrial Applications, pp. 179–182 (1988)
14. Yoshioka, Y., Tsukada, Y.: Actual cases of medical charts and clinical records (Chap. 2). In: Murata, M., Yagasawa, K. (eds.) Handbook for Reading Medical Records Cards, 4th edn. Jiho Inc., Tokyo (2007)
15. All Japan Hospital Association (ed.): Manual for Preparation and Administration of Standard Clinical Documents. Jiho Inc., Tokyo (2004)
16. Otsu, N.: A threshold selection method from gray-level histograms. IEEE Trans. Syst. Man Cybern. (SMC) **9**(1), 62–66 (1979)

Structural and Perceptual
Based Approaches, Grouping

An Algorithm for Grouping Lines Which Converge to Vanishing Points in Perspective Sketches of Polyhedra

Pedro Company[1(✉)], Peter A.C. Varley[1], and Raquel Plumed[2]

[1] Institute of New Imaging Technology, Universitat Jaume I, Castellón, Spain
{pcompany, varley}@uji.es
[2] Department of Mechanical Engineering and Construction,
Universitat Jaume I, Castellón, Spain
plumed@emc.uji.es

Abstract. We seek to detect the vanishing points implied by design sketches of engineering products. Adapting previous approaches, developed in computer vision for analysis of vectorised photographic images, is unsatisfactory, as they do not allow for the inherent imperfection of sketches. Human perception seems not to be disturbed by such imperfections. Hence, we have designed and implemented a vanishing point detection algorithm which mimics the human perception process and tested it with perspective line drawings derived from engineering sketches of polyhedral objects. The new algorithm is fast, easily-implemented, returns the approximate locations of the main vanishing points and identifies those groups of lines in 2D which correspond to groups of parallel edges in the 3D object.

Keywords: Sketches · Perspective · Vanishing points · Parallel edges

1 Introduction

Our area of interest is creating computer-based tools to help design engineers during conceptual design (the first stage of the design process). For sketch-based modelling (SBM) systems to become a valid alternative to both current WIMP-based CAD systems and traditional paper and pencil sketching, they must cope with the full range of conceptual design sketches. Although most such sketches are done in orthographic projection style [1], it is also important to allow for perspective projection.

As explained in Sect. 2, some of the most popular vanishing point detection algorithms are compatible with human interpretation and may be tuned to mimic human perception [1–3], but none of them copes satisfactorily with the inherent imperfection of sketches. Hence, we have designed and implemented a new algorithm, specifically aimed at finding vanishing points (VPs) in sketches of engineering design products. Our algorithm clusters candidate vanishing points instead of clustering lines, and measures cluster similarity by angular difference in orientation. This deals naturally with sketching errors, as, when judging where VPs should be located, people are far more tolerant of discrepancies in distance than discrepancies in orientation [4].

B. Lamiroy and J.-M. Ogier (Eds.): GREC 2013, LNCS 8746, pp. 77–95, 2014.
DOI: 10.1007/978-3-662-44854-0_7

Section 3 describes our algorithm. Section 4 presents our test results. Section 5 presents conclusions and recommendations for future work.

2 Related Work

The input to our algorithm is a set of lines. In discussing related work, we only consider approaches which takes lines as input (we exclude those such as Barnard [5] and Magee and Aggarwal [6] which require bitmaps). We also exclude those such as Varley [7] which use (or attempt to deduce) higher semantic level information.

We note that most methods for detecting VPs are intended for 2D camera images. The errors they deal with (lens imperfections and noise in line segment extraction) are much smaller than typical sketching errors. Of these methods, the clustering approach of McLean and Kotturi [2] is most tolerant to noisy data.

Tardif [8] is interesting as it deals with one of the problems we consider here: its input is a set of N sparse edges, and its output is a set of VPs and a classification for each edge (assigned to a VP or marked as an outlier). It also includes a clustering strategy which improves on McLean and Kotturi [2]. However, it uses the J-Linkage algorithm, which is (a) computationally expensive and (b) non-deterministic, so only produces "probable" rather than "definite" results.

Rother [3] is a recent and representative example of a group of approaches which explore all candidate VPs, a reasonable choice when the aim is to detect VPs in a line drawing with a small number of strokes. This has the major drawback that its accumulation step only works well for geometrically perfect inputs—errors in geometry would result in a set of neighbouring cells each being visited only once, resulting in a set of non-dominant cells instead of the single dominant cell which the algorithm requires to predict the location of the dominant VP. Figure 1 illustrates that a coarse grid only returns "the vanishing point is somewhere around here", while a fine grid does not work at all—each vote is in a different box.

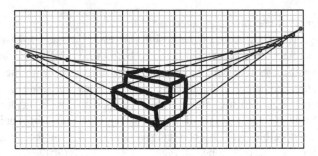

Fig. 1. Grid cannot cope with sketching imperfections

A further problem is that it only works well for the "Manhattan world" of normalons, and cannot reliably find oblique VPs. Nevertheless, [3] is representative of approaches which consider all pairwise intersections of the detected line segments. This technique is impractical for online analysis of photographic images, as it is very time consuming, but it may be useful for sketches, which contain fewer lines.

A recent study by Plumed et al. [4] gives criteria and metrics for implementing algorithms which mimic human perception in detecting vanishing points in design sketches. Although these have proved useful during the design and implementation of our algorithm, we must highlight a substantial difference between [4] and the approach we propose here. Since the interviewed people were aware of the nature of the depicted object, they first perceived the object (as a "step", a "house", ...), then spontaneously grouped edges which they know to be parallel in 3D, and finally checked whether the corresponding 2D lines were parallel or converged to a VP. However, our algorithm begins with a set of unclassified 2D lines—there is no high semantic level information about the object—and determining groups of parallel edges is one intended output of the algorithm.

We note that first grouping the lines and then finding VPs could be a valid alternative, although it is not as straightforward as it seems. Approaches for grouping 2D lines that represent edges parallel in 3D have been reported in the literature. However, the problem has proved difficult as no general solution has been developed so far. For instance, a naïve algorithm may group lines A and D—instead of A, B and C—in Fig. 2 (Varley [7]).

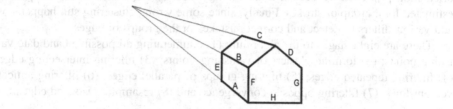

Fig. 2. Which lines should be parallel?

3 Algorithm

The input for Sketch-Based Modelling approaches is a sketch and the output is a 3D model. We assume that the sketch depicts a single object. This paper deals with one intermediate stage of the process, in which a line drawing is parsed to get higher semantic-level information. The input for this stage is a list of lines (where a line is defined by two endpoints, each of which is an (x-y) coordinate pair). The output is a set of groups of lines in 2D which correspond to groups of parallel edges in the 3D object; each group has either one vanishing point (perspective projection) or none (parallel projection).

We do not discuss *vectorisation*, the conversion of strokes (time-stamped lists of 2D points) (Fig. 3 left) into lines (Fig. 3 centre). But we note that vectorisation does not correct geometrical imperfections inherent in sketching. Vectorisation strategies also affect our clustering algorithm: segmented edges (upper red lines in Fig. 1 centre) produce more candidate VPs (and more "votes") than their unsegmented equivalent (lower red line). Our algorithm uses minimal vectorisation—for example, it does not use junctions (Fig. 3 right), because fitting line endpoints into a common junction produces undesired line rotations which corrupt the parallelism intended in the sketch.

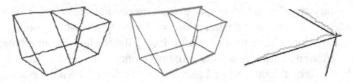

Fig. 3. Strokes (left), collinear edges (centre), and detail of endpoints (right) (Color figure online)

We have followed the idea used by Rother [3] of exploring all candidate VPs, and the idea of clustering present in McLean and Kotturi [2] and Tardif [8]. Two key ideas make our algorithm different from previous approaches. (1) We cluster candidate vanishing points, instead of clustering lines as in [9]. This prevents the need for repeatedly measuring complex distances (as in the voting distance in [3] or the vanishing point estimator in [8]), and allows clustering in a way more tolerant of imperfections in the sketched lines. (2) We use a polar coordinate system whose origin is the image centroid, and measure cluster similarity as difference in the orientation (angle), regardless of the distance (radius)—sketching imperfections produce far more uncertainty in distances than in orientation [4]. Thus we deal in a natural way with discrepancies in the VP position estimated for a group of strokes. Finally, since some wrong clustering still happens, we add various filters to detect and correct mistakes in the groups of edges.

There are eight stages to the algorithm: (1) enumerating all possible candidate vanishing points; (2) forming clusters of vanishing points; (3) filtering intersecting edges; (4) filtering repeated edges; (5) filtering groups of parallel edges; (6) filtering anticonvergent lines, (7) filtering opposite convergence and (8) resampling isolated edges.

3.1 Enumerating Candidate Vanishing Points

A candidate VP is created wherever the extensions of two lines cross. The data stored for each VP are the two lines and the position, calculated in polar coordinates R_{VP} and θ_{VP} relative to the drawing centroid. R_{VP} is scaled to the size of the drawing ($R_{VP} = 1$ is the largest distance between the centroid and any line endpoint).

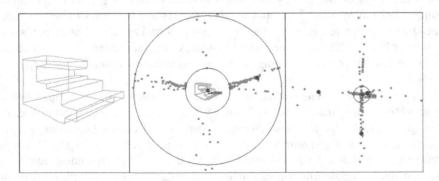

Fig. 4. Sketch (left), ring with candidate VPs (orange dots) in two zooms (centre and right) (Color figure online)

According to [4], humans generally only perceive candidate VPs where R_{VP} is between an *inner ring* (Ri) of 1.5 and an *outer ring* (Ro) of 5. Thus, for the purpose of detecting VPs, only candidate VPs within this ring should be output from this stage and should be passed on to the clustering process (Fig. 4 shows an example sketch and its ring in two different zooms).

However, we also wish to identify non-convergent groups of lines. In practice, groups of nearly-parallel lines also produce clusters of candidate VPs, but the clouds of such clusters are longer and their centroids are typically more distant to the object than those of convergent lines. In order to allow for these, we first calculate all VPs, regardless of outer radius, and only later classify them as true VPs or spurious VPs (groups of parallel lines).

3.2   Clustering

A cluster of VPs is a list of one or more VPs, together with a mean orientation angle θ_C.

Initially, each VP is its own cluster; larger clusters are grown by merger of two smaller clusters. Iteratively, we identify the closest pair of nearest-neighbour clusters and merge them, until the smallest difference between any pair of neighbouring θ_C is greater than a cutting-distance threshold "*CD*".

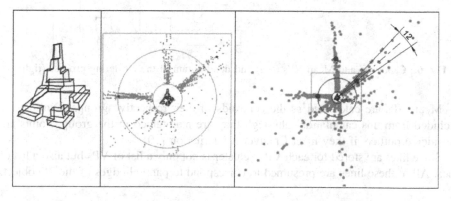

Fig. 5. Sketch (left), candidate VPs and clustering (centre and right)

The pseudo-code for the clustering algorithm is as follows:

1. Get the θ angles for each of the NumCandidateVP candidate VPs
2. Create two paired lists (whose initial length is NumCandidateVP):

   - Orientations list of θ angles
   - Cluster list, which is a meta-list where each item is a list which starts having just one candidate VP (the candidate VP whose angle is stored in the paired member of Orientations list)

3. Sort the paired lists in ascending order of θ
4. Define NumClusters = NumCandidateVP;

5. Repeat while NumClusters > 1:

   (a) Find the position of the smallest MinGap (i.e. min(Gap[i] = Orientation [i + 1] − Orientation[i]) ∀i)
   (b) Finish if smallest gap (MinGap) is bigger than CD
   (c) Add all the candidate VPs from Cluster[i + 1] to Cluster[i]
   (d) Recalculate Orientation[i] as the angle of the centroid of all candidate VPs in Cluster[i]
   (e) Remove Cluster[i + 1] and Orientation[i + 1] from the list
   (f) NumClusters = NumClusters − 1

Figure 6 displays the clusters for a simple drawing, and shows that the algorithm does not produce a full dendrogram, but a "truncated" one. A suitable CD parameter guarantees that Mean VPs are not clustered together, as would happen with a full clustering process. Note that the dendrogram is out of scale in the figure to highlight the cutting-distance. We set CD to 12° (Fig. 5), as suggested in [4].

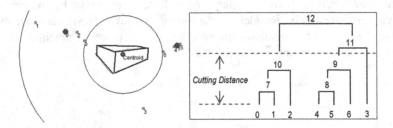

Fig. 6. Candidate and Mean VPs (left) and dendrogram of the clustering process (right)

Mean VPs are calculated as the centroids of their respective groups. Outliers are excluded from this calculation, although they are maintained in the group. Points are considered outliers if they meet Chauvenet's Criterion [10].

Since lines are stored for each VP, a cluster is not only a list of VPs but also a list of lines. All of these lines are presumed to correspond to parallel edges of the 3D object.

3.3   Filtering Intersecting Lines

Clearly, any pair of lines which cross within the object cannot be parallel in 3D and thus should not appear in the same cluster. We use a filtering process to remove lines (and VPs) from clusters when this rule is breached.

Figure 7 shows an example where this filter is required: the intersection points of line 11 with lines 4 and 12 are internal, but the intersections of 11 with 5, 6 and 9 meet the criteria for valid candidate VPs and have been clustered with the intersections of 4, 5, 6, 9 and 12. Line 11 must be removed from this cluster.

When detecting intersecting lines, we must consider sketching imperfections. Our algorithm marks two lines as crossing within the object if they are not collinear and: (a) their endpoints are close to one other (up and down lines in Fig. 3 right), or (b) their endpoints are close to their intersection (up and left lines in Fig. 3 right). We implement both criteria as thresholds: the distances (between the endpoints or between the intersection and either endpoint) are less than 0.1 times the length of the original edges (parameter SnapD).

Similarly, we have included a tolerance angle for accepting two nearly-parallel lines sharing an endpoint as collinear (collinear lines may meet at a K-junction [7]), since they are not always sketched as perfectly parallel (Fig. 1 centre). We set this TolCol tolerance to 5°.

These tolerances are appropriate for our test examples, but will require adjustment for better-quality or poorer-quality sketches.

When deciding which line to exclude, we apply two rules: (1) the line contributing to more VPs in the cluster is retained; (2) where the conflicting lines contribute to the same number of VPs, the line with VPs closer to the centroid is retained.

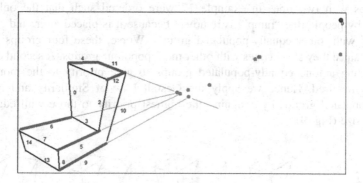

Fig. 7. Vanishing points from intersecting lines

Lines intersecting the extrapolations of other lines are also removed (unless *nearly* parallel), as the edges they depict cannot be parallel to the rest of the group (for example, the edge depicted by line 10 could never be parallel to the edges depicted by lines 5 or 6 in Fig. 7).

3.4   Filtering Repeated Lines

Most lines produce more than one candidate VP, and clustering VPs often results in some lines appearing in more than one cluster. See, for example, Fig. 8.

Since each cluster corresponds to a group of 3D-parallel edges, each line may belong to no more than one group. We add a filter to remove repeated lines.

We order clusters in descending order of (number of VPs + number of lines), following the heuristic that the most populous clusters are the best perceived ones [4]. For each cluster after the first, we remove any lines which also appear in any more populous cluster. Where this results in a cluster with fewer than two lines, the cluster itself is deleted. Thus, in the example in Fig. 5, only the first three clusters would remain.

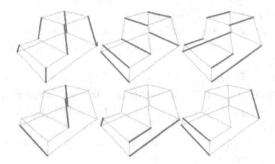

Fig. 8. Clustering output, with lines in more than one cluster

In some cases, retaining the most populous groups is insufficient. For example, the five groups with two lines in example 17 were ordered such that the only group perceived by people (the "ramp") is removed because it is placed after, and shares its two edges with, other equally-populated groups. Worse, these four groups are later discarded, since they share edges with other more populous groups. A second criterion, discriminating among equally-populated groups to give priority to the more useful groups, is required. Hence we apply the Gestalt Law of Similarity and rearrange equally populated groups by assigning the highest priority to those with edges most similar in size (Fig. 9).

Fig. 9. Equally sized groups rearranged in decreasing order of similarity between lengths of lines

3.5   Filtering Parallel Edges

The outer ring was ignored in Sect. 3.1, so as to detect groups of parallel edges. Once all groups have been detected, groups of parallel edges must be labelled as such. Two criteria must be met for labelling genuinely parallel groups: (i) if the centroid of the VPs is within the outer radius, the group is convergent; if the centroid of the VPs is beyond the outer radius, the group might be parallel; (ii) parallel groups are disperse; hence, the group might be parallel if the standard deviation of distances between each VP and the centroid of the cloud is greater than 15 times the radius of the bounding box of the drawing (parameter MinDisp). Groups with only two lines are considered to depict parallel edges whenever their VPs are outside the outer ring.

3.6   Filtering Anticonvergent Lines

It is only after filtering parallel edges that we filter anticonvergent lines for convergent groups. We find the Mean Line (the line which passes through the centroid of the drawing and the Mean VP of the group). Anticonvergent lines intersect the Mean Line of the group to which they supposedly belong on the side opposite to the Mean VP. Figure 10 left illustrates two converging lines which intersect the Mean Line near the Mean VP of the group; Fig. 7 right illustrates how line 2 converges to the other side.

Fig. 10. True convergence (left) and anticonvergence (right) for line 2

Figure 11 illustrates an actual example, in which anticonvergence merges red edges (which clearly converge to the right) with green ones (converging to the left). Our algorithm removes red lines from the group of green lines by repeatedly removing lines (a) which intersect the Mean Line on the opposite side to the Mean VP (marked as a blue dot in Fig. 8), and (b) whose VP is farthest from the Mean VP (which is recalculated after removing every line). Lines nearly collinear with the Mean Line are considered parallel and are not removed, irrespective of their actual orientation.

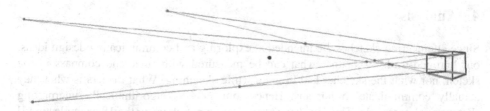

Fig. 11. Red edges do not converge to the left side, where the Mean VP is located (Color figure online)

3.7   Filtering Opposite Convergence

Nearly-parallel lines pose the question: were they intended to meet at a single VP, or at two opposed VPs, or were they intended to be parallel?

We have already seen (in Fig. 4) that, even when convergence is intended, poor sketch quality can create artefacts: line orientations all close to, but not exactly, the intended angle α produce some candidate VPs located around α and others located around $\alpha + 180°$ (Fig. 12). For clearly convergent lines this "opposite convergence" does not affect the results as the superfluous clusters are removed by the filtering stage of repeated edges. In this stage, we only merge genuinely parallel groups.

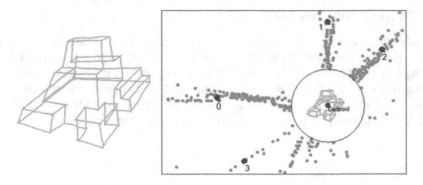

Fig. 12. Example of opposite VPs (#2 and #3)

3.8   Resampling Isolated Edges

After running previous filters, some lines may remain ungrouped. To allow for this, where an isolated line is nearly parallel to a group of parallel lines, and does not intersect the group, we add the isolated line to the group. We implement this *resample of isolated parallel lines* as a threshold: the orientation of the isolated line differs by less than CD from the orientation of the group of parallel lines. In the *resample of isolated convergent lines*, any remaining isolated line is grouped into a nearby convergent group if (a) the line orientation differs by less than CD from the mean line of the group and (b) the line does not intersect any line of the group.

4   Analysis

Since engineering sketches are intended at exploring and communicating design ideas, our "ground-truth" is neither what can be measured with ruler and compass in the sketch, nor what the sketcher had in mind while sketching. What matters is what they actually communicate to humans. Hence, our goal is algorithmically interpreting sketches as humans do. Thus, we have tested our approach using the 18 examples in [4] (Fig. 13). It can be seen that some of these are natural line drawings, while others are wireframes—the algorithm should (and does) work equally well for both.

We have also tested two variants of an angle bracket, with respectively zero and three perceptual VPs (19 and 20 in Fig. 14), and five more complex drawings (21 to 25 in Fig. 14).

The dataset tests demonstrate that our algorithm is limited neither by the number of VPs, nor by the number of lines in the sketches, and replicates human perception, as it locates VPs and groups lines representing sets of parallel edges in the same way humans did in the experiments described in [4]. For most test drawings, the results are the same as human perception. Quantitative results are available in the annex.

For drawing 6, very poor quality sketching prevents vectorisation from creating a valid line drawing (e.g. the short line highlighted in Fig. 15), so our algorithm fails to group one edge (although even if the missing line were vectorised from junction to

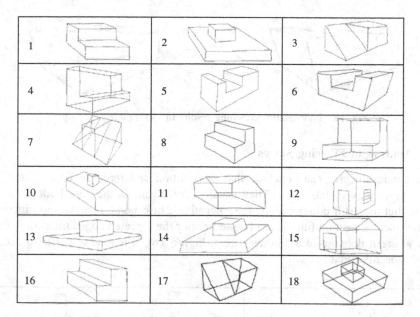

Fig. 13. Test examples

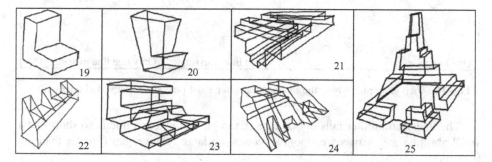

Fig. 14. Additional test drawings

junction, it would be discarded by the anticonvergence filter). The same happens with drawings 9 and 13. In all three cases, a slightly better sketch results in the correct grouping. We note that humans can group correctly even these poor quality sketches, but this is because they use high semantic level information (candidate edges are collinear with other edges in the group, or are opposite other edges in the group in the same quadrilateral face) which is not available to the algorithm—the algorithm is designed to be independent of other perceptual cues (such as collinearity or faces) as it may precede detection of such cues.

Fig. 15. Poor quality sketching results in incomplete grouping

4.1 Analysis of Filtering Stages

From our results, we can conclude that intersection and repeated edges filters are necessary to prevent false VPs. They usually work well, as they are built on sound criteria, but they still produce some false negatives. In general, it makes no difference whether the intersection filter is run before or after the repeated edges filter. In the few cases where it does make a difference (e.g. Figure 16), it is always better to run the intersection filter first.

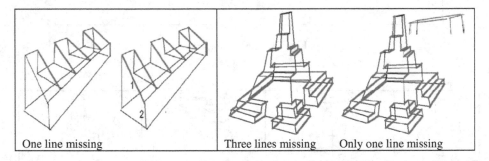

| One line missing | Three lines missing | Only one line missing |

Fig. 16. Two examples where the intersection filter must precede the repeated edges filter

The intersection filter fails in one case (Example 25) where a line is so short that a small absolute gap between endpoints becomes a large relative gap (greater than the 0.15 threshold).

In examples 7, 8, 9 and 16 opposite VPs appear. The filter for merging them into single groups does not detect them because they do not constitute a group. Instead, the complementary filter for isolated lines nearly-parallel to groups of parallel lines adds them to the group of nearly-parallel lines where they belong.

Occasional lines clearly non-parallel belong to parallel groups (example 10). They are there because they intersect at least one of the parallel lines outside the inner circle. A parallelism check removes them. In such cases, filtering repeated edges after filtering anticonvergent lines reduces the number of wrong lines.

4.2 Sensitivity Analysis

Our experiments do not support the proposed outer radius of 5.0 as a rigid limit for filtering parallel groups. Some examples switch from parallel to convergent for outer radii in the range 7.0–10.0. Since this value was fixed though an experiment aimed only at finding how people perceive convergent lines, an experiment aimed at determining how people distinguish between convergent and parallel lines is still required. The dispersion threshold should be tuned too. However, the combination of Ro = 5 and MinDisp = 15 (Sect. 3.5) usually allows the algorithm to determine which groups are parallel and which are convergent.

Example 13 illustrates two problems. Firstly, since the aspect ratio is so high, the mean lines to the two opposed vanishing points are almost parallel. The anticonvergence filter sometimes fails for lines which are both (a) poorly-sketched and (b) nearly collinear with mean lines. This problem is shared with lintel lines in examples 12 and 15. Secondly, the high aspect ratio makes intersection points more sensitive to small sketching errors, increasing the likelihood of internal intersections being accidentally located outside the inner ring and thus being wrongly listed as candidate VPs.

In order to determine how robust our algorithm is to the values of its tuning parameters, we carried out a sensitivity analysis. The algorithm uses the six parameters described previously: inner radius Ri and outer radius Ro (Sect. 3.1); Cutting-distance CD (Sect. 3.2); snapping distance SnapD and tolerance angle TolCol (Sect. 3.3); and minimum dispersion MinDisp (Sect. 3.5).

We varied all parameters in steps around their recommended values to find the ranges within which the parameters still work reasonably well (Table 1), and determined how many more mistakes the algorithm makes. We conclude that for parameter Ri the algorithm is very sensitive, as it makes many more mistakes with different values (see examples 13, 15, 17, 23, 24 and 25 in the annex). It is also sensitive to parameter CD (see examples 13, 15 and 22 in the annex). The algorithm is robust to varying the other four parameters (Ro, MinDisp, SnapD and TolCol).

Table 1. Parameters of the algorithm and their recommended range of values

	Tested		Recommended						Tested	
	Min	Errors	Min	Errors	Default	Errors	Max	Errors	Max	Errors
Ri	0.4	16/25	1.0	13/25	1.5	5/25	2.0	11/25	12	25/25
Ro	1.0	0	4.0	0	5.0	0	7.0	2/25	62	25/25
CD	2°	25/25	8°	8/25	12°	3/25	20°	6/21	95°	25/25
MinDisp	1.0	4/25	7.0	2/25	10.0	1/25	15.0	5/25	77.0	25/25
SnapD	0.005	8/25	0.05	6/25	0.15	1/25	0.3	6/25	1.0	23/25
TolCol	1°	4/25	3°	2/25	5°	1/25	15°	5/25	180°	21/25

Very close VPs (those which correspond to a "fish eye perspective") may require Ri values smaller than 1 (see example 23 in annex), which fail for more usual perspectives.

Increasing SnapD beyond 0.3 raises the risk of detection of false intersections, particularly for dense sketches. TolCol also depends on the sketch quality and density: smaller values should only be used for quite accurate sketches; poor quality sketches would not be correctly processed by increasing TolCol beyond 15°, as this increases the number of false collinearities (e.g. lines 1 and 2 in Fig. 16).

4.3 Running Time

We can compare our approach with a reduced set of approaches which are represented by the work by Tardiff [8]. They are computationally more expensive than our own approach, and were not tuned to mimic human perception.

Our algorithm is polynomial (it is a variant of agglomerative hierarchical clustering), and counting loops shows it to be $O(n^4)$ in theory. Its practical time complexity is illustrated in Fig. 17 (where run time is in milliseconds): for typical engineering sketches (orange line), it is around $n^{1.97}$; for sketches with more lines (green line), the $O(n^4)$ clustering algorithm dominates and the time complexity is around $n^{3.64}$. Figure 17 uses the 25 examples illustrated in Figs. 13 and 14, plus 13 other examples (not shown) with 134–247 lines.

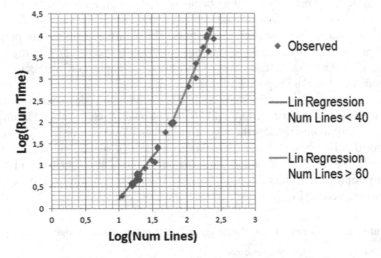

Fig. 17. Practical time complexity (Color figure online)

We conclude that the algorithm is fast enough for an interactive approach for drawings of up to 100 lines, but may be impractical beyond that.

4.4 Other Considerations

Our algorithm always detects the correct three groups of lines for normalon ("Manhattan-like") shapes where all edges and face normals are aligned with one of three main perpendicular axes, except for very poor quality sketches and cases of opposite convergence. The algorithm succeeds irrespective of the number of actual vanishing points, and also succeeds when lines represent edges intended to be parallel. For example, the different representations of the angle bracket have been perceived by humans as having one (examples 1, 9, 16), two (4 and 8), three (20) and zero (19) VPs.

At first sight, these results appear similar to those reported for other approaches currently used in SBM for grouping parallel lines. However, such approaches fail when the 2D lines corresponding to parallel edges span angles as big as 28°, as in Fig. 18. Our new algorithm processes this and similar drawings correctly. We know of no previous approach which can do this.

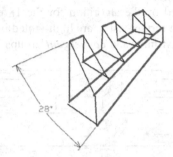

Fig. 18. Grouping parallel edges represented by converging lines

5 Conclusions

We have presented a new approach for finding vanishing points, tailored to sketches of polyhedral objects. Our approach improves on previous approaches in two ways: (1) it allows for inherent sketching errors, which defeat approaches designed for nearly-perfect line segments extracted from cameras images from cameras; (2) it derives from a study of human perception rather than arbitrary geometric criteria. The new algorithm uses perceptual criteria for tuning thresholds based on the following conclusions from [4]: (1) humans generally perceive vanishing points for sets of lines spanning 12° or more; (2) humans agree about the orientation angle of the VP relative to the sketch, while they often do not agree about the distance of the VP from the sketch; (3) VPs are easiest to perceive and to locate if they are neither too close nor too far away from the sketch—ideally, at distances not much more than the size of the sketch; (4) enforcement of the acceptance criteria should be tolerant to imperfections inside the main region (1.6x to 3x), and stricter outside (3x to 5x).

Our preliminary tests show that the algorithm is reasonably successful in matching human interpretation. Where humans do better, it is by making use of high semantic level information.

During tests, we have frequently noted that failure to vectorise results in failure to detect vanishing points. Future developments should address those typical vectorisation faults which greatly affect the vanishing points algorithm. However, state-of-the-art vectorisation algorithms produce reasonably good input drawings which may be used by our algorithm to detect those vanishing points clearly perceived by humans, together with their associated groups of converging lines that depict parallel edges.

Acknowledgments. This work was partially funded by financial support from the Ramon y Cajal Scholarship Programme and by the "Pla de Promoció de la Investigació de la Universitat Jaume I", project P1 1B2010-01.

Annex

A C++ implementation of our algorithm is available at www.regeo.uji.es, where the set of examples can also be found.

Groups of edges detected by the algorithm for the 18 examples in reference [1], plus the 7 examples added to further test it, are highlighted in the table (*parallel* groups are highlighted in thick *green* lines and *convergent* groups in thick *red* lines):

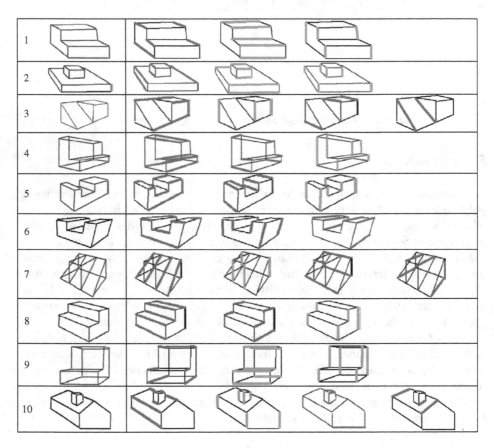

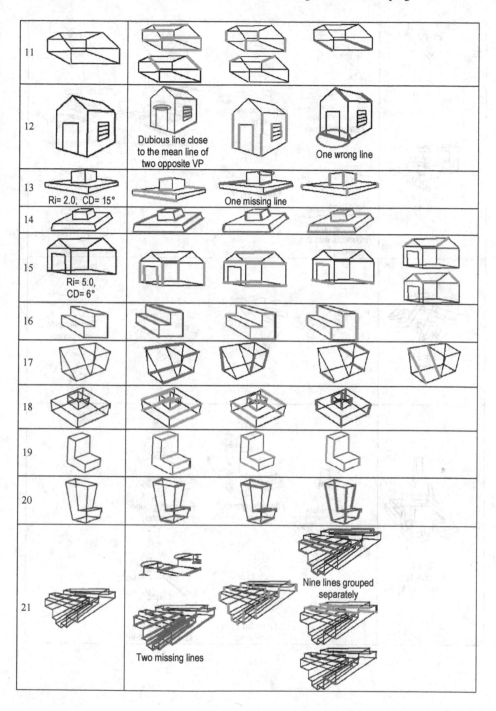

11			
12	Dubious line close to the mean line of two opposite VP		One wrong line
13	Ri= 2.0, CD= 15°	One missing line	
14			
15	Ri= 5.0, CD= 6°		
16			
17			
18			
19			
20			
21	Two missing lines	Nine lines grouped separately	

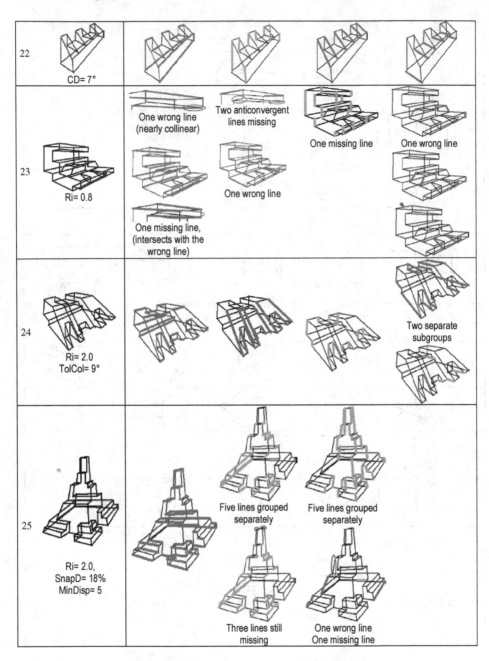

| 22 | CD= 7° | | | | |

References

1. Plumed, R., Company, P., Piquer, A., Varley, P.A.C.: Do engineers use convergence to a vanishing point when sketching? In: Proceedings of the International Symposium on Distributed Computing and Artificial Intelligence 2010 (DCAI'10), pp. 241–250 (2010)
2. McLean, G.F., Kotturi, D.: Vanishing point detection by line clustering. IEEE Trans. Pattern Anal. Mach. Intell. **17**(11), 1090–1095 (1995)
3. Rother, C.: A new approach to vanishing point detection in architectural environments. Image Vis. Comput. 20(9-10), 647–655 (2002)
4. Plumed, R., Company, P., Varley, P.A.C.: Metrics of human perception of vanishing points in perspective sketches. In: 21st International Conferences in Central Europe on Computer Graphics, Visualization and Computer Vision, WSCG 2013, pp. 59–68 (2013)
5. Barnard, S.T.: Interpreting perspective images. Artif. Intell. **21**(4), 435–462 (1983)
6. Magee, M.J., Aggarwal, J.K.: Determining vanishing points from perspective images. Comput. Vis. Graph. Image Process. **26**(2), 256–267 (1984)
7. Varley, P.A.C.: Automatic creation of boundary-representation models from single line drawings. Ph.D. thesis, Cardiff University (2003)
8. Tardif, J.P.: Non-iterative approach for fast and accurate vanishing point detection. In: 12th International Conference on Computer Vision, pp. 1250–1257. IEEE (2009)
9. Almansa, A., Desolneux, A., Vamech, S.: Vanishing point detection without any a priori information. IEEE Trans. Pattern Anal. Mach. Intell. **25**(4), 502–507 (2003)
10. Lin, L., Sherman, P.D.: Cleaning data the Chauvenet way. In: The Proceedings of the SouthEast SAS Users Group, SESUG Proceedings, Paper SA11 (2007)

Visual Saliency and Terminology Extraction for Document Classification

Duthil Benjamin, Coustaty Mickael[⊠],
Courboulay Vincent, and Jean-Marc Ogier

Laboratoire d'Informatique, Image et Interactions, Université de La Rochelle,
Avenue Michel Crepeau, 17042 La Rochelle, France
{bduthil,mcoustat,vcourbou,jmogier}@univ-lr.fr

Abstract. The document digitization process becomes a crucial economical issue in our society. Then, it becomes necessary to be able to organize this huge amount of documents. The work proposed in this paper tends to propose a new method to automatically classify documents using a saliency-based segmentation process on one hand, and a terminology extraction and annotation on the other hand. The saliency-based segmentation is used to extract salient regions and by the way logo, while the terminology approach is used to annotate them and to automatically classify the document. The approach does not require human expertise, and use *Google Images* as a knowledge database. The results obtained on a real database of 1766 documents show the relevance of the approach.

1 Introduction

The digitization of administrative documents and correspondences become economical and ecological issues in our society. Electronic mail, Intranet, Internet and document scanners can radically reduce paper use, while also saving time and money. Considering the interest to easily, efficiently and smartly acquire important documents of the daily life (invoice, payslip, credit card tickets ...). Imagine that you can store and protect such administrative documents, but besides all, imagine that you can navigate inside your database to find documents sended by specific organization. One of the oldest clue to facilitate this navigation, classification inside documents is *logo*. In France, *"La Marianne"* is the seal of state documents, and *a map of the world centered on the North Pole, inscribed in a wreath consisting of crossed conventionalized branches of the olive tree* is the famous symbol of the united nations. Thus the role of logo inside a document is crucial. It influences our decision concerning its importance.

According to the Oxford Dictionary, a logo is a *symbol or other small design adopted by an organization to identify its products, uniform, vehicles, etc.* By the way, they correspond to an important information to retrieve, classify and analyze documents (like one can observe in Fig. 1). Facing to the dramatic explosion of number of documents to process, logo spotting and recognition have evolved

© Springer-Verlag Berlin Heidelberg 2014
B. Lamiroy and J.-M. Ogier (Eds.): GREC 2013, LNCS 8746, pp. 96–108, 2014.
DOI: 10.1007/978-3-662-44854-0_8

as a practical and reliable supplement to the OCR. Indeed, without understanding a foreign language, we can easily classify documents by using their logos. It is also possible to cluster birth-certificate or marriage contract by recognizing the logo of the city. For instance, imagine Mr Washington that got married with Ms Paris in London, it could be difficult to disambiguate these names by only using an OCR approach.

Then, we assume that a logo conveys enough information to understand the main purpose of the emitting company (line of business, company name, etc.). Thus, in the context of content based image retrieval (CBIR), the logo spotting techniques provides an important cues to allow document recognition. But generally, most of the techniques for document classification or retrieval have been applied to binary documents.

In this paper, we propose an original administrative documents classification process based on the cooperation between a visual saliency approach and a terminology extraction. The paper is organized as follows: Sect. 1.1 presents the related works, and Sect. 2 describes the global scheme of the proposed approach. Section 3 presents the experimental results while Sect. 4 draws a conclusions and some perspectives.

Fig. 1. Different logos (French republic, United Nation Organization, London city, Paris city, Washington DC)

1.1 Related Works

Numerous approaches on logo localization and detection have been reported in the literature over the last decades. If the first trials done on binary documents [2,10,15–17], more and more approaches tend to apply these techniques to color documents [1,7]. One of the first approach, initiated by Pham [10] in 2003, was developed for logos detection in grayscale document images. The computational schemes involved segmentation, and the calculation of the spatial density of the defined foreground pixels. Detection is based on the hypothesis that the spatial density of the foreground pixels within a given windowed image that contains a logo is greater than those of non-logo regions.

Alajlan introduced an approach for retrieving the envelope of logo [2]. Motivated by studies in Gestalt theory, he used a hierarchical clustering and a fusion stage on a set of 110 black and white logos. Two major drawbacks can be mentioned: the first one is the absence of color cues, and the second one is the particular family of tested logo. Only logos that can be grouped with a same particular spatial proximity, area, shape features and orientation were used, which is quite restrictive. In 2007, Zhu and Doermann [18] proposed an approach for logo detection and extraction that classifies and localizes logos using a boosting strategy across multiple image scales. An initial two-classes classification process was performed using a Fisher classifier at a coarse image scale on each connected component. A logo was then identified as a candidate region, and successively classified at finer image scales by a cascade of simple classifiers. These classifiers allowed false alarms to be quickly rejected, and the detected logo to be more precisely localized.

In 2008, Zeggari [1] developed a logo extraction algorithm based on two properties of logos: spatial compactness and colorimetric uniformity. First, the image content is reduced and transformed using mathematical morphology operators to decrease the distance between the identical logo parts. Afterwards the logo regions of spatial and chromatic densities are detected.

Rusinol and Llados proposed in [12] to use a bag of words approach to categorize document. Categorization is performed in terms of the presence of certain graphical logo detected and spotted in the document. Logos are described by a set of local features and the categorization of the documents is performed by the use of a bag-of-words model. Authors reinforce the correct category hypothesis by using spatial coherence rule. They developed their approach in [6].

More recently, in 2011, [7] proposed a method for logo detection in color documents. The proposed rotation and scale invariant method is based on the Gaussian Mixture Markov Random Field which labels the pixels in the documents as foreground or background with respect to the query logo. Then a shape descriptor is applied to the foreground regions to verify the presence of the logo. As a conclusion authors mentioned the advantage of color for detecting logos for document classification without any heuristic information.

In 2012, Sahbi et al. [13] design a novel variational framework able to match and recognize multiple instances of multiple reference logos in image archives. Authors considered logos as constellations of local features and matched by minimizing an energy function. This function takes into account a fidelity term that measures the quality of feature matching, a neighborhood criterion which captures feature geometry and a regularization term that controls the smoothness of the matching solution. These last method based on interest points and local descriptors appears much more appropriate to support detection and recognition of graphic logos in real world images. Besides it supposed a database of existing logo.

Most of the mentioned methods are quite restrictive in the hypothesis they used and are time consuming, besides they only used low levels features. Our target is to propose a method that performs either on black and white but also on color document, correctly scanned or degraded image, and that performs with unknown logo. Besides all, we want to propose a method that combine image and text mining techniques, two communities rarely and hardly combined.

2 Proposed Approach

Our approach relies on a three steps process summarized in Fig. 2. First, we analyze the document saliency to extract the most salient areas (called thumbnails hereafter). In this work, we assume that a logo is a salient part of a document, and it can be extracted using a saliency-based segmentation process (see Sect. 2.1). Secondly, we learn the vocabulary (terminology) associated to each thumbnail of the document. For this, we use *Google Images API* to get some information associated to each thumbnail from web pages. Thus, some keywords and a set of documents are associated to each thumbnail. Finally, based on the documents returned, we extract the terminology associated to each thumbnail of original document using text-mining techniques. One of our main motivations is actually to reduce the semantic gap by proposing an original cooperation between low level image processing and text mining techniques.

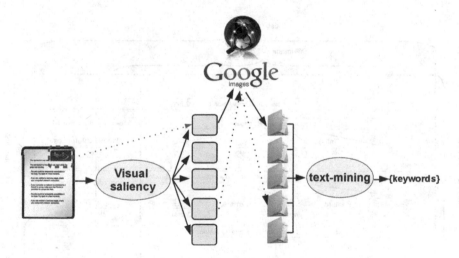

Fig. 2. Global diagram

2.1 Visual Saliency Approach

Recenlty, Perreira Da Silva et al. [9] proposes a new hybrid model which allows modeling the temporal evolution of the visual focus of attention and its validation. As shown in Fig. 3, it is based on the classical algorithm proposed by Itti in [4], in which the first part of its architecture relies on the extraction of three conspicuity maps based on low level characteristics computation. These three conspicuity maps are representative of the three main human perceptual channels: color, intensity and orientation. In [8] Perreira Da Silva et al. propose to substitute the second part of Itti's model by an optimal competitive approach: a preys/predators system. They have demonstrated that it is an optimal way of extracting information. Besides, this optimal criteria, preys/predators equations are particularly well adapted for such a task:

- preys/predators systems are dynamic, they include intrinsically time evolution of their activities. Thus, the visual focus of attention, seen as a predator, can evolve dynamically;
- without any objective (top-down information or pregnancy), choosing a method for conspicuity maps fusion is hard. A solution consists in developing a competition between conspicuity maps and waiting for a natural balance in the preys/predators system, reflecting the competition between emergence and inhibition of elements that engage or not our attention;
- discrete dynamic systems can have a chaotic behavior. Despite the fact that this property is not often interesting, it is an important one in this case. Actually, it allows the emergence of original paths and exploration of visual scene, even in non salient areas, reflecting something like curiosity.

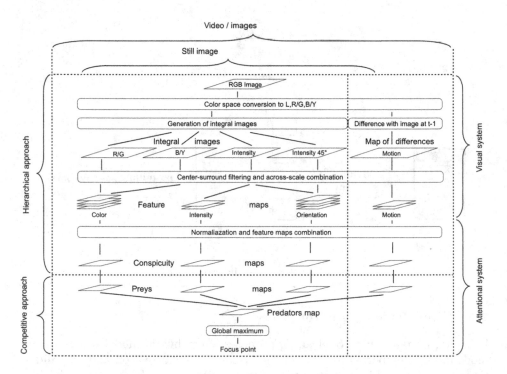

Fig. 3. Architecture of the computational model of attention

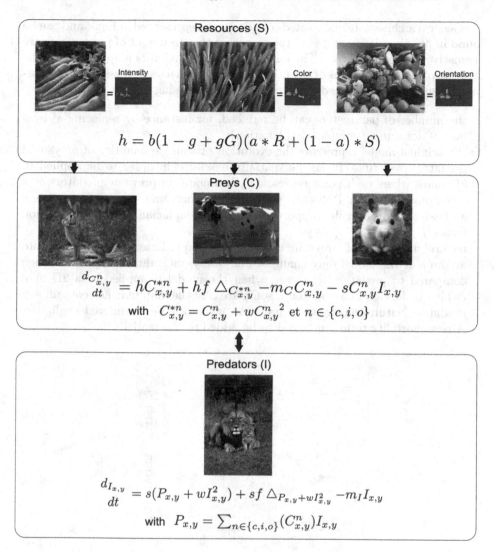

Fig. 4. Competitive preys/predators attention model.

Reference [9] shows that despite the non deterministic behavior of preys/predators equations, the system exhibits interesting properties of stability, reproducibility and reactiveness while allowing a fast and efficient exploration of the scene. We applied the same optimal parameters used by Perreira Da Silva to evaluate our approach.

The attention model is computationally efficient and plausible [8]. It provides many tuning possibilities (adjustment of curiosity, central preferences, etc.) that can be exploited in order to adapt the behavior of the system to a particular context.

General architecture and related equations are represented in Fig. 4 and can be found in [9]. Singularity maps are the resources that feed a set of preys which are themselves eat by predators. The maximum of the predators map represents the location of the current focus of attention. Starting from a basic version of predator-preys equations, they have decided to enhance processing in several ways:

– the number of parameters can be reduced, for instance by replacing s' by s (see [9] for a more complete explanation).
– the original model represents the evolution of a single quantity of preys and predators over time. It can be spatially extended in order to be applied to 2D maps where each point represents the amount of preys or predators at a given place and time. Preys and predators can then "move" on this map using a classical diffusion rule, proportional to their Laplacian $\triangle_C$ and a diffusion factor f.
– natural mortality of preys in the absence of predation is not taken into account. If the model only changes temporally, mortality is negligible when compared to predation. However, when the model is applied to a 2D map (which is the case in our system), some areas of the map may not contain any predator. Natural mortality of prey can no longer be considered negligible. A new mortality term $-m_c$ need to be added to the model.

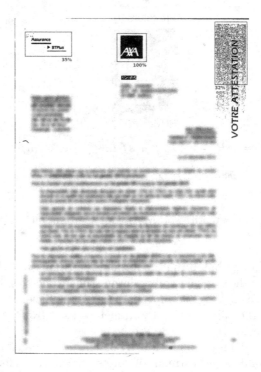

Fig. 5. Example of thumbnails extracted using the proposed saliency-based segmentation process (Color figure online)

This yield to the following set of equations, modeling the evolution of preys and predators populations on a two dimensional map:

$$\begin{cases} \frac{d C_{x,y}}{dt} = b C_{x,y} + f \, \triangle_{C_{x,y}} - m_C C_{x,y} - s C_{x,y} I_{x,y} \\ \frac{d I_{x,y}}{dt} = s C_{x,y} I_{x,y} + s f \, \triangle_{P_{x,y}} - m_I I_{x,y} \end{cases} \tag{1}$$

In order to illustrate the results obtained with this saliency-based segmentation process, the Fig. 5 propose an example of administrative document treated during our process, and the most salient thumbnails proposed (surrounded in red).

2.2   Corpus Constitution

The objective of this step is to built a corpus of web documents for each thumbnail identified by our visual saliency approach. This corpus is used in the next step (c.f. Sect. 2.3). We use the *Google Images*[1] web search engine in order to link some web pages to each thumbnail extracted. If the input image is recognized, *Google Images* provides the name N of the logo (generally, the company name). This information is used during the learning phase to set up the learning words close to N. The direct identification or recognition by Google of a logo or a thumbnail is not mandatory. This can happen where either the document definition is too low, or if this image is not a logo (the logo in that case could correspond to an area with a fewer saliency), or if *Google Images* doesn't know this logo. However, *Google Images* also offers a list of links related to web pages containing similar images. From these links, we build a corpus $C = \{c_1, \ldots, c_k\}$ of web documents associated to each thumbnail. Let s_q be the different thumbnails extracted from an image. Then, each thumbnail will be associated to a corpus c_q composed of k documents (with $\{q = 1 \ldots k\}$ for an image where k equals to the number of links returned by *Google Images*).

2.3   Terminology Extraction

The objective of this step is to extract from the web corpus (HTML pages) built in Sect. 2.2, the terminology related to the original document. All the thumbnails identified in step 1 have not the same degree of importance in the document. Indeed, each thumbnail have a weight P_q that corresponds to the saliency level sensed by our saliency segmentation process (between 0 and 100 %) That is why it is necessary to take this weight into account during the learning step. The final score assigned to a word is then weighted by this value.

Moreover, in order to ensure the learning of the descriptors related to the logo, we use a window [3,11] to guarantee the semantic proximity between the name of the logo and the keywords associated. More formally, the words in the immediate neighborhood of the name N_q of the logo are first selected inside a window $\mathcal{F}$ of size sz in a document doc:

$$\mathcal{F}(N, sz, doc) = \{w \in doc / d_{noun}(N, w) \leq sz\} \tag{2}$$

---

[1] Google Images: http://images.google.fr/

with $d_{noun}(r, w)$ being the distance corresponding to the number of nouns (considered as meaningful terms [5]) separating a word w from N in the document doc [3] and sz the number of noun at right of N and the number of noun at left of N.

The use of window $\mathcal{F}$ allows filtering and limiting the scope of the semantic distance between the name of the logo and the other terms in the window. To consider the name returned by *Google Images* as a "germ" [3,11] implies that the web search engine was able to identify the logo. The thumbnails where no logo are identified by *Google Images* are ignored at this time.

The representativity $X(W, sz)$ of a word is computed using tf-idf measure [14], saliency weight and considering only the words (nouns) include in $\mathcal{F}$. For each thumbnail s_q where *Google Images* has identified a logo with his associate name N_q, representativity (tf-idf) of a each word (noun) W is weighted using the saliency weight related to the considered thumbnail. So, the more a thumbnail is prominent and characteristic for the original document, the more important the words related to this thumbnail will be. For all thumbnails, the calculated frequencies of each word W are added and a lexicon of word is created. This lexicon is sorted and allows identifying the most representative words for a logo. Some examples of automatically extracted keywords from thumbnails is presented in Table 1.

Table 1. Example of words automatically learned

Logo	associated words	Logo	associated words	Logo	associated words
	AGPM		**IAPR**		**Banque Postale**
	AGPM Group		Association		bank
	Housing contract		Pattern		client
	insurance		Vison		services
	risk		Recognition		financing
	contract		Image		management
	life insurance				advisor

3 Experimental Results

In this section we evaluate the method on a corpus composed of 1766 administrative documents distributed in 4 classes of documents (marriage act (M-A), birth certificate (B-C), insurance certificate (I-C), bank account details (B-A-D)) such as is described in Table 2. This database was provided by one of a world-class Document Capture solution vendor. Each document contains one of the 196 logos identified in the corpus. Documents are scanned in 200 dpi black and white. We used classical indicators to evaluate classification such as *Precision* and *Recall*. *Precision* is computed by considering the error in the identification of a logo: the system identifies a logo that is not the real logo. *Recall* is computed using the number of logos correctly identified by the system. Our results are presented in Table 3.

Table 2. Classes repartition

	Number of logos	Number of documents
Marriage act	36	40
Birth certificate	113	169
Insurance certificate	30	822
Bank account details	15	735

Table 3. Classification results for each classe of the 1766 documents: marriage act (M-A), birth certificate (B-C), insurance certificate (I-C), bank account details (B-A-D)

	I-C	M-A	B-C	B-A-D	All classes
Recall	**95.5**	22.5	60.4	**71.7**	*80.6*
Precision	100	100	100	100	*100*

The results show the relevance of the approach. The differences between each class is explained by the document quality (c.f. Table 4). For example, the quality of "marriage act" documents is very poor which explains the low *recall*. In addition, the number of different logos to identify is different in each class and increases the difficulty. However, the results are remarkable, we obtain an average *recall* of **80.6** and a *precision* of **100**. The *precision* (100) highlights the robustness of the approach.

Table 4. Example of unidentified logos

4   Conclusion and Perspectives

To conclude, we have presented a new automatic classification method based on a salient area segmentation process on one hand, and on a terminology extraction and annotation on the other hand. The saliency-based segmentation is used to extract the logo and some salient regions, while the terminology approach is used to annotate them and to automatically classify the document. The approach does not require human expertise. The use of *Google Images* avoids the construction of a local database. In addition, when a new logo is found, the system is able to provide a classification, which is impossible even if the local database is updated.

In perspectives, we planned to use OCR information to improve document classification. On one hand to make the system able to classify documents without logo, and on the other hand we target to render the classification of document with very poor quality logo. For this task, it's necessary to consider the terminology associated to each logo using *Synopsis* approach and the keywords as germs [3] in order to refine the terminology extraction and reduce the semantic gap between the image and the terminological concepts it contains. Moreover, considering image as concept and the thumbnails as germs, it is possible to make the parallel with Synopsis approach: it should be possible to link a lexicon of words to an image.

Another perspective for this work is to extend it to natural scene images, in order to automatically annotate them and to propose a conceptual synopsis of the scene. Figure 5 illustrates an example of this, in which a picture of a desktop has been shooted with a mobile phone. Started from our works, we planned to automatically extract the most salient regions, and to automatically associate some keywords (in this example, some examples of keywords are proposed in the table near from the Fig. 6).

Associated keywords
Senseo
Vittel
Black-Berry

Fig. 6. Example of natural scene picture, the most-salient thumbnails associated and the automatically extracted keywords

References

1. Ahmed, Z.: Logos extraction on picture documents using shape and color density. In: IEEE International Symposium on Industrial Electronics, ISIE, pp. 2492–2496 (2008)
2. Alajlan, N.: Retrieval of hand-sketched envelopes in logo images. In: Kamel, M.S., Campilho, A. (eds.) ICIAR 2007. LNCS, vol. 4633, pp. 436–446. Springer, Heidelberg (2007)
3. Duthil, B., Trousset, F., Roche, M., Dray, G., Plantié, M., Montmain, J., Poncelet, P.: Towards an automatic characterization of criteria. In: Hameurlain, A., Liddle, S.W., Schewe, K.-D., Zhou, X. (eds.) DEXA 2011, Part I. LNCS, vol. 6860, pp. 457–465. Springer, Heidelberg (2011)
4. Itti, L., Koch, C., Niebur, E.: Others: a model of saliency-based visual attention for rapid scene analysis. IEEE Trans. Pattern Anal. Mach. Intell. **20**(11), 1254–1259 (1998)
5. Kleiber, G.: Noms propres et noms communs: un problme de dnomination. Meta **41**, 567–589 (1996)
6. Rusinol, M., Poulain D Andecy, V., Karatzas, D., Llados, J.: Classification of administrative document images by logo identification. In: Ninth IAPR International Workshop on Graphics RECognition - GREC, pp. 3–6 (2011)
7. Nourbakhsh, F., Karatzas, D., Valveny, E., Llados, J.: Color logo detection and retrieval in document collections. In: Ninth IAPR International Workshop on Graphics RECognition - GREC (2011)
8. Da Silva, M.P., Courboulay, V., Prigent, A., Estraillier, P.: Evaluation of preys/predators systems for visual attention simulation. In: VISAPP 2010 - International Conference on Computer Vision Theory and Applications, pp. 275–282. INSTICC, Angers (2010)
9. Da Silva, M.P., Courboulay, V.: Implementation and evaluation of a computational model of attention for computer vision. In: Developing and Applying Biologically-Inspired Vision Systems: Interdisciplinary Concepts, pp. 273–306. IGI Global, Hershey (2012)
10. Pham, T.D.: Unconstrained logo detection in document images. Pattern Recogn. **36**(12), 3023–3025 (2003)
11. Ranwez, S., Duthil, B., François Sy, M.F., Montmain, J., Ranwez, V.: How ontology based information retrieval systems may benefit from lexical text analysis. In: Oltramari, A., Vossen, P., Qin, L., Hovy, E. (eds.) New Trends of Research in Ontologies and Lexical Resources. Theory and Applications of Natural Language Processing, pp. 209–231. Springer, Heidelberg (2013)
12. Rusinol, M., Llados, J.: Logo spotting by a bag-of-words approach for document categorization. In: 2009 10th International Conference on Document Analysis and Recognition, pp. 111–115 (2009)
13. Sahbi, H., Ballan, L., Serra, G., Del Bimbo, A.: Context-dependent logo matching and recognition. IEEE Trans. Image Process. (a publication of the IEEE Signal Processing Society) **22**(3), 1018–1031 (2012)
14. Salton, G., Yang, C.S.: On the specification of term values in automatic indexing. J. Doc. **29**(4), 351–372 (1973)
15. Seiden, S., Dillencourt, M., Irani, S., Borrey, R., Murphy, T.: Logo detection in document images. In: Proceedings of the International Conference on Imaging Science, Systems, and Technology, pp. 446–449 (1997)

16. Wang, H., Chen, Y.: Logo detection in document images based on boundary extension of feature rectangles. In: 2009 10th International Conference on Document Analysis and Recognition (c), pp. 1335–1339 (2009)
17. Zhu, G., Doermann, D.: Automatic document logo detection. In: Ninth International Conference on Document Analysis and Recognition (ICDAR 2007), September 2007, vol. 2, pp. 864–868 (2007)
18. Zhu, G., Jaeger, S., Doermann, D.: A robust stamp detection framework on degraded documents. In: Taghva, K., Lin, X. (eds.) SPIE 6067, Document Recognition and Retrieval XIII, January 2006, pp. 60670B–60670B-9 (2006)

Unsupervised and Notation-Independent Wall Segmentation in Floor Plans Using a Combination of Statistical and Structural Strategies

Lluís-Pere de las Heras[✉], Ernest Valveny, and Gemma Sánchez

Computer Vision Center - Universitat Autònoma de Barcelona,
Campus UAB, 08193 Bellatera, Barcelona, Spain
{lpheras,ernest.valveny,gemma.sanchez}@cvc.uab.es
http://www.cvc.uab.cat

Abstract. In this paper we present a wall segmentation approach in floor plans that is able to work independently to the graphical notation, does not need any pre-annotated data for learning, and is able to segment multiple-shaped walls such as beams and curved-walls. This method results from the combination of the wall segmentation approaches [3,5] presented recently by the authors. Firstly, potential straight wall segments are extracted in an unsupervised way similar to [3], but restricting even more the wall candidates considered in the original approach. Then, based on [5], these segments are used to learn the texture pattern of walls and spot the lost instances. The presented combination of both methods has been tested on 4 available datasets with different notations and compared qualitatively and quantitatively to the state-of-the-art applied on these collections. Additionally, some qualitative results on floor plans directly downloaded from the Internet are reported in the paper. The overall performance of the method demonstrates either its adaptability to different wall notations and shapes, and to document qualities and resolutions.

Keywords: Graphics recognition · Floor plan analysis · Object segmentation

1 Introduction

Wall detection is a crucial step in floor plan interpretation because walls globally define the structure of buildings. Nevertheless, due to the lack of a standard graphical notation in architectural documents, there is a big variability on how these elements are lineally drawn; they can be represented by thick black lines, parallel lines, hatched textures, colored patterns, etc... (some real instances are shown in Fig. 1). This issue provokes that classical approaches, which are very ad-hoc for a small set of notations, fail to generalize and become useless for multiple graphical representations.

© Springer-Verlag Berlin Heidelberg 2014
B. Lamiroy and J.-M. Ogier (Eds.): GREC 2013, LNCS 8746, pp. 109–121, 2014.
DOI: 10.1007/978-3-662-44854-0_9

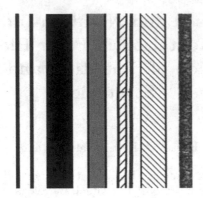

Fig. 1. Vertical walls cropped from real floor plans.

In the literature, several approaches have been presented to segment walls on a predefined notation. In [1,7,12,14], different strategies are proposed for segmenting walls modeled by thick black lines. Both, [1,7], apply morphological filtering to thin-thick line separation. Contrarily, [6,12] use the Hough Transform on the vectorized images to detect parallel lines with black texture in between. Finally, [14] spots the walls on the polylines generated after vectorizing the thick lines in the image.

All of these floor plan recognition systems need to redefine their wall segmentation steps when dealing with images of different notations, as the ones represented by simple parallel lines in [11], or a hatched texture in [4]. This fact leads to the impossibility of comparing their efficiency since most of them are significantly oriented to their own private collections. With the aim of finding a solution to this problem, our group has put the effort in the recent years to create an effective method to detect walls in real floor plans of different notations.

The first attempt was inspired by the existent methods on appearance-based object detection in real scenes. As a result, the authors presented in [4] a bag of visual patches model that learns the graphical appearance of walls when labeled data is available. This system was refined and its performance enhanced in [5], showing a great adaptability to the existent graphical variability. Subsequently in [2], this technique was used to build the first floor plan interpretation system able to deal with different graphical notations. Even though this approach demonstrated its suitability on real images, the need of generating ground-truth for each new collection was added to the system, pushed us to rethink the whole strategy.

The second attempt on wall detection was tackled under structural point of view. In [3], the authors presented an unsupervised approach that drives the detection based on six structural assumptions on general building properties. The results demonstrated that this method is able to segment walls in different collections with similar results to the ones obtained by [5]. With all, the method still has some restrictions inherent to the structural properties, e.g. "walls are usually straight" or "they are longer than thicker".

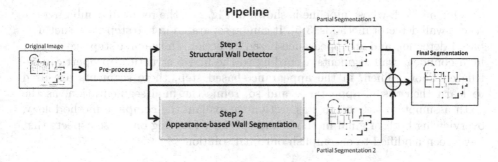

Fig. 2. Pipeline of the method

In this paper we close the circle by proposing a new approach based on the combination of these two strategies mentioned above. This new method is able to detect walls independently to their notation and structure, and does not need of any labeled data to learn their graphical appearance. Firstly, a modified version of [3] outputs a preliminary segmentation. Then, a revisited version of [5] learns their appearance and refines the initial segmentation. The proposed method has been tested on 4 available datasets presented in [2] and some Internet images. Moreover, it is compared to the recent strategies that have reported their results on these collections.

In Sect. 2 we explain the method, revisiting the two approaches combined. Section 3 is devoted to present the experimental evaluation. Finally, in Sect. 4 we conclude the paper.

2   Methodology

The detection method is driven by the following 6 general assumptions on walls structure in architectural drawings:

1. Walls are drawn by parallel lines.
2. They appear in orthogonal directions.
3. Walls are rectangularly shaped, usually they are longer than thicker.
4. They define the structure of the building; appearing naturally distributed in the plan.
5. Different thicknesses are used to model internal and external walls.
6. The walls in a document are filled by the same pattern (hatched, tiled, solid, etc.).

These assumptions cannot be seen as a complete pack of unbreakable statements for all existing floor plans. For instance, there are floor plans with diagonal or curved walls, buildings with the same thickness for interior and exterior walls, etc. Nevertheless, a relaxed combination of them enhances the flexibility of the system, leading to a good final segmentation that works fine independently on the building or document complexity.

Our method, whose pipeline is shown in Fig. 2, is the result of combining the recent wall detector methods [3,5]. It can be separated in two steps: a structural-based detection and an appearance-based detection. In the first step, we extract high confident wall segments according to the first 5 structural properties postulated above. Then, in the appearance-based step, these segments are used to learn their visual appearance and so, refine the final segmentation, as the sixth assumption asserts. In this section we explain the complete methodology, overviewing both original methods and specially focusing on those aspects that have been modified to accomplish our final solution.

2.1   Step 1: Structural Detection

The first stage of the method is devoted to detect wall segments by their structural properties, similarly to [3]. The detection starts by detecting elements formed by parallel lines, according to *assumption 1*. The confidence of the resulting wall segments is determined by their agreement with the *assumptions 2, 3, 4*, and *5*. This process is divided into *Preprocessing, Black-wall detection, Wall-segment candidates* and *Confident wall segmentation*.

Preprocessing
The images are binarized and the textual information is filtered out using [15]. Possible deviations in the floor plan modeling are corrected by an adaptation of [13]; a method for handwritten deskewing. This is done to facilitate the detection of parallel lines in the orthogonal directions, as *assumption 2* asserts. Even though the segmentation strategy is scale-invariant, for efficiency issues the images with resolutions higher than 4000×4000 pixels are down-scaled.

Black-Wall Detection
Some old documents contain walls modeled by thick black lines as the ones shown in Fig. 4a. Since the preliminary detection is based on finding parallel lines, an automatic ad-hoc preprocessing has designed to detect and transform these sort of documents to a more suitable input. Firstly, horizontal and vertical runs of foreground pixels are quantized in a histogram. Documents with thick walls present sparser histograms with far more outliers in higher positions than the rest. Then, they are easily detected by thresholding the sigma parameter on the Gaussian mixture fitted to the histogram by EM. Images with thick black walls are replaced by their edge image, obtained using the Canny edge detector.

Wall-Segment Candidates
Wall-segment candidates are seek in a first step according to *assumption 1*; looking for parallel lines in the document. These lines are encountered by only considering those runs of foreground pixels of a certain minimum length. They are quested in multiple orientations of the image according an angle α. The distances between lines are quantized in a histogram, where bins with higher

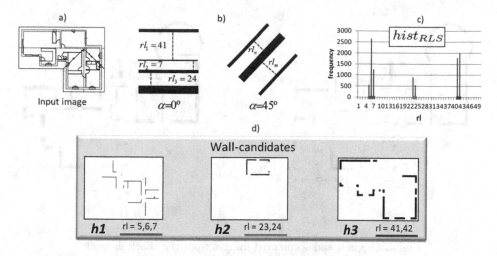

Fig. 3. Wall candidate generation. The input image is shown in a). In b), the run extraction process at two different orientations α is zoomed. This runs are quantized in the histogram shown in c), generating three colored clusters that belong to common parallel line thickness in the input image. For each cluster, the parallel lines of their corresponding thickness are retrieved in three different candidates h.

frequencies stand for common parallel line distances. The histogram is smoothed in order to filter out irrelevant information. Then, for each non zero bin, a candidate segmentation image is generated by retrieving the areas according the corresponding distances between parallel lines. In other words, each segmentation image contains wall segments of the same thickness. This process is detailed in Fig. 3.

Confident Wall Segmentation

To extract the segments with the highest degree of confidence, we firstly rank the wall image candidates before spreading them into the final segmentation. This is done oppositely from the original approach [3], where all possible wall candidates were combined to posteriorly rank them regarding their confidence. The reason is following this strategy is that the wall's texture will be learned from these segments and used to recover lost instances that do not agree with the structural *assumptions*. Thus, at this point the precision on wall segmentation has to be maximized to enhance the subsequent visual learning step. It is also worth to point out that most of the confident segmentations tend to rely on exterior and interior walls, as it is assumed in 5.

Let H be the set of wall image candidates h, where the segment thickness $thick(h_i) \neq thick(h_j)$ for all $i \neq j$. Agreeing to *assumption 4*, walls are elements that appear repeatedly in floor plans. The score Ncc accounts the number of connected components (CC) in the segmentation image:

$$\mathrm{Ncc}_{h_i} = \#\mathrm{CC}(h_i). \tag{1}$$

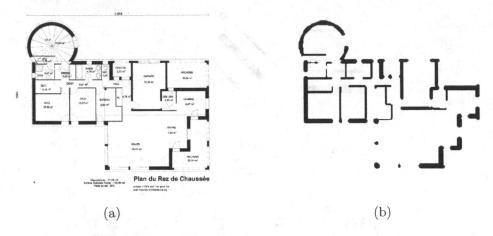

(a)   (b)

Fig. 4. Original and segmented images from the Black dataset

Likewise, according to the *assumption 3*, walls are longer than thicker and then, segmentations with longer segments are more likely to belong to wall elements. Thus:

$$\text{AR}_{h_i} = \overline{\text{long}(\text{CC}_j(h_i))/\text{width}(\text{CC}_j(h_i))}, \forall j | CC_j \in h_i \tag{2}$$

where AR_{h_i} bears the aspect ratio of the segments.

Finally, also according to *assumption 4*, **DiffD** enforces segmentations with similar black pixel distributions to the input image:

$$\text{DiffD}_{h_i} = \sum_{n=1}^{r} \sum_{m=1}^{r} p_{nm} - p_{nm}^{h_i}. \tag{3}$$

where p_{nm} and $p_{nm}^{h_i}$ are the percentage of the black pixels in the nm^{th} region r of the original image and h_i respectively.

The final ranking is calculated by sorting in a descend order the candidates regarding their global score, which is calculated as:

$$W(h_i) = \text{Ncc}_{h_i} + \text{AR}_{h_i} + \text{DiffD}_{h_i}. \tag{4}$$

Once the ranking of the segmentation candidates is done, the top n are combined into the final segmentation image. The number of selected images n depends on a experimentally calculated boundary over the confidence score. This boundary is thought to not only enforce final segmentations with more than only one candidate *assumption 5*, but also discard completely impossible segmentations.

2.2   Step 2: Appearance-Based Detection

Up to now we have an image out of the combination of wall segments that we call segment-image for clarity. The aim in this step is to regard the *assumption*

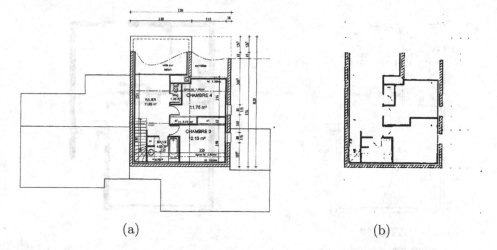

(a)   (b)

Fig. 5. Original and segmented images from the Textured dataset

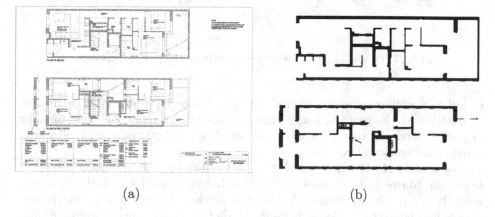

(a)   (b)

Fig. 6. Original and segmented images from the Textured2 dataset

6 and therefore, to learn the visual appearance of the already segmented walls to refine the final segmentation. The process here is similar to the one from [5], but reconsidering the learning step; it is done from the segment-image instead from a preannotated corpus of images. In this section we explain the learning procedure and summarize the classification.

Learning
The original image is split into squared equal-sized and overlapped patches. This procedure is repeated for the image rotations 45°, 90° and 135° with two purposes: to get more learning instances and to achieve rotation-invariableness. Patches falling into segmented regions in the segment-image are labeled as positive examples $c = \{Wall\}$, the rest as negative $c = \{Background\}$ meanwhile

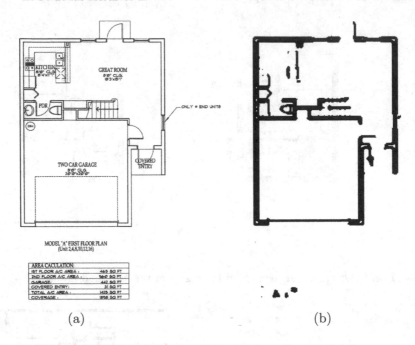

(a)   (b)

Fig. 7. Original and segmented images from the parallel dataset

completely white patches are filtered out. The image descriptor BSM [9] is used to describe all the patches, and a subset of them containing the same number of positive and negative instances is clustered into a dictionary of visual words using a fast version of Kmeans [8].

Once the dictionary is created, the probability of each vocabulary word w belonging to every object classes $C = \{\text{Wall}, \text{Background}\}$ is calculated as follows. Every patch-descriptor pd_i that has already a label to one of the two classes is assigned to its closest word in the dictionary w_j. Then, the conditional probability of a word to belong to each one of the classes is given by:

$$p(c_i|w_j) = \frac{\#(pd_{w_j}, c_i)}{\#pd_{w_j}}, \forall i, j. \tag{5}$$

Where $\#(pd_{w_j}, c_i)$ states for the number of patch descriptors with the label c_i assigned to codeword w_j, and $\#pd_{w_j}$ is the total number of patch-descriptors assigned to w_j.

Recognition

Every patch-descriptor from the overlapped grid on the input image inherits the class probabilities of its nearest word in the dictionary. This classification is performed by the 1-NN hard assignment on the Euclidean space. Lastly, the final pixel categorization depends on the multiple patches that fall on it.

The *Mean Rule* on the theoretical framework of combining multiple classifiers [10] is adapted to calculate the final segmentation for every pixel px in the image:

$$class(px) = \arg \max_i \Big(mean(P(c_i|pd)) \Big), \forall pd \mid px \in pd. \qquad (6)$$

Table 1. Wall segmentation results

	#images	[1]		[4]		[5]		[3]		New method	
		JI	Rec.	JI	Rec.	JI	Rec.	JI	Rec.	JI	Rec.
Dt. Black	90	0.90	0.92	0.97	0.99	0.97	0.99	0.93	0.97	0.95	0.99
Dt. Textured	10	–	–	0.83	0.98	0.86	0.99	0.82	0.97	0.82	0.98
Dt. Textured2	18	–	–	0.81	1	0.82	1	0.77	0.91	0.79	0.96
Dt. Parallel	4	–	–	0.70	0.84	0.71	0.86	0.66	0.98	0.67	1
Average per dataset	–	–		**0.83**	**0.95**	**0.84**	**0.96**	**0.80**	**0.96**	**0.80**	**0.98**

3 Experiments

In this section we explain the experimental evaluation performed to our new method presented in this paper. We firstly overview the datasets and the evaluation protocols, and then we present the results quantitatively and qualitatively.

3.1 Datasets

The database used to evaluate our method is the one presented in [2]. It contains 4 freely available datasets of real floor plans containing different graphical notations. Moreover, we have evaluated our approach on some images randomly picked from the Internet[1]. In the following, we summarize the content of the 4 datasets:

- **Black.** This dataset contains 90 images of real floor plans and has been used for evaluation of wall detection in [3–5]. Walls are modeled by thick black lines of different thicknesses whether they belong to interior or exterior instances. An example image of this dataset is shown in Fig. 4a.
- The **Textured** collection contains 10 real floor plan documents on a lower resolution. Here, interior and exterior walls are modeled with different textures as it can be seen in Fig. 5a.
- **Textured2.** This dataset contains 18 high resolution real floor plans. Walls are of multiple thicknesses depending they are interior, exterior, or main instances. Moreover, they are drawn by a hatched pattern as it is shown in Fig. 6a.
- The **Parallel** dataset contains 4 real floor plans. Walls are modeled by simple parallel lines, without any texture in between. An image of this set is shown in Fig. 7a.

---

[1] https://www.google.es/imghp?q=floor%20plan

3.2   Evaluation Protocol

The evaluation protocol is the same used in the last wall detection works [3–5]: the Jaccard Index (JI). As in [3], the global recall is also taken into account for the experimental evaluation. The reason is that, if we consider the detection of walls as a crucial step in floor plan interpretation, higher recall results are preferred since false positive instances are easily postprocessed than lost instances. The JI and Recall are calculated respectively as:

$$JI = \frac{TruePos}{TruePos + FalsePos + FalseNeg},$$

$$Recall = \frac{TruePos}{TruePos + FalseNeg}.$$

3.3   Experimental Results

Our method is inherently affected by the same parameters than the original approaches. In the first step of our method, the parameter values considered in [3] are also adopted here for comparison purposes. Hence, rl_{min}^{b}, which indicates the minimum length of the runs on black pixels to be considered as lines, is set to 10 pixels. The rotation angle interval α that defines the orientation where the lines are seek is set to 15°. The boundary value of σ^{thw} to discriminate floor plans with thick black walls is 25. And finally, the number of equal-sized squared divisions r to calculate the difference on the pixel distribution (DiffD) is 9.

On the other hand, the parameters in the second step have been restudied and recalculated experimentally since the learning origin is completely different from [5]. The parameters that affect the behavior of our method are 3 inherited from the original approach: the size of the patches PS, the distance between patches ϕ^{ov}, and the dictionary size K. Additionally, there is a fourth parameter generated by the new learning framework, which accounts on the amount of patches used in the creation of the vocabulary Spd. Regarding PS, only proportional values to the highest wall thickness in the segment-image have been tested, adopting finally 0.5 times the size of the thickest segment. ϕ^{ov} measures the distance between the centers of the patches. In other words, it defines the grid overlapping. Here, several proportional values to the patch-size have been tested, being $1/2 \times PS$ the one leads to the best performance. In terms of the dictionary size K, smaller dictionaries proved to generalize better. Thus, just 300 words are enough to learn the wall texture. Finally, the experiments have shown that the greater value for Spd, the better results obtains the method. Nevertheless, we have detected a learning saturation point at 75.000 patch-descriptors.

The Table 1 shows the quantitative results obtained by our new approach compared with the most recent state-of-the-art methods tested on the same sets of images. From this table we can observe that our new unsupervised approach performs better than the original [3]. Not only overperforms it in terms of average recall but also obtains better JI scores in two of the datasets. On the other hand, even the higher recall, our new method still behaves slightly worse in JI terms

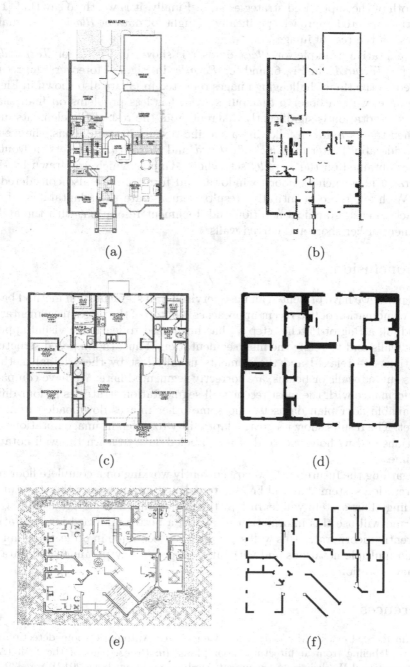

Fig. 8. Qualitative results for images extracted from the Internet. In (b), (d) and (f), the segmented walls are shown from their corresponding original images (a), (c) and (e).

than both of the supervised strategies [4,5]. Finally, it is worth to say that [1] is a notation-oriented approach specifically thought for dataset *Black*, which makes it useless in the rest of images.

A qualitative example for *Black* dataset is shown in Fig. 4, for *Textured* in Fig. 5, for *Textured2* in Fig. 6, and for *Parallel* in Fig. 7. Moreover, the results obtained on the three challenging images reported in [3] are also shown in Fig. 8. At a glance, we can observe that our system has less problems on floor plans where wall notation is significantly different from the rest of the elements; usually when they are drawn following a specific textual pattern. Thus, the results are considerably better on *Black, Textured* and *Textured2* datasets in front of the ones obtained on the *Parallel* set, where symbols which are drawn by simple parallel lines such as doors, windows, and furniture are also considered as walls. With all, these quantitative results demonstrate the adaptability of our approach to each graphical notation and document resolution, with the ability to segment either short and curved walls.

4   Conclusion

In this paper we have presented an unsupervised wall segmentation method based on the combination of two recent approaches. On top of the original segmentation method [3], a Bag-of-Patches step [5] has been used to learn the visual appearance of walls and to refine the final segmentation. Thus, the imposed structural restrictions are relaxed and the elements usually lost by the original method, such as curved walls or beams, are correctly segmented here. We have compared its performance with the most recent wall segmentation strategies in four different available floor plan datasets, and some other images downloaded from the Internet. The results show its great adaptability to different image notations and resolutions and without the need of any labeled data to learn the wall notation each time.

Regarding the future work, we are currently working on a complete floor plan interpretation system that will be able to extract automatically the structure of a building. This system will learn how the structural elements are usually composed and will use this information to obtain a better informed interpretation. It currently incorporates this wall segmentation technique in order to be able to work on multiple notations and without the need of any preannotated data for each new notation.

References

1. Ahmed, S., Liwicki, M., Weber, M., Dengel, A.: Automatic room detection and room labeling from architectural floor plans. In: Proceedings of the 10th IAPR International Workshop on Document Analysis Systems (DAS-2012), pp. 339–343 (2012)
2. de las Heras, L.-P., Ahmed, S., Liwicki, M., Valveny, E., Sánchez, G.: Statistical segmentation and structural recognition for floor plan interpretation. Int. J. Doc. Anal. Recogn. **17**, 221–237 (2014)

3. de las Heras, L.-P., Fernández, D., Valveny, E., Lladós, J., Sánchez, G.: Unsupervised wall detector in architectural floor plans. In: 2013 12th International Conference on Document Analysis and Recognition (ICDAR), pp. 1245–1249 (2013)
4. de las Heras, L.-P., Mas, J., Sánchez, G., Valveny, E.: Wall patch-based segmentation in architectural floorplans. In: Proceedings of the 11th International Conference on Document Analysis and Recognition, pp. 1270–1274 (2011)
5. de las Heras, L.-P., Mas, J., Sánchez, G., Valveny, E.: Notation-invariant patch-based wall detector in architectural floor plans. In: Kwon, Y.-B., Ogier, J.-M. (eds.) GREC 2011. LNCS, vol. 7423, pp. 79–88. Springer, Heidelberg (2013)
6. de las Heras, L.-P., Sánchez, G.: And-or graph grammar for architectural floor plan representation, learning and recognition. a semantic, structural and hierarchical model. In: Vitrià, J., Sanches, J.M., Hernández, M. (eds.) IbPRIA 2011. LNCS, vol. 6669, pp. 17–24. Springer, Heidelberg (2011)
7. Dosch, P., Tombre, K., Ah-Soon, C., Masini, G.: A complete system for the analysis of architectural drawings. Int. J. Doc. Anal. Recogn. 3, 102–116 (2000)
8. Elkan, C.: Using the triangle inequality to accelerate k-means. In: The Twentieth International Conference on Machine Learning, pp. 147–153 (2003)
9. Escalera, S., Fornes, A., Pujol, O., Escudero, A., Radeva, P.: Circular blurred shape model for symbol spotting in documents. In: 2009 16th IEEE International Conference on Image Processing (ICIP), pp. 2005–2008 (2009)
10. Kittler, J., Hatef, M., Duin, R.P.W., Matas, J.: On combining classifiers. IEEE Trans. Pattern Anal. Mach. Intell. 20(3), 226–239 (1998)
11. Lu, T., Yang, H., Yang, R., Cai, S.: Automatic analysis and integration of architectural drawings. Int. J. Doc. Anal. Recogn. 9, 31–47 (2007)
12. Macé, S., Locteau, H., Valveny, E., Tabbone, S.: A system to detect rooms in architectural floor plan images. In: Proceedings of the 9th IAPR International Workshop on Document Analysis Systems, pp. 167–174 (2010)
13. Ouwayed, N., Belaid, A.: A general approach for multi-oriented text line extraction of handwritten document. Int. J. Doc. Anal. Recogn. 14(4), 297–314 (2011)
14. Shi, Z., Govindaraju, V.: Line separation for complex document images using fuzzy runlength. In: Proceedings of the First International Workshop on Document Image Analysis for Libraries, pp. 306–312 (2004)
15. Tombre, K., Tabbone, S., Pélissier, L., Dosch, P.: Text/Graphics separation revisited. In: Lopresti, D.P., Hu, J., Kashi, R.S. (eds.) DAS 2002. LNCS, vol. 2423, pp. 615–620. Springer, Heidelberg (2002)

Detecting Recurring Deformable Objects: An Approximate Graph Matching Method for Detecting Characters in Comics Books

Hoang Nam Ho, Christophe Rigaud, Jean-Christophe Burie[✉],
and Jean-Marc Ogier

L3i Laboratory, University of La Rochelle, Avenue Michel Crépeau,
17042 La Rochelle Cedex 1, France
{hoang_nam.ho,christophe.rigaud,jcburie,jmogier}@univ-lr.fr

Abstract. Graphs are popular data structures used to model pair wise relations between elements from a given collection. In image processing, adjacency graphs are often used to represent the relations between segmented regions. The comparison of such graphs has been largely studied but graph matching strategies are essential to find, efficiently, similar patterns. In this paper, we propose a method to detect the recurring characters in comics books. We would like to draw attention of the reader. In this paper, the term "character" means the protagonists of the story. In our approach, each panel is represented with an attributed adjacency graph. Then, an inexact graph matching strategy is applied to find recurring structures among this set of graphs. The main idea is that the same character will be represented by similar subgraphs in the different panels where it appears. The two-step matching process consists in a node matching step and an edge validation step. Experiments show that our approach is able to detect recurring structures in the graph and consequently the recurrent characters in a comics book. The originality of our approach is that no prior object model is required the characters. The algorithm detects, automatically, all recurring structures corresponding to the main characters of the story.

Keywords: Comics · Character detection · Attributed adjacency graph · Approximate graph matching · Spatial relation

1 Introduction

Nowadays, with the development of information technology and communication, the digital information is becoming increasingly popular. It is a great challenge for computer science to develop applications to help the user to process this information. Born in the 19th century, comics spread worldwide and became an important industry. Although hundreds of thousands comics albums have been digitized around the world, few researches have been carried out in order to exploit the content of digitized comics.

© Springer-Verlag Berlin Heidelberg 2014
B. Lamiroy and J.-M. Ogier (Eds.): GREC 2013, LNCS 8746, pp. 122–134, 2014.
DOI: 10.1007/978-3-662-44854-0_10

Some works have been done to analyze the layout of Japanese mangas [25], to extract panels [7,8,12,19], to localize speech balloons [2,8] or to detect text [2,19]. In [24], authors are able to detect faces, in Japanese mangas, as regions of interests to detect illegal copies. But, the detection of the characters, the differents objects drawn by the author, or even, the elements of the background, represents a big challenge to be able to index efficiently the comics books. To our knowledge, no research has been done to analyze the graphical content of color comics books.

If we consider the characters illustrated in the panels of a comics book, their representation changes because the artist usually draws the characters with different sizes or from different point of view, with various face expressions or in diverse positions. Usual pattern recognition methods would try to match a candidate area with a given model of a character. But the main problem to solve would be to define a model of this character since there are almost as many models as character representations.

The first question is how to represent a character? Each character corresponds to a set of regions with different colors which represent clothes, head, skin, eyes, hair and so on... More generally, each panel is a set of color regions which represent the parts of the characters, but also the ones of the background. Graphs are popular data structures used to model pair wise relations between elements from a given collection. In document analysis, or more generally, in image processing, adjacency graphs are often used to represent the relations between segmented regions. The comparison of such graphs and especially the search of frequent subgraphs has been largely studied [11,13,14,27] but in our research graph matching strategies are essential to find, efficiently, similar patterns corresponding to the characters.

We propose to represent each panel with an attributed adjacency graph and to extract recurring structures. The main idea is that the same character will be represented by similar subgraphs in the different panels where it appears. Thus, an inexact graph matching strategy has been developed to find these recurring structures among this set of graphs.

The paper is organized as follow. The second section gives an overview of comparison methods between graphs. The method used to represents comics panels with graphs is detailed in Sect. 3. Section 4 describes the inexact graph matching approach. The experiments and results are given in Sect. 5. Finally, conclusion and future works end this paper.

2   Overview of Graph Comparison Methods

A graph $G = (V, E)$ is a set of vertices (nodes) V, E is a set of edges (links). In model-based pattern recognition problems, two graphs are given, the model graph G_M and the data graph G_D. The procedure for comparing them involves checking whether they are similar or not. Generally speaking, we can state the graph matching problem as follows: given two graphs $G_M = (V_M, E_M)$ and $G_D = (V_D, E_D), with |V_M| = |V_D|$, the problem is to find a one-to-one mapping

$f : V_D \rightarrow V_M$ such that $(u, v) \in E_D$ *iff* $(f(u), f(v)) \in E_M$. The inverse correspondance is given by $(u, v) \in E_M$ *iff* $(f^{-1}(u), f^{-1}(v)) \in E_D$. When a mapping f exists, this is called an isomorphism, and G_D is said to be isomorphic to G_M. This type of problem is known as exact graph matching. On the other hand, the term "inexact" applied to graph matching problems means that it is not possible to find an isomorphism between the two graphs. This is the case when the number of nodes is different in both the model and the data graphs. Therefore, in these cases no isomorphism can be expected between both graphs, and the graph matching problem does not consist in searching for the exact way of matching nodes of a graph with nodes of the other, but in finding the best matching between them. This leads to a class of problems known as inexact graph matching. In that case, the matching aims at finding a non-bijective correspondence between a data graph and a model graph [4,18]. If one of the graphs involved in the matching is larger than the other, in terms of the number of nodes, then the matching is performed by a subgraph isomorphism. A subgraph isomorphism from G_M to G_D means finding a subgraph s_g of G_D such that G_M and s_g are isomorphic.

Two drawbacks can be stated for the use of graph matching. First, the computational complexity is an inherent difficulty of the graph-matching problem. A research effort has been made to develop computationally tractable graph-matching algorithms [6,21]. The second drawback is dealing with noise and distortion. The encoding of an object of an image may not be perfect due to noise and errors introduced in low-level stages. In such situations, the graph representation of identical objects may not exactly match. To overcome this shortcoming, some methods propose to define a distance between graphs. The edit distance is often used to measure the distance between graphs [26]. The edit distance is a dissimilarity measure that represents the minimum-cost sequence of basic editing operations to transform a graph into another graph by means of insertion, deletion and substitution of nodes or edges. The flexibility of the edit distance allows to use this approach on a large diversity of graphs with no constraint on the labels or the topology. However, its application is generally limited to small graphs to keep a reasonable computation time. However, efficient heuristics have been proposed recently [6].

Another approach, to overcome computational time and dimensionality problems, consists in embedding graph in vector spaces. Different graph embedding procedures have been proposed. Some of them are based on pattern numeration such as graph probing [15], Graphlet [22], Non isomorphic patterns [23], Fuzzy graph embedding [17] or based on spectral graph theory [16]. Others take advantage of typical similarity measures to perform the embedding tasks [3]. The main advantage of this approach is that the comparison of graphs becomes a comparison of vectors, euclidian distance can be used and computational time depends on the vector size. Moreover all classification methods based on vectors are available to the graph domain. However, graph embedding lacks the capabilities to address the problem of graph matching. This is because of the strict limitation of the resulting feature vector which is not capable of preserving the matching between nodes of graphs.

In our work, we have considered the search of redundant structures as an inexact graph matching problem. The approach will be detailed in Sect. 4.

3   Graph Representation of Comics

We introduce in this section an approach to represent a comics panel by a graph. First, we extract the color regions and their features, second the graph is constructed in three steps: node labeling, edge construction and edge labeling.

3.1   Pre-processing

The first step consists in extracting panels from a comics page with the method proposed in [19]. Each panel is then processed separately as shown in Fig. 1. To obtain regions, any color segmentation method can be used in this stage. However to avoid over-segmentation, a color reduction in 16 most significant colors is applied to the page. In this work, the color reduction is carried out with the k-means algorithm ($k = 16$). In order to limit noise and distortion in the graph, three filtering steps are applied to remove:

- The text inside the balloons with the method given in [20]
- The small regions to limit the number of regions and consequently the size the graph.
- The black lines surrounding the color regions.

The black lines are a feature of most color comics but are not interesting in our approach since they create no significant region and break the adjacency relationship between meaningful color regions. Since a black line surrounds all the regions of the panel, it produces the biggest connected component in the panel. This component can easily be ignored in the rest of process.

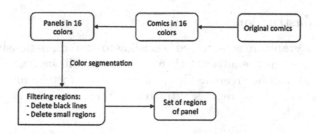

Fig. 1. Process from comics page to panels

After this pre-processing stage, a set of regions is obtained. Each region is characterized by the following features: color, surface area, compactness, shape and its adjacent regions.

3.2   Node Labeling

In our approach, the regions are represented as the nodes of the graph. Each node is described by the following attributes:

- **Color.** The color is defined in CIE L*a*b* color space [1]. L*a*b* is a uniform color space based on the human perceptual system. It has been specially designed so that the calculated euclidian distances between colors correspond to the differences perceived by the human eye. The region color is represented by a vector of three dimensions where each element corresponds respectively to L (luminance), a and b (chromatic components).
- **Compactness.** This value is calculated in the segmentation step.
- **Shape.** The shape of the regions is characterized by Hu moments [9] which are invariant under translation, changes in scale, and also rotation. These properties are essential in our case because the characters can be drawn with different size or orientation. This attribute is defined by a vector with the 7 values of Hu moments.

Finally, by combining these attributes, each region is characterized by an 11-dimensional vector. Since the magnitude of each component of this vector can be very different, a normalization process is applied to give the same weight to each component and to be able to compare vectors objectively. Let X_i be the value of one component, $\overline{X_i}$ the average value and Γ the standard deviation. The average value $\overline{X_i}$ and the standard deviation Γ are computed from the components of the whole dataset. The normalization is performed as follows: $(X_i - \overline{X_i})/\Gamma$. This normalized vector will be used to compare the regions. It should be noted that currently the same weight is given to each component of the 11-dimensional vector. The objective was, indeed, validating the global approach to extract the recurring characters. To improve the comparison process, a complementary study will be done in order to evaluate the relevance of each attribute (color, compactness, shape).

3.3   Edge Construction

The edges of the graph are constructed according to spatial relationships between regions. If two regions are adjacent then their nodes will be linked by an edge otherwise no link will be created. This strategy allows to take into account the spatial organization of the regions extracted in the comics panel and provides an adjacency graph.

3.4   Edge Labeling

The last step consists in giving labels to the edges in order to quantify the relationship between two regions. This measure should be invariant to rotation and scaling change to take into account that a character can be drawn with different size and position. We propose to use the surface area ratio between adjacent regions. Indeed, we assume that the proportions between regions will be preserved, whether the character is viewed from near or far. Let S_{R1} and S_{R2} be respectively the area of regions $R1$ and $R2$. Since the ratio S_{R1}/S_{R2} is the reciprocal number of the ratio S_{R2}/S_{R1}, an orientation is given to the edge indicating how the ratio has been computed. So, an edge is oriented from the node corresponding to the region $R1$ toward the node corresponding to the region $R2$ if the label given to the edge is S_{R1}/S_{R2} and reciprocally from $R2$ toward $R1$ if the label is S_{R2}/S_{R1}.

Finally, each panel is transformed into an attributed adjacency graph where nodes, labeled with an 11-dimensional vector, correspond to the regions and the oriented edges quantify the relationships between adjacency regions in terms of surface ratio.

4   Inexact Graph Matching Approach

In this section, the approach to compare two graphs is presented. First, the algorithm description is discussed and then the algorithm is detailed.

4.1   Algorithm Description

Panels are transformed into graphs with the method presented above. In order to find recurrent structures in the comics book, a specific method is necessary to compare graphs and to extract similar subgraphs. Let G_1 and G_2 be two graphs to compare. This algorithm consists of two steps:

- The first one concerns the node matching. The distance between each node of G_1 and each node of G_2, characterized respectively by an 11-dimensional vector, is computed. The lowest distances are selected to provide a list of matched nodes.
- The goal of the second step is to verify, for each pair of matched nodes, the compatibility of the edges that connect them, in order to extract the common subgraphs.

Node Matching to match the regions of 2 panels represented respectively by two graphs G_1 and G_2, we define a matrix P of size $n_1 \times n_2$ where n_1 and n_2 are respectively the node number in G_1 and G_2. Each element p_{ij} in P corresponds to the euclidian distance between attributes of node i in G_1 and node j in G_2 with $i \in \{1, ..., n_1\}$ and $j \in \{1, ..., n_2\}$.

In each row i' of P, we select the element j' with the minimal value. The indices i' and j' of the selected element match the node i' in G_1 with the node j' in G_2. However, to avoid wrong matching, this minimal value has to be lower than a threshold λ, defined experimentally here. Consequently, a node i in G_1 may not have corresponding node in G_2.

When all the rows of P have been processed, this first step provides a set of pairs of matched nodes between the graphs G_1 and G_2. Let $(N_{G_1}^k, N_{G_2}^k)$ be a pair of matched node between G_1 and G_2 with $k \in \{1, ..., l\}$ and where l is the number of matched nodes. An example of pairs of matched nodes is given in Fig. 2. The result shows that the region (node) 1 of the panel (graph) G_1 is similar to region (node) A of the panel (graph) G_2.

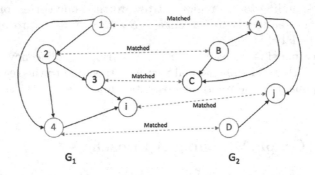

Fig. 2. Node matching for two graphs

Edge Compatibility. The node matching is not enough, the relationships between regions, represented by the edges, have also to be compatible in order to extract similar subgraph. Let $(N_{G_1}^i, N_{G_2}^i)$ and $(N_{G_1}^j, N_{G_2}^j)$ be two pairs of matched node with $i, j \in \{1, ..., l\}$: If $N_{G_1}^i$ is connected with $N_{G_1}^j$ AND $N_{G_2}^i$ with $N_{G_2}^j$, the edge labels are compared. If the two conditions are not true, the match is ignored. As mentioned above, the edge label is the ratio between the surface areas of adjacent regions. If the two edges have the same orientation, the labels can be compared as they are. Otherwise, the reciprocal number of one of the label has to be computed before comparing them. The compatibility of the edges and therefore the similarity is established if the distance between the 2 labels is lower than a threshold ω. This threshold is chosen to be quite tolerant since variations of the ratio of 20 % are accepted to consider that the edges are compatible.

4.2   Algorithm and Complexity

Algorithm. We present here the algorithm used for graph matching.
Input : two attributed adjacency graphs G_1 and G_2
Output : the common subgraph to G_1 and G_2
Pre-condition : the node number n_1 of G_1 is lower than the one n_2 of G_2

Initialize P as follows $p_{ij} = \mathrm{d}(N_{G_1}, N_{G_2})$: Euclidian distance between the attributes of the two nodes N_{G_1} and N_{G_2}.
Node matching between G_1 and G_2
   for all $i = 0$ to $n_1 - 1$ **do**
      for all $j = 0$ to $n_2 - 1$ **do**
         if $p_{ij} < \lambda$ **then**
            Keep the lowest value p_{ij}
            Save i and j, it means that the node i is similar to the node j

else
    Do nothing (there is no matching between the node j and the node i)
  end if
  end for
end for
Search for the similar elements (nodes and edges) between G_1 and G_2
Set l as the matching number founded in below
for all $i = 0$ to $l - 1$ **do**
  for all $j = i + 1$ to $l - 1$ **do**
    Set a as edge between the node i and node j of G_1
    Set b as edge between the node i and node j of G_2
    Call **Verification** (a, b)
  end for
end for
Verification (a,b)
Check whether a and b are in the same direction, and calculate D_{edge}, the distance between a and b
if $D_{edge} < \omega$ **then**
  keep the nodes and the edges, they correspond to a common subgraph between G_1 and G_2
end if

Complexity. The complexity of the algorithm is $O(n_1 \times n_2 \times l)$ where n_1 is the number of nodes of G_1, n_2 is the number of nodes of G_2 and l is the number of matching nodes.

4.3   Recurrence

The approach detailed above allows to compare two graphs (panels) in order to extract common subgraphs (similar objects). But, our purpose is to extract recurring objects drawn in the comics. So, how to define the recurrence of an object? The strategy consists in comparing panels (or rather their graphs) two by two and in counting the number of times a given subgraph is detected. Let f be the frequency of appearance of an object in the panels and N_p the total number of panels. An object (or subgraphs) is called recurring if it verifies the following expression: $f \geq N_p/2$. In this approach no model is given, the algorithm finds by itself the recurring subgraphs and consequently the characters in our case.

5   Experiments and Results

Two experiments have been carried out to evaluate the performance of the proposed approach. The first one searches the same characters in two panels. The second one consists in the analysis of a whole comics album to extract the recurring characters. For each experiment, the panels are first extracted and transformed into graphs with the method described in Sect. 3. Note that the text of speech balloons has been removed [19] to avoid the introduction of noise in the process. The two thresholds used in this method are set to $\lambda = 10$ and $\omega = 0.2$. These thresholds have been determined experimentally. The dataset used in this experiments can't be shared for copyright issues but, as it is a webcomics, the images are available on the author's blog [10].

5.1 Comparison of Two Panels

The aim of the first experiment is to test the ability of the algorithm to detect the similarity between two panels. A data set with 200 panels extracted from a comics album has been created. Then, the 200 panels have been transformed in 200 distinct graphs. From these 200 graphs, 100 pairs of graphs have been selected randomly. 76 pairs contain similar elements, 24 pairs have no similar elements. In this study, the time required to execute the comparison is also considered. Figure 3 shows an example where the algorithm detects similar objects (here a character) in two panels. To visualize the results a bounding box has been drawn around the similar subgraph found in the panels.

Fig. 3. Detection of similar objects (Image credit: Cyb [5])

In some cases, only partial detections of the characters are carried out. An example is shown on Fig. 4. The algorithm detects similarities between the parts corresponding to the hair and the upper body, but no similarity is found for the face (Note that the result for the left character is not displayed on this figure). This result can be explained because the facial features (mouth, eyes) are different. The structure of the two corresponding graphs being different, no matching between the nodes is found. This creates an ambiguity in the detection. If we consider the character detection process, the algorithm failed. However it succeeded to find recurring structures. This example shows the capabilities of our approach to extract similar parts of the panels, but the method needs to be improved to take into account the fact that characters can show bigger variations.

To evaluate the detection results we consider that a pair is valid if a character has been correctly found in the two panels. Table 1 shows a confusion matrix, which is the result of the comparison of 100 pairs of graphs. 54 pairs have been well detected. Among the 22 pairs detected as non valid, 7 correspond to partial detections of the characters. 5 non valid pairs have been detected as valid because

Fig. 4. Partial detections of a character (Image credit: Cyb [5])

similar regions, in terms of shape and color, are drawn in the panels. As the algorithm considers that recurring structures are characters, they have been evaluated as valid. The recall and precision are respectively 71.05 % and 91.5 %.

Table 1. Results of comparison of two graphs

		Estimated class	
		Valid	Non valid
Real class	Valid	54	22
	Non valid	5	19

The computation time to process a pair of graphs is about 2 s on regular machine without any optimization. The computation time depends on the number of nodes of the graphs (i.e. the number of segmented regions in each panel). For example, on the Fig. 3, the graph corresponding to the panel on the left is constituted by 30 nodes and the graph of the right one by 48 nodes. In our experiments, the average number of regions and consequently the number of nodes was about 58.

5.2 Recurring Character Detection

The second experiment was carried out with a set of 42 pages of comics. All pages contain at least one recurring character. Each page consists of 4 panels. To limit computation time, the purpose of this test is to verify if the algorithm is able to detect redundancies in each comics page and not in the whole album. Redundancy (see Sect. 4.3) is defined by the frequency of occurrence of an object. For a page of 4 panels as shown in Fig. 5, a recurring character is a character that appears at least twice. To evaluate algorithm performance, the detection is considered as valid if this redundancy condition is true. Table 2 presents the results. At least one recurring character has been detected in 71.4 % of the pages. Partial detections have been detected in 9.6 % of the 42 pages. Non valid pages correspond to pages where the redundancy criterion is not verified. The characters have been detected but only once.

Table 2. Results of comparison for a page of comics

Valid page	Non valid page	Page with partial detection
71.4%	19%	9.6%

Fig. 5. Recurring character detection (Image credit: Cyb [5])

The average computation time for one comics page with 4 panels is about 4 s. The results of this experiment are encouraging for the detection of recurring objects but improvements are necessary to solve the problem of partial detections.

6   Conclusion and Future Works

In this paper, we have presented an approach to detect recurring structures in comics books. Each panel is transformed in an attributed adjacency graph where the nodes represent the regions and the edges the relationships between adjacency regions. A specific inexact graph matching has been developed to extract similar subgraphs. This approach has been used to detect recurring characters drawn in comics but it could be used to detect any recurring objects. The originality of this approach is that the definition of a prior object model is not required. The algorithm detects all the recurring structures without using any model. In this paper, the experimentations have been done on each page separately. However, the same approach can be applied on a whole album. The additional redundancy may allow more robust detection of recurring characters. On the other hand, scaling up could be very difficult due to CPU-time-complexity of graph matching, and due to increased possibility of false positives. However, the method should be able to detect characters even with complex backgrounds. Indeed, the background changes during the story but the characteristics of the character don't change. So, the method should be able to extract the recurring structures corresponding to the main characters of the comics books.

Future works will concentrate on the problem of partial detections to improve the rate of recognition of characters. We will also study the possibility to extract other objects or scenery elements for comics book indexation. Finally the tests will be done on a bigger dataset to check the robustness of the approach.

Acknowledgement. This work was supported by the European Regional Development Fund, the region Poitou-Charentes (France), the General Council of Charente Maritime (France) and the town of La Rochelle (France).

References

1. Commission Internationale de l'Eclairage, Colorimetry, CIE 15.2 (1986)
2. Arai, K., Tolle, H.: Automatic e-comic content adaptation. Int. J. Ubiquitous Comput. (IJUC) **1**(1), 1–11 (2010)
3. Bunke, H., Riesen, K.: Recent advances in graph-based pattern recognition with applications in document analysis. Pattern Recogn. **44**(5), 1057–1067 (2011)
4. Bunke, H.: Error-tolerant graph matching: a formal framework and algorithms. In: Amin, A., Pudil, P., Dori, D. (eds.) SPR 1998 and SSPR 1998. LNCS, vol. 1451, pp. 1–14. Springer, Heidelberg (1998)
5. Cyb: Cosmozone, vol. 1. Studio Cyborga (2009)
6. Fischer, A., Suen, C.Y., Frinken, V., Riesen, K., Bunke, H.: A fast matching algorithm for graph-based handwriting recognition. In: Kropatsch, W.G., Artner, N.M., Haxhimusa, Y., Jiang, X. (eds.) GbRPR 2013. LNCS, vol. 7877, pp. 194–203. Springer, Heidelberg (2013)
7. Chan, C.H., Leung, H., Komura, T.: Automatic panel extraction of color comic images. In: Ip, H.H.-S., Au, O.C., Leung, H., Sun, M.-T., Ma, W.-Y., Hu, S.-M. (eds.) PCM 2007. LNCS, vol. 4810, pp. 775–784. Springer, Heidelberg (2007)
8. Ho, A.K.N., Burie, J.C., Ogier, J.M.: Panel and speech balloon extraction from comic books. In: DAS 2012, Tenth IAPR International Workshop on Document Analysis Systems, Gold Coast, Australia (2012)
9. Hu, M.K.: Visual pattern recognition by moment invariants. IRE Trans. Inf. Theor. **8**(2), 179–187 (1962)
10. Le blog bd de cyb. http://www.cosmozone.fr/tag/Cosmozone%20p%C3% A9riode%201/
11. Inokuchi, A., Washio, T., Motoda, H.: An apriori-based algorithm for mining frequent substructures from graph data. In: Zighed, D.A., Komorowski, J., Żytkow, J.M. (eds.) PKDD 2000. LNCS (LNAI), vol. 1910, pp. 13–23. Springer, Heidelberg (2000)
12. Ishii, D., Watanabe, H.: A study on frame position detection of digitized comics images. In: Proceedings of Workshop on Picture Coding and Image Processing, PCSJ2010/IMPS2010, Nagoya, Japan, December 2010, pp. 124–125 (2010)
13. Kuramochi, M., Karypis, G.: Frequent subgraph discovery. In: Proceedings of the 2001 IEEE International Conference on Data Mining, pp. 313–320 (2001)
14. Kuramochi, M., Karypis, G.: Finding frequent patterns in a large sparse graph. Data Min. Knowl. Discov. **11**, 243–271 (2005)
15. Lopresti, D., Wilfong, G.: A fast technique for comparing graph representations with applications to performance evaluation. Int. J. Doc. Anal. Recogn. **6**(4), 219–229 (2003)

16. Luo, B., Wilson, R.C., Hancock, E.R.: Spectral embedding of graphs. Pattern Recogn. **36**(10), 2210–2230 (2003)
17. Luqman, M.M., Ramel, J.Y., Llads, J., Brouard, T.: Fuzzy multilevel graph embedding. Pattern Recogn. **46**(2), 551–565 (2013)
18. Messmer, B.T., Bunke, H.: A new algorithm for error-tolerant subgraph isomorphism detection. IEEE Trans. Pattern Anal. Mach. Intell. **20**(5), 493–504 (1998)
19. Rigaud, C., Karatzas, D., Van de Weijer, J., Burie, J.C., Ogier, J.M.: Automatic text localisation in scanned comic books. In: Proceedings of the 8th International Conference on Computer Vision Theory and Applications (VISAPP), pp. 814–819 (2013)
20. Rigaud, C., Tsopze, N., Burie, J.-C., Ogier, J.-M.: Robust frame and text extraction from comic books. In: Kwon, Y.-B., Ogier, J.-M. (eds.) GREC 2011. LNCS, vol. 7423, pp. 129–138. Springer, Heidelberg (2013)
21. Shapiro, L., Haralick, R.: Structural descriptions and inexact matching. IEEE Trans. Pattern Anal. Mach. Intell. **3**(5), 504–519 (1981)
22. Shervashidze, N., Vishwanathan, S.V.N., Petri, T., Mehlhorn, K., Borgwardt, K.M.: Efficient graphlet kernels for large graph comparison. In: Twelfth International Conference on Artificial Intelligence and Statistics, pp. 488–495 (2009)
23. Sidere, N., Héroux, P., Ramel, J.Y.: Embedding labeled graphs into occurence matrix. In: Proceedings of the IAPR Workshop on Graphics Recognition, GREC 2009, La Rochelle, France, pp. 44–50 (2009)
24. Sun, W., Kise, K.: Similar manga retrieval using visual vocabulary based on regions of interest. In: Proceedings of the 11th International Conference on Document Analysis and Recognition (ICDAR2011), October 2011, pp. 1075–1079 (2011)
25. Tanaka, T., Shoji, K., Toyama, F., Miyamichi, J.: Layout analysis of tree-structured scene frames in comic images. In: Proceedings of International Joint Conference on Artificial Intelligence, IJCAI-07, Hyderabad, India, January 2007, pp. 2885–2890 (2007)
26. Tsai, W.H., Fu, K.S.: Error-correcting isomorphisms of attributed relational graphs for pattern analysis. IEEE Trans. Syst. Man Cybern. **9**(12), 757–768 (1979)
27. Yan, X., Han, J.: Span: graph-based substructure pattern mining. In: Proceedings of the 2002 IEEE International Conference on Data Mining, pp. 721–725 (2002)

Runlength Histogram Image Signature for Perceptual Retrieval of Architectural Floor Plans

Lluís-Pere de las Heras[✉], David Fernández, Alicia Fornés, Ernest Valveny, Gemma Sánchez, and Josep Lladós

Computer Vision Center, Universitat Autònoma de Barcelona, Campus UAB, 08193 Bellaterra, Barcelona, Spain
{lpheras,dfernanez}@cvc.uab.es
http://www.cvc.uab.cat

Abstract. This paper proposes a runlength histogram signature as a perceptual descriptor of architectural plans in a retrieval scenario. The style of an architectural drawing is characterized by the perception of lines, shapes and texture. Such visual stimuli are the basis for defining semantic concepts as space properties, symmetry, density, etc. We propose runlength histograms extracted in vertical, horizontal and diagonal directions as a characterization of line and space properties in floorplans, so it can be roughly associated to a description of walls and room structure. A retrieval application illustrates the performance of the proposed approach, where given a plan as a query, similar ones are obtained from a database. A ground truth based on human observation has been constructed to validate the hypothesis. Additional retrieval results on sketched building's facades are reported qualitatively in this paper. Its good description and its adaptability to two different sketch drawings despite its simplicity shows the interest of the proposed approach and opens a challenging research line in graphics recognition.

Keywords: Graphics recognition · Graphics retrieval · Image classification

1 Introduction

Aesthetics is a branch of philosophy devoted to beauty, scientifically defined as the study of sensory or sensori-emotional values, sometimes called judgements of sentiment and taste. Visual aesthetics is an emerging topic in computer vision [1,8]. The general idea is to use machine learning techniques to score the aesthetics of images in terms of visual cues as color, shape and texture, given a subjective human characterization. In document analysis, and in particular in graphics recognition, to the best of our knowledge the concept of aesthetics has not been developed. Some promising approaches have been proposed on perceptual document analysis to segment text lines [7], or to interpret sketches [9].

B. Lamiroy and J.-M. Ogier (Eds.): GREC 2013, LNCS 8746, pp. 135–146, 2014.
DOI: 10.1007/978-3-662-44854-0_11

In these works the structure of the document is analyzed in terms of salient objects, following perceptual grouping rules. We propose the use of perceptual organization, i.e. concepts like saliency, closure, repetition, alignment of geometric primitives, etc. as the basis of aesthetics in graphical documents.

Architecture is a visual art where a creative process results in a design that encompasses aesthetics and function. Hence, a composition is influenced by the standards of beauty that can vary depending on the social, cultural and temporal context, but also by the function of the building and its parts. In the conceptualization stage, architects use CAD software or just sketching interfaces for designing new constructions, projecting it in different views, namely the floor plan or the facade. In this stage, a blank paper is considered as a canvas, and the line drawings are like a painting. The language of architecture consists of basic visual tokens as lines, shapes and texture. Lines can be thick or thin, straight or curved, jagged or smooth, dotted or continuous. Shapes define symbols (structure, furniture, utilities). Texture describes materials and object surfaces. The perception of the spatial arrangement and combination of the basic visual elements gives rise to concepts as symmetry, balance, rhythm, proportion, space, etc. A style is characterized by these concepts, influenced by cultural, societal and temporal trends. Roughly speaking, gothic constructions have geometrically ordered and dense ornaments and vertical emphasis; American colonial house plans feature symmetry in doors and windows; Mediterranean style plans include big spaces like patios or courtyards.

This paper is an early attempt to introduce visual aesthetics in graphics recognition, in particular in line drawings of architectural plans in a retrieval scenario. In this context, aesthetics can be also seen as a drawing style of the architect. Our hypothesis is that an architect can cast queries in large databases in terms of a sample document and retrieve the architectural drawings from the database having a similar style. The state of the art on floor plan retrieval consists in formulating queries in terms of the functional view of the building. Hence, using ontology models, the user can search for similar designs in terms of the number of rooms, the building symbols, etc. [11]. The approach presented in this paper is appearance-based, so we don't recognize building elements, but correlate perceptual semantic concepts with features extracted from raw images. We focus on two topics, namely spaces and lines. Space refers to the size, the layout, or the shape of rooms. Lines in a broader sense give information of the walls width, texture, or length. Perceptually, spaces and lines give an idea of the building structure (e.g. big squared rooms with thick external walls could be stated as a query in terms of spaces and lines). The structure can be associated to the function of the building (a public theater will have big spaces, a bungalow small ones and thin lines defining the walls).

We propose a very simple image signature model, but descriptive enough to represent semantic topics related to some space and line properties. We propose a runlength histogram descriptor. The intuitive idea is that thick lines representing orthogonal walls generate a high frequency of the codeword of long runs in vertical and horizontal direction, and another high frequency in the codeword of

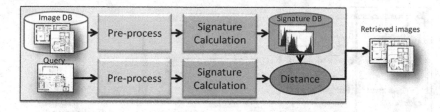

Fig. 1. Pipeline of the method

runlengths corresponding to the width of the walls. On the other hand, big rooms (spaces) are represented by histogram maxima in the runlengths corresponding to their size. The retrieval model proposed is a query by example framework. Given a query architectural image, we retrieve images that are similar in terms of the space and line topics.

This model has also been tested for retrieving similar sketch drawings of building facades. Qualitative results on arbitrarily downloaded images from the Internet are reported in the paper. Our signature is able to describe in a similar way not only buildings of a similar architectural style, but also in terms of the drawing technique.

The rest of the paper is organized as follows. In Sect. 2 we first review the runlength histogram descriptor and afterwards the approach for retrieving architectural drawings is described. In Sect. 3 the performance evaluation protocol and the experiments are presented. Finally Sect. 4 draws the conclusions and outlines the future work.

2   The Runlength Histogram Representation

A runglenth is the number of linewise consecutive pixels with the same value in a given direction. Given a direction d that defines the scanpath, the *runlength histogram*, denoted as H_d, encodes the length frequencies of the runs in the image extracted linewise at direction d. Thus, $H_d[i]$ counts the number of runs of length i at direction d. Runs can be extracted from foreground or background images. Thus, separate histograms can be considered, or they can be accumulated in a single one depending on the application. To avoid confusions, we will denote as H_d^f, H_d^b or H_d the foreground, background or joint histograms respectively.

Runlength analysis has been used in document analysis with different purposes. Due to the simplicity in the computation, vertical and horizontal runs are the most usually used. In [5], runlength histograms are used to classify between textual and non-textual blocks in administrative documents. Lately, in [10], runlength projections are used to detect page frames in double-page scanned documents. More recently, in [2], the authors suggest the use of runlengths in the detection of potential wall-elements in architectural floor plans. Finally, in [4], runlength histograms are introduced as whole page document description. Here, foreground runlengths at different scales using spatial pyramids are concatenated

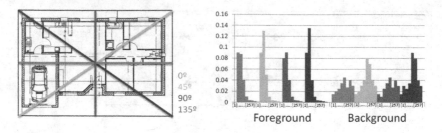

Fig. 2. Signature extraction

and used as signature for efficient classification and retrieval tasks in large-scale collections. Strongly based in this idea, we use runlength projections as a perceptual signature model for architectural floor plans.

The pipeline of the process, shown in Fig. 1, can be seen as a specific case of existing CBIR strategies. Firstly, all the images are preprocessed for ease of computation. Then, for every floor plan, its signature is calculated by generating the runlength histogram. Given a query example, the method returns a ranked list of the most similar images. Let us further describe the steps of the process.

Preprocess. Floor plan images are first binarized using the Otsu method to be able to extract runs. Afterwards, text-graphic separation is performed to filter out text components, because do not appear in all the images and can slightly bias their global perception. In addition to that, images are resized. Thus, the height of the images has been fixed to 1200 pixels meanwhile the width is rescaled dynamically to keep the aspect ratio. With this, we preserve the same image proportions as the ones used to generate the ground truth, in which the images were shown to the observers in a fixed screen resolution of 1900×1200. The details of the ground truth generation are explained in Sect. 3.1.

Signature Model. The signature model to describe every image is extracted as it is shown in Fig. 2. A histogram of runs is calculated in the horizontal, vertical and both diagonals for both, foreground and background layers. Histograms are quantized in bins, experimentally determined, distributed in a logarithmic scale as follows:

$$[1], [2], [3-4], [5-8], [9-16], \ldots, [257, -].$$

Then, the signature S of an image j is the concatenation of its directional histograms ordered as follows:

$$S_j = [H_{0^\circ}^f : H_{45^\circ}^f : H_{90^\circ}^f : H_{135^\circ}^f : H_{0^\circ}^b : H_{45^\circ}^b : H_{90^\circ}^b : H_{135^\circ}^b]$$

Each signature contains $2 \times 4 \times 10 = 80$ dimensions. Notice that differently than [4], no spatial information is included in the histogram since there is a lack of correlation between the building structure and its location within the floor plan; as common office-documents do (logos and titles at the top, signatures at the bottom, etc). In addition to that, foreground and background histograms are L1 normalized separately. Our intention is to equilibrate the relevance of the information conveyed by the background and foreground runs, with much higher frequencies in the background ones.

Retrieval. Let P and Q be the signatures of two different floor plan images. Their similarity is calculated by means of the χ^2 distance:

$$\chi^2(P,Q) = \frac{1}{2} \sum_i \frac{(P_i - Q_i)^2}{(P_i + Q_i)}. \tag{1}$$

Given a query instance, the system ranks the rest of the images in the collection according to their affinity to the query, being the first the most similar and the last the most dissimilar.

3 Experiments

3.1 Formulation of the Experimental Framework

The starting hypothesis of this work is that similarity between architectural plans can be formulated in terms of perceptually dominant visual cues, without interpreting building elements. The runlength histogram descriptor proposed in this paper is a computational model for the perceptual concepts of space and lines. In a retrieval scenario, given a query floorplan image, the proposed method ranks the database images in terms of the runlength histogram similarity. To validate this output in terms of the visual perception, a ground truth based on subjective human assessment was required. This ground truth was constructed with the participation of human observers that classified images in terms of visual aesthetics. Although it is a subjective assessment, we aimed at statistically corroborate that our computational model validates the hypothesis.

A key issue of the ground truth creation is the design of the procedure to collect the user classification of images. A number of considerations must be made. First, since the goal of the users is to classify images with perceptual features and without interpreting the building elements of the architectural drawings, a pre-attentive experiment was conducted. In cognitive vision, pre-attentive processing is the unconscious accumulation of visual information. To force the users to classify images in a pre-attentive way, they have to be displayed in a short lapse of time (no more than a second). A second consideration in the procedure is the way how images are shown to users. Pairwise learning is usually used in the literature [3]. It consists in decomposing a multi-class classification problem into a set of pairwise problems. Therefore given a query, instead of ranking or classifying the whole set of images it is simpler to compare alternatives in a pairwise way. Finally, a third consideration is the question that is made to the users. They can just be asked to assess if a pair of images are similar or not, or a more focused question that affects the observation of the observer (e.g. "do you consider that images are similar in terms of space distribution?", or "don't consider the external shape of the plan when assessing the similarity between images").

Taking into account the above considerations, our ground truth creation was conducted as follows. 20 users participated in the experiment. A database of 39 floor plan images drawn by different architects was used. 6 query images were selected. Each run (different user) showed 234 pairs of images. One of the images was always a query image. Each pair of images was displayed during a second. The user was requested to label each pair of images regarding whether they were very similar, fairly similar or completely dissimilar. At the end, the different labels given by the users to the images where combined averaging the labels so a ranking was generated for each query image.

The human observers selected for generating the ground truth were people aged between 25 and 35 (5 of them were PhD, 14 were PhD students and one had College Studies). None of the volunteers had studied the degree in Architecture and Urban Planning or had any knowledge related with floor plans.

We have formulated two different questions to the users. The question **A**, formulated to 10 observers, was: *"Do you consider that these floor plans are from the same architect or architecture studio?"*. The objective of this question was to cluster the floor plans according to the different architectural styles. On the other hand, to the rest of the observers we asked the question **B**: *"Do you consider that these floor plans are similar?"*. Inversely from question **A**, here the aim is to give more freedom to the observers when considering the meaning of *similar*. Nevertheless, in order to narrow the limits, we suggested to disregard the exterior shape of the building and the size of the plan.

Both formulated questions allowed us to generate three different ground truth rankings. The *gtA*, taking into consideration the answers from the observers asked with question A. The *gtB*, considering the answers to question B. And *gtAB* considering the answers from all the observers that have participated in the experiment, independently of the question formulated to them.

3.2   Performance Evaluation Protocol

Once the ground truth has been collected after the different user observations as described in the previous section, let us describe how the performance of the proposed approach has been measured. A retrieval process consists in sorting the images of the database according to the similarity to the query. The upper is an image in the ranked list, the more similar is to the query. The ground truth has collected subjective assessments of similarity between the six queries and the database images. These scores given by the users can be turned into ranked lists, so given a query, the performance of the approach is measured in terms of ranked list comparison.

A number of distances between rankings have been proposed in the literature [6]. Let S and S' be two ranked lists of items with the particularity of S' being a permutation of S, i.e. both lists contain exactly the same set of items. Let $\sigma(i)$ denote

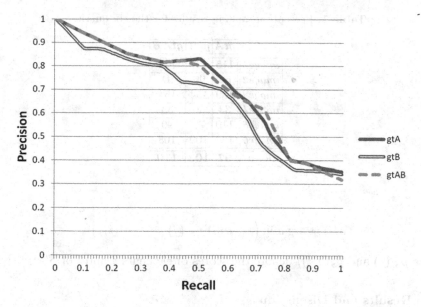

Fig. 3. Precision and recall curves for the three ground truth models.

the rank in S' of the element i in S. The *Spearman's footrule* distance between two rankings measures the total element-wise displacement and is given by:

$$F(S, S') = \sum_i |i - \sigma(i)|;$$

This measure only takes into account the order of the elements to assess the similarity between two lists. The order of the elements is given by their similarity score. Hence, if two elements have the same score value, an arbitrary technique has to decide which element is sorted first. This issue can lead to a random-like ranking when several elements are equally scored in a list and then strongly influence in the ranking distance.

This is the case of our ground truth ranking. The affine answers obtained from the observers lead to a ranking with many repeated scores for different images. In order to avoid this problem, we have adapted the distance function between two ranking, considering the same distance value for images with the same score. Thus, let S be a ranking obtained by the system, given a query, and S' its corresponding ground truth, the distance measurement between both rankings is given by:

$$F(S, S') = \sum_i min(|i - \hat{\sigma}(i)|),$$

where $\hat{\sigma}(i)$ denotes the class of equivalence in S' of the element i in S, i.e. a representative among the different images in S' having the same score. Formally:

Table 1. Perceptual ranking results for the six queries.

	gtA	*gtB*	*gtAB*
image1	115	137	154
image2	64	96	94
image3	139	154	154
image4	33	50	53
image5	110	72	99
image6	123	109	108
mean	**97**	**103**	**110**

$$\hat{\sigma}(i) = \arg\min_{j \in S'} \left(i - \sigma(j) | p_{S'}(j) = p_{S'}(\sigma(i)) \right),$$

where $p_{S'}(j)$ and $p_S(\sigma(i))$ denote the scores of elements j and i of S'.

3.3 Results and Discussion

In Table 1 we show the ranking results obtained for six different queries. The numerical values denote the distance between the system retrieval and the three different ground truth rankings: *gtA*, *gtB* and *gtAB*. In the hypothetical case of a resulting list sorted inversely to the ground truth the score would be 760. When studying the results, the main sorting differences occur in lasts positions of the lists, where most dissimilar images are ranked. Meanwhile, in the first positions, the most similar images are matched for all the queries, a fact that is corroborated by the precision and recall curves extrapolated for all the queries shown in Fig. 3. In addition to that, we also observe that results are slightly different depending on the groundtruth compared with, being *gtA* the one that leads to the best ranking. In retrieval terms, the mean average precision (mAP) obtained also varies depending on the ground truth model. Thus, the mAP scores are 0.67 when compared to *gtA*, 0.63 to *gtB*, and 0.66 to gtAB.

In qualitative terms, we show in Fig. 4 the six queries and their three respectively most similar images retrieved by the system. As it can be seen in every case, the three retrieved images belong to the same collection of the query – share the same drawing style–, a fact that ratifies the fact just mentioned above regarding the matching accuracy in the first positions of the ranking.

Analysing the experiment performed, we realized about the impact on the system performance of the question formulated to the observers in the ground truth generation time. It can strongly determine their perception in terms of *similarity*. As it has been shown, different ways to formulate a question aiming for the same answer can imply different interpretations from the observers. Thus, the system performance varies when it is compared with *gtA*, *gtB* or *gtAB*. Furthermore, a hight population of observers is needed to generate a trustful ground truth able to smooth the high impact of biased perceptions from certain individuals.

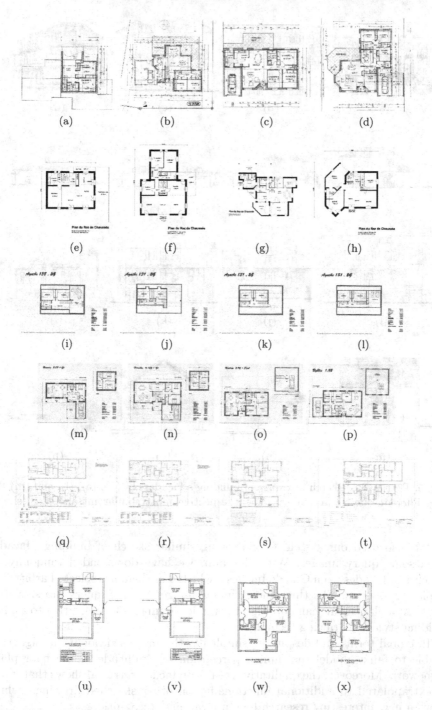

Fig. 4. Floor plan retrieval. The 6 different queries are shown in left column: (a), (e), (i), (m), (q), and (u). Their respective 3 most similar images sorted by similarity are shown row-wise.

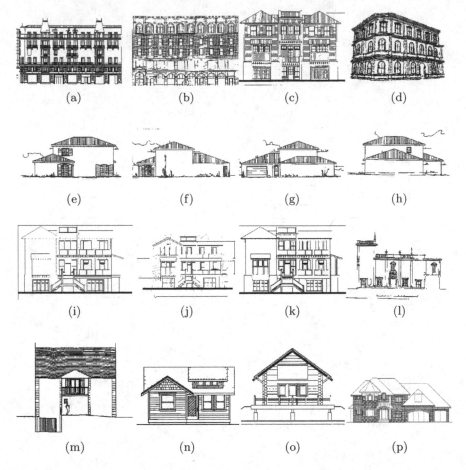

Fig. 5. Retrieval of sketch drawings of building's facades. In (a), (e), (i), and (m) the four different queries are shown. Their respective most similar instances are shown row-wise.

We also used our system for retrieving similar sketch of building's facades given some query images. With this aim, we have downloaded randomly 58 sketches of facades from Google Images[1], which 4 of them are selected arbitrarily to play as queries. The three most similar images to each query are shown in Fig. 5. At a glance, one can note that the retrieved images belong either to similar building styles or drawing technique.

In global terms and despite its simplicity, the proposed document signature is able to fairly model the human perception of similitude in the floor plans framework. Moreover, the qualitative results on facade retrieval shows that it can be extrapolated to additional functionality on other sketched drawings, which opens a new interesting research line in Graphics Recognition.

---

[1] http://www.google.cat/imghp

4   Conclusions

In this paper we have proposed a perceptual model to describe the drawing style in architectural plans. We have considered that semantic concepts associated to lines and space can make two plans similar to the eyes of a human observer in a pre-attentive process. A simple descriptor based in runlength histograms has been proposed. This signature has the ability to roughly capture the properties of the lines (mainly walls) and the spaces (room aspect) of a floorplan design. In a retrieval framework, this descriptor allows to search for perceptually similar plans into a database. The main contributions of the paper have been: first a pioneer approach of graphical document retrieval based on perceptual cues, without interpreting the building elements, i.e. symbols, of the drawing; and second the design of an experimental setup inspired in the pre-attentive theories of cognitive vision.

Although the work is in a preliminary stage, the obtained results are promising. We have only focused on a few number of perceptual features. A complete system that wants to model the style of an architectural drawing combining function and aesthetics should consider other features representing density, proportion, symmetry, etc. The results presented in Sect. 3 allow to conclude that runlength histograms appear as a simple and promising descriptors to capture the intended concepts related to lines and space. When floor plans present orthogonal walls, runlengths characterizing the width or filling texture of walls present high frequencies. On the other hand, big rooms correspond to long high frequent runlengths, and small rooms correspond to mid-length ones.

To validate our model, we have collected ground truth based on human observation. A pre-attentive experiment has been conducted, resulting in ranked lists of floor plan images according to the human assessment of their similarity to a given query. We have noticed the subjectivity of this procedure, which corroborates the complexity of human perception in visual aesthetics. We have experimentally observed the relevance of the question made to the users when they are asked to score images.

Additionally, we have shown qualitatively that our model can be extrapolated to other sketch-based drawing retrieval problems. It has been tested successfully to capture similar drawing styles and building types from randomly downloaded facade sketches.

As a continuation of the work, we will focus on enhancing our descriptor for architectural drawings. We are considering to describe other semantic concepts to have a more complex model of visual aesthetics characterizing styles of this kind of documents. Although some exchanges have been done with architects, a rigorous validation should be carried on with experts. It is necessary to translate the semantic concepts that guide their perception to visual features, making the proposed model usable in professional tools.

Acknowledgement. This work has been partially supported by the Spanish projects TIN2009-14633-C03-03, TIN2011-24631, TIN2012-37475-C02-02, and by the research grants of the Universitat Autònoma de Barcelona (471-01-8/09) and (471-02-1/2010).

References

1. Datta, R., Joshi, D., Li, J., Wang, J.Z.: Studying aesthetics in photographic images using a computational approach. In: Leonardis, A., Bischof, H., Pinz, A. (eds.) ECCV 2006. LNCS, vol. 3953, pp. 288–301. Springer, Heidelberg (2006)
2. de las Heras, L-P., Fernández, D., Valveny, E., Lladós, J., Sánchez, G.: Unsupervised wall detector in architectural floor plan. In: Proceedings of the 12th International Conference on Document Analysis and Recognition (accepted) (2013)
3. Fürnkranz, J., Hüllermeier, E.: Preference learning and ranking by pairwise comparison. In: Fürnkranz, J., Hüllermeier, E. (eds.) Preference Learning, pp. 65–82. Springer, Heidelberg (2011)
4. Gordo, A., Perronnin, F., Valveny, E.: Large-scale document image retrieval and classification with runlength histograms and binary embeddings. Pattern Recogn. **46**(7), 1898–1905 (2013)
5. Keysers, D., Shafait, F., Breuel, T.M.: Document image zone classification - a simple high-performance approach. In: Proceedings of the 2nd International Conference on Computer Vision Theory and Applications, pp. 44–51 (2007)
6. Kumar, R., Vassilvitskii, S.: Generalized distances between rankings. In: Proceedings of the 19th International Conference on World Wide Qeb, pp. 571–580 (2010)
7. Lemaitre, A., Camillerapp, J., Coüasnon, B.: A perceptive method for handwritten text segmentation. In: Proceedings of Document Recognition and Retrieval, pp. 1–10 (2011)
8. Moorthy, A.K., Obrador, P., Oliver, N.: Towards computational models of the visual aesthetic appeal of consumer videos. In: Daniilidis, K., Maragos, P., Paragios, N. (eds.) ECCV 2010, Part V. LNCS, vol. 6315, pp. 1–14. Springer, Heidelberg (2010)
9. Saund, E.: Finding perceptually closed paths in sketches and drawings. IEEE Trans. Pattern Anal. Mach. Intell. **25**(4), 475–491 (2003)
10. Stamatopoulos, N., Gatos, B., Georgiou, T.: Page frame detection for double page document images. In: Proceedings of the 9th IAPR International Workshop on Document Analysis Systems, pp. 401–408 (2010)
11. Weber, M., Langenhan, C., Roth-Berghofer, T., Liwicki, M., Dengel, A., Petzold, F.: a.SCatch: semantic structure for architectural floor plan retrieval. In: Bichindaritz, I., Montani, S. (eds.) ICCBR 2010. LNCS, vol. 6176, pp. 510–524. Springer, Heidelberg (2010)

Low Level Processing

A Stitching Method for Large Document Images

Ludovic Paulhac and Jean-Philippe Domenger[✉]

LaBRI, UMR 5800, University of Bordeaux, 33400 Talence, France
{ludovic.paulhac,jean-philippe.domenger}@labri.fr

Abstract. In this paper, we are interested in stitching specific types of images such as schemes, cartographies, documents or drawings that have been acquired using a scanner. Because of the size of these documents, it is not possible to make one acquisition even using large scanners. The result of the acquisition is then an image mosaic that needs to be stitched to obtain the entire image. For that purpose, we propose an adaptation of feature based methods that are not directly usable with the images we want to process. Indeed, points of interest (POIs) extraction on the entire image requires too much memory and matching are not always pertinent because of the particularity of these documents. To demonstrate the good performance of our proposition, we present quantitative and qualitative results obtained using two datasets: a set of images divided synthetically and a set of images that have been acquired manually using a scanner.

Keywords: Image stitching · Document imaging · Points of interest

1 Introduction

Several methods have been proposed for image mosaicing where multiple correlated images are stitched to generate a larger wide-angle image of a scene [1–4]. These methods are widely used for panorama construction and several software already exist on computers but also on mobile devices [2,5]. In this paper, we are interested in using these techniques to stitch specific types of images such as schemes, cartographies, documents or drawings that have been acquired using a scanner. Because of the size of these documents, it is not possible to make one acquisition even using large scanners. The result of the acquisition is then an image mosaic that needs to be stitched to obtain the entire image. Some examples are displayed in Fig. 1.

In order to be efficient, mosaicing methods should preserve different properties [6,7]:

- **Structure preservation.** The result should not create new structures and break the existing ones.
- **Intensity alignment.** Luminosity and contrast of the stitched images should be balanced to obtain natural transitions after the stitching process.
- **Image context consideration.** During the stitching process, the context information of the objects inside the input images should be preserved.

© Springer-Verlag Berlin Heidelberg 2014
B. Lamiroy and J.-M. Ogier (Eds.): GREC 2013, LNCS 8746, pp. 149–160, 2014.
DOI: 10.1007/978-3-662-44854-0_12

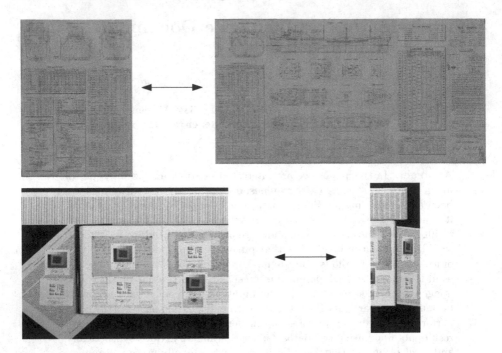

Fig. 1. Examples of images we need to stitch. The first image is a plan that describe the properties of a boat. The second one is a mix between a book and articles.

To address the above issues, several algorithms have been proposed in the literature such as: transition smoothing [3,8], optimal seam finding [4,5] and matching methods [1,2,9–11].

Transition smoothing approaches try to reduce color differences between source images by smoothing or combining informations in the intersection area. The most simple approaches use a bilinear weighting function to blend the overlapped regions [12]. More sophisticated methods propose to use gradient domain operations to smooth color transitions [13–16]. Methods using optimal seam try to find a path in the overlapped regions where differences between input images are minimal. To compute an optimal partition, techniques such as dynamic programming [5,17] or Graph Cuts [4,18] are usually used. The optimal seam finding and the transition smoothing methods are often combined [5] and obtain good stitching results. Nevertheless, they consider the overlapped area of the source images as known which is not the case in the problematic presented in this paper. Matching methods do not consider this intersection area. Two families of matching methods have been proposed in the literature: direct methods [1,9] and feature based methods [1,2,11]. Direct methods use all the available image and have the advantages of providing very accurate measures. However, they are not the most adapted for a large misalignment between source images and when the overlapped region is small [1]. This is why feature based methods have been mainly used for panorama problems [1,2,11]. With the emergence of new features partially invariant under affine change [19,20], these methods allow to obtain very good results with a low complexity.

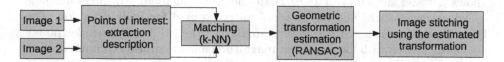

Fig. 2. Scheme of the standard process to stitch two images. (1) POIs are detected and associated with a set of features that describe input images. (2) POIs are matched to their k nearest neighbors in feature space. (3) The geometric transformation is estimated using matching. (4) Images are stitched according to the estimated transformation.

In this paper, we propose an adaptation of feature based methods that are not directly usable with the images we want to process. POI extraction on the entire image requires too much memory and matching are not always relevant because of the particularity of these documents.

In Sect. 2, feature based methods for geometric transformation estimation are presented. In Sect. 3, we describe our proposition to adapt feature based methods to large document images. Section 4 presents quantitative and qualitative results using two datasets: a set of images divided synthetically and a set of images that have been acquired manually using a scanner. We conclude with a summary of our research and prospects for future work.

2   Feature Based Methods for Geometric Transformation Estimation

This section presents how feature based methods estimate geometric transformations between two images. The methodology can be seen on Fig. 2. For each of the input images, points of interest (POIs) are detected and associated with a set of features that describe the image. Once the POIs have been extracted, they are matched to their k nearest neighbors in feature space. The geometric transformation between the two images is estimated using the RANSAC algorithm [21]. This estimation is then used to stitch the two input images. In the next sub-sections, a brief explanation of these steps is exposed.

2.1   Points of Interest Extraction and Description

The extraction and description of POIs are two primordial steps in this kind of stitching algorithms. Descriptors have to be robust to potential transformations and well adapted for input data description. In our method, POIs have been detected and described using SIFT [19] and SURF [20].

For POIs detection, the SIFT method extracts local extrema of a difference of Gaussian set computed from the initial image. The detected points are filtered removing points with low contrast responses and removing points along edges. To describe the detected POIs, the SIFT method proposes to study gradient magnitude and orientation in the region around the POI location. SURF method allows a faster detection of POIs than the SIFT method. An integral image speed up calculations and the Hessian matrix is used for POIs detection. The POI description using SURF is very similar to the SIFT one since keypoints are characterized with local gradient magnitude and orientation computed using the Haar wavelet.

2.2   Image Matching and Geometric Transformation Estimation

Once the POIs have been extracted, they are matched to their k nearest neighbors in feature space. Each POI in the first image is matched to its nearest neighbors in the second one and inversely. In our implementation, we used the euclidean distance to compare the feature vectors of each point. As proposed in [2], a k-d tree has been used ($k = 4$). It approximates nearest neighbors in $O(n \log n)$ time.

Now that we have computed a set of matching, we want to identify good matchings i.e. the ones that allows to identify the transformation parameters we need to stitch the two input images. This can be done using the RANSAC algorithm. According to a given application, different kinds of transformations can be considered (translation, homography for instance). In the case of panorama applications, a special group of homographies are considered assuming that the camera rotates around its optical centre. Each camera is parametrized using a rotation vector $\Theta = [\theta_1, \theta_2, \theta_3]$ and a focal length f. Thus, the following relation $u_i = H_{ij}u_j$ is obtained with

$$H_{ij} = K_i R_i R_j^T K_j^{-1} \tag{1}$$

where u_i and u_j are the coordinates of images I and J. K_i and R_i are defined as follows:

$$K_i = \begin{bmatrix} f_i & 0 & 0 \\ 0 & f_i & 0 \\ 0 & 0 & 1 \end{bmatrix} \tag{2}$$

and

$$R_i = [\Theta_i]_\times = \begin{bmatrix} 0 & -\theta_{i3} & \theta_{i2} \\ \theta_{i3} & 0 & -\theta_{i1} \\ -\theta_{i2} & \theta_{i1} & 0 \end{bmatrix} \tag{3}$$

Once the geometric transformation to estimate has been chosen, the RANSAC algorithm is used to identify inliers i.e. the maximum number of matching whose projections are consistent with a set of parameter transform. In our implementation, the RANSAC parameters proposed in [2] have been used. For each iteration of RANSAC, 4 features are randomly chosen and used to compute the parameters of the geometric transformation between them. Then, the other elements validating the transformation are searched. This operation is repeated $n = 500$ times and the solution with the maximum number of inliers is selected. To validate a matching, the RANSAC method uses a threshold d that represents the maximum distance between the expectation position of matching given by the transformation and the real position of matched point. As in [2], the value $d = 3$ has been used. In Fig. 3, we show matching before and after using RANSAC to illustrate the impact of this algorithm.

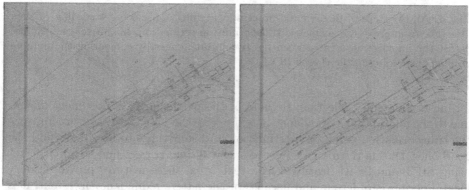

(a) Matching obtained after the k nearest neighbors in feature space

(b) Matching obtained after the RANSAC method

Fig. 3. Examples of the obtained matching before and after using the RANSAC algorithm. The matching in (b) are inliers and their projections are consistent with a set of transform parameters.

3   Image Stitching Adapted to Large Document Images

In this section, we present our proposition to adapt the feature based-method scheme (Fig. 2) to our problematic. Our methodology can be seen Fig. 4. Region of interests (ROIs) are extracted from the input images and POIs are detected in these areas. These points are then exploited to detect inliers as presented in the previous section. To obtain a more robust detection of inliers, we also add a matching selection step that takes their directions into consideration. Our method (Fig. 4) also proposes to estimate the overlapped regions to improve geometric transformation parameters estimation and to preserve memory consuming.

3.1   Matching Selection Using Direction

In our method (Fig. 4), we propose to select a set of matches according to their direction. A graphical interface allows the user to indicate a global direction. Using this information, we define a direction interval that must be respected

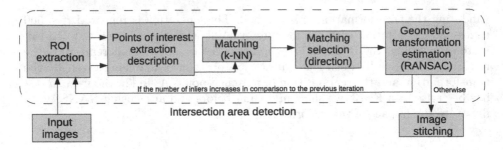

Fig. 4. All the steps of the adapted process. Matching are selected according to their direction to improve the geometric transformation estimation. In this scheme we also detect the intersection area between the two input images by comparing the number of inliers according to the chosen ROIs.

during the matching selection. Because of the particularity of document images due to the information redundancy in text areas, this step is necessary to improve the transformation parameters estimation and sometimes to be able to find the good ones. During the matching process, the system tries to find a similar letter using SIFT and SURF features. In a text area, these features provide a very local description of letters and because of the letters redundancy in a text, it is not guaranteed that a matching of two similar letters is correct. In other words, it is possible to match a letter of an image I with a bad one in an image J even if the features are similar. An example is given (Fig. 5) where we have tried to find the homography parameters without using the matching selection step. After the RANSAC algorithm, it is possible to see that some letters "c" and "e" in the first image have been connected to letters "c" and "e" in the second image but not the correct ones.

Without using a matching selection according to the direction, the RANSAC algorithm is sometimes able to find an acceptable transformation but most of the time including a lack of precision. It becomes even more difficult when considering an homography because of the number of parameters to estimate. If a great number of matching are not correct, it is very probable for the RANSAC algorithm to find an homography that do not corresponds to the one we need to stitch correctly the two processed images.

3.2   Detection of the Overlapped Regions

Because of the important size of images that we need to stitch, POI extraction on the entire image requires too much memory. To avoid this problem, we propose to detect the overlapped regions by analyzing the evolution of the number of inliers according to the size of two ROIs defined in the input images. During the acquisition process, these documents are scanned horizontally or vertically. Therefore, the intersection area corresponds to a rectangular region positioned in one of the image sides. Currently, the user provides the acquisition direction (horizontal or vertical) to our system that uses this information to choose the

Fig. 5. Matching obtained after the RANSAC method and without using the matching selection according to the direction. Letters "c" and "e" in the first image have been connected to letters "c" and "e" in the second image but not the good ones.

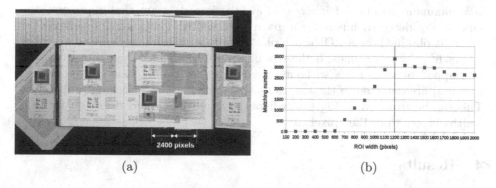

Fig. 6. Example that illustrates the detection of the overlapped regions. (a) is the used image to detect the overlapped regions. Green lines correspond to inliers detected for a ROI width of 1200 pixels. (b) is a diagram that represents the number of matching detected for a given ROI width. The maximum number of matches is obtained for a ROI width of 1200 that corresponds to the case presented in (a) (Color figure online).

sides where the overlapped regions are located. Then, as presented in Fig. 4, two ROIs with the same size are considered in each of the images to stitch. POIs are extracted in these regions and matched with their k nearest neighbors in feature space. These matching are selected according to their direction and the RANSAC algorithm return a geometric transformation estimation and the corresponding inliers. Then, the system increases the ROIs size and computes the

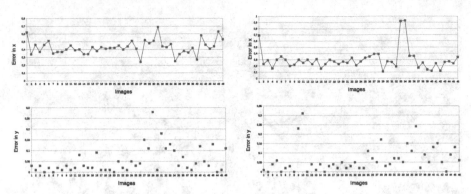

(a) Quantitative results obtained using our proposition with the SIFT method   (b) Quantitative results obtained using our proposition with the SURF method

Fig. 7. Diagrams that represent translation errors in x and y (in pixels) in comparison to the ground truth for 46 different images.

inliers once again. This step is repeated until the number of inliers decreases in comparison to the previous iteration. The geometric transformation parameters used to stitch the two images are the ones that correspond to the ROIs with the maximum number of inliers. Figure 6(b) is a diagram that represents the numbers of detected inliers for a given ROI width. The maximum number of inliers is obtained for a ROI width of 1200 pixels. These inliers are represented in Fig. 6(a) by green lines. If the size of the ROI is bigger than the size of the overlapped regions, POIs without correspondence (points that can be related to noise) are detected in the two ROIs that increase bad matching probability. This can be observed on Fig. 6(b) where the number of inliers decreases for ROI widths bigger than 1200 pixels.

4   Results

In this section, we apply the previously described methodology to stitch a set of images divided synthetically and a set of images that have been obtained manually using a scanner.

The first set of images have been constructed synthetically by dividing 46 different images in two sub-images by applying a translation transformation. Figure 8 presents one example of this set. Our method has been used to stitch these images using the SIFT and SURF methods for POIs extraction and description. Figure 7 presents the errors in x and y in comparison to ground truth for each of the 46 images. Figure 7(a) shows the results obtained using the SIFT method and Fig. 7(b) shows the results obtained using the SURF method.

Regarding the measures obtained in these tables, one can observe that our proposition estimates precisely the translation parameters whatever the POIs extraction and detection methods used (SIFT or SURF). Average errors in x

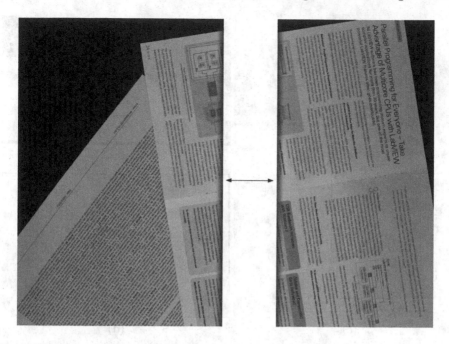

Fig. 8. Example of an image we propose to stitch to provide quantitative experiments (Fig. 7). The two sub-images are two parts of a same image (with overlapped regions) that have been separated using a translation.

and y are 0.42 and 0.05 pixels using the SIFT method and 0.29 and 0.06 pixels using the SURF method. By comparing results obtained with SIFT and SURF in these experiments, one can see that the SURF method is a little bit more precise than SIFT method for translation estimation.

By using the classical approach presented in Sect. 2, it is not possible to stitch this type of images. Indeed, POI extraction on the entire image requires too much memory. Each sub-image to stitch have a size of 7000×20000 pixels and as depicted on Fig. 8, the number of potential POIs to detect is very important.

The second set of images has been obtained manually using a scanner. In that case, we tried to estimate an homographic transformation because the scanned documents are not flat (different perspectives). In addition, a manual image acquisition often results in rotations between the images we want to stitch. Since the acquisition was manual, it was not possible to construct a ground truth. That is why we propose in this paper the previous experiments to provide quantitative results. This second set of images contains 40 different images and some of the stitching results are presented in Fig. 9. The images depicted on Fig. 9(a) and (b) have been obtained after the stitching of images presented on Fig. 1. The images (Fig. 9(c) and (d)) represent a street map and a building plan respectively. As in the quantitative experiments presented previously, one can observe the good quality of the stitching results obtained using our method.

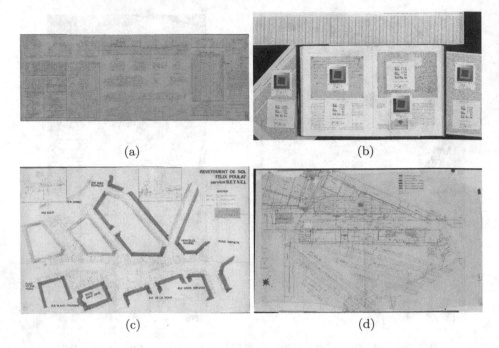

(a)

(b)

(c)

(d)

Fig. 9. Qualitative results obtained using our proposition with the SIFT method. (a) and (b) have been obtained after stitching of images presented in Fig. 1. (c) and (d) represent a street map and a building plan respectively.

5   Conclusion

In this paper, we propose an adaptation of the feature-based methods to stitch specific types of images such as schemes, cartographies, documents or drawings. Indeed, feature based methods are not directly usable with these images: interest point extraction on the entire image requires too much memory and matching are not always pertinent because of the specificity of these documents (information redundancy).

In our method, we propose to detect the overlapped regions by analyzing the evolution of the number of inliers according to the size of two ROIs defined in the images to stitch. By considering POIs only in the overlapped region, our proposition preserves memory consuming and improves the quality of the stitching results. To provide a solution to the information redundancy problem, we also propose to select the matching according to their direction. A direction interval is defined manually using a graphical interface in our software.

To evaluate our proposition, we present a quantitative evaluation where a set of 46 images divided synthetically are stitched using our methodology. For each of the tested images, the translation parameters are estimated very precisely and are very similar to the ground truth. We also provide qualitative results by stitching a set of images that have been obtained manually using a scanner.

These results are presented in Fig. 9 and show the good performance of our method.

Of course, several improvements could be made in future works. Currently, the SIFT and SURF methods have been used to provide a characterization of keypoints and we believe that these features that describe gradient magnitude and orientation in the region around the POI location are not the most adapted for all the regions in these images. As pointed out by Uchitama and Saito [22], methods like SIFT and SURF are not the most efficient to handle repetitive binary patterns such as text. That is why in a future work, we are interested to segment the intersection areas (once they have been detected) to propose a characterization of POIs adapted to the type of regions (text, logo, image). Methods such as [23] that exploit texture descriptors could be used to segment the regions of the intersection areas. Finally, to provide a characterization adapted for each region, it will be necessary to determine the zones content type [23,24].

Acknowledgments. The piXL project is supported by the "Fonds national pour la Société Numérique" of the French State by means of the "Programme d'Investissements d'Avenir", and referenced under PIA-FSN2-PIXL. For more details and resources, visit http://valconum.fr/index.php/les-projets/pixl

References

1. Szeliski, R.: Image alignment and stitching: a tutorial. Technical report, Microsoft Research (2006)
2. Brown, M., Lowe, D.G.: Automatic panoramic image stitching using invariant features. Int. J. Comput. Vis. **74**(1), 59–73 (2007)
3. Xiong, Y., Pulli, K.: Mask based image blending approach and its applications on mobile devices. In: MIPPR'09: International Symposium on Multispectral Image Processing and Pattern Recognition (2009)
4. Gracias, N., Mahoor, M., Negahdaripour, S., Gleason, A.: Fast image blending using watersheds and graph cuts. Image Vis. Comput. **27**, 597–607 (2009)
5. Xiong, Y., Pulli, K.: Fast panorama stitching for high-quality panoramic images on mobile phones. IEEE Trans. Consum. Electron. **56**, 298–306 (2010)
6. Jia, J., Tang, C.K.: Image stitching using structure deformation. IEEE Trans. Pattern Anal. Mach. Intell. **30**, 617–631 (2008)
7. Zhi, Q., Cooperstock, J.R.: Toward dynamic image mosaic generation with robustness to parallax. IEEE Trans. Image Process. **21**, 366–378 (2012)
8. Levin, A., Zomet, A., Peleg, S., Weiss, Y.: Seamless image stitching in the gradient domain. In: Pajdla, T., Matas, J.G. (eds.) ECCV 2004. LNCS, vol. 3024, pp. 377–389. Springer, Heidelberg (2004)
9. Irani, M., Anandan, P.: About direct methods. In: Triggs, B., Zisserman, A., Szeliski, R. (eds.) ICCV-WS 1999. LNCS, vol. 1883, pp. 267–277. Springer, Heidelberg (2000)
10. Torr, P., Zisserman, A.: Feature based methods for structure and motion estimation. In: Triggs, B., Zisserman, A., Szeliski, R. (eds.) ICCV-WS 1999. LNCS, vol. 1883, pp. 278–294. Springer, Heidelberg (2000)

11. Brown, M., Szeliski, R., Winder, S.: Multi-image matching using multi-scale oriented patches. In: CVPR'05: Proceedings of the Computer Society Conference on Computer Vision and Pattern Recognition (2005)
12. Uyttendaele, M., Eden, A., Szeliski, R.: Eliminating ghosting and exposure artifacts in image mosaics. In: CVPR'01: Proceedings of the IEEE International Conference on Computer Vision and Pattern Recognition (2001)
13. Pérez, P., Gangnet, M., Blake, A.: Poisson image editing. ACM Trans. Graph. **22**(3), 313–318 (2003)
14. Agarwala, A.: Efficient gradient-domain compositing using quadtrees. ACM Trans. Graph. **26**(3), 94:1–94:5 (2007)
15. Kazhdan, M.M., Hoppe, H.: Streaming multigrid for gradient-domain operations on large images. ACM Trans. Graph. **27**(3), 1–10 (2008)
16. Farbman, Z., Hoffer, G., Lipman, Y., Cohen-Or, D., Lischinski, D.: Coordinates for instant image cloning. ACM Trans. Graph. **28**(3), 67:1–67:10 (2009)
17. Efros, A.A., Freeman, W.T.: Image quilting for texture synthesis and transfer. In: SIGGRAPH'01: Proceedings of the Conference on Computer Graphics and Interactive Techniques (2001)
18. Agarwala, A., Dontcheva, M., Agrawala, M., Drucker, S., Colburn, A., Curless, B., Salesin, D., Cohen, M.: Interactive digital photomontage. ACM Trans. Graph. **23**, 294–302 (2004)
19. Lowe, D.G.: Distinctive image features from scale-invariant keypoints. Int. J. Comput. Vis. **60**, 91–110 (2004)
20. Bay, H., Ess, A., Tuytelaars, T., Gool, L.V.: Surf: speeded up robust features. Comput. Vis. Image Underst. **110**(3), 346–359 (2008)
21. Fischler, M., Bolles, R.: Random sample consensus: a paradigm for model fitting with application to image analysis and automated cartography. Commun. ACM **24**, 381–395 (1981)
22. Uchiyama, H., Saito, H.: Augmenting text document by on-line learning of local arrangement of keypoints. In: ISMAR'09: IEEE International Symposium on Mixed and Augmented Reality (2009)
23. Vieux, R., Domenger, J.P.: Hierarchical clustering model for pixel-based classification of document images. In: ICPR'12: Proceedings of the IEEE International Conference on Pattern Recognition (2012)
24. Wang, Y., Phillips, I.T., Haralick, R.M.: Document zone content classification and its performance evaluation. Pattern Recogn. **39**, 57–73 (2006)

Filtering Out Readers' Underline
in Monochromatic and Color Documents

Ricardo da Silva Barboza[1,2(✉)], Rafael Dueire Lins[1(✉)],
and Luiz W. Nagata Balduino[2(✉)]

[1] Universidade Federal de Pernambuco, Recife–PE, Brazil
{rsbarboza, rdl.ufpe}@gmail.com
[2] Universidade do Estado do Amazonas, Manaus–AM, Brazil
luiz.nagata@gmail.com

Abstract. Text "underlining" is a practice of many interested readers, but it may be seen as a noise inserted by the user that damages the physical integrity of a document. This paper presents two different algorithms for underline removal. The first one addresses the case of monochromatic document images. The second algorithm is applied to remove the underline noise in recent and aged documents written on a blank sheet of white paper. Underline information is also used to automatically generate summaries of documents.

Keywords: Underline · Noises · Algorithms · Documents

1 Introduction

Underlining textual documents is a frequent attitude of interested readers and it was quite usual before the advent of the modern felt-tip marker, invented by Yukio Horie in Japan in 1962, when people started to highlight documents. There is a personal outlook in document underlining and highlighting. The same reader may be interested in different aspects of a document every time he reads it. What one reader may stress and emphasize may be considered irrelevant to another. Thus, in general, highlighting may be perceived as a "noise" physically damaging the document [1].

Straight-line removal, such as the ones on forms and notebook lines, has been addressed by several authors in the technical literature [2–5]. Text underlining by readers is far more complex as readers very seldom use rulers to underline texts and often the line segment either touches or crosses the textual areas. Figure 1 presents an example of a "free-hand" underlined document. The deleterious effect of underlining in OCR transcription may be of great proportions.

One may find a few references in the literature for underline removal. Castro Pinto and his colleagues [6] propose integrating fuzzy clustering of color properties of original images and mathematical morphology and they say that such technique was successfully applied to books of the 19th Century. Yoshihiro Shima and three others [13] propose a technique for removing an underline on a character string existing on a business form image. The algorithms presented in references [6] and [13] are not suitable for removing underline when it touches the text. Zhen-Long Bai and

© Springer-Verlag Berlin Heidelberg 2014
B. Lamiroy and J.-M. Ogier (Eds.): GREC 2013, LNCS 8746, pp. 161–175, 2014.
DOI: 10.1007/978-3-662-44854-0_13

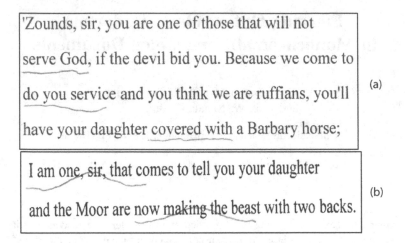

'Zounds, sir, you are one of those that will not serve God, if the devil bid you. Because we come to do you service and you think we are ruffians, you'll have your daughter covered with a Barbary horse;   (a)

I am one, sir, that comes to tell you your daughter and the Moor are now making the beast with two backs.   (b)

Fig. 1. (a) Underline does not touch text. (b) Underline crossing printed text.

Qiang Huo [14] present and algorithm suitable for underline removal in monochromatic images that may only have text and underline.

In 28 May 2013, Hitachi Solutions Ltd. got granted the patent US 8452133 B2 Underline removal apparatus [15]. The patent "provides an underline removal apparatus that removes an underline area from binary image data including the underline area touching a character string, the underline removal apparatus comprising: an underline search processing unit that executes a line template matching process by setting a point on the binary image data as a starting point to set a rectangular line template, tracing pixels included in the line template, and extracting a polyline indicating underline position coordinates; and an underline removal processing unit that uses the polyline to execute a process of obtaining background borderline coordinates between the underline area and a background area and character borderline coordinates between the underline area and the character string obtained by applying an interpolation process to a part in the underline area touching the character string and to execute a process of replacing an area surrounded by the background borderline coordinates and the character borderline coordinates by a color of pixels of the background area."

This paper presents two new algorithms for underline removal. The first algorithm presented here deals with underline removal of monochromatic documents, i.e. documents that were either scanned in monochromatic version or binarized after the underline had been done. The second one addresses the case of documents originally written on a sheet of white paper background, in which the underlining was made either with pencil or pen that may be of different colors, and the original paper document was scanned in true color (RGB 24-bits per pixel). The proposed algorithm works well in the aged version of similar documents, despite of the darkening of the paper background. A scheme to generate summaries of the original document with the underlined text is also presented.

2   Monochromatic Documents

The image of monochromatic documents is poor in information. Filtering in such kind of document is restricted to the recognition of its graphical elements and is shape and/or size dependant. Readers' underline may be observed in the binary document shown in Fig. 2.

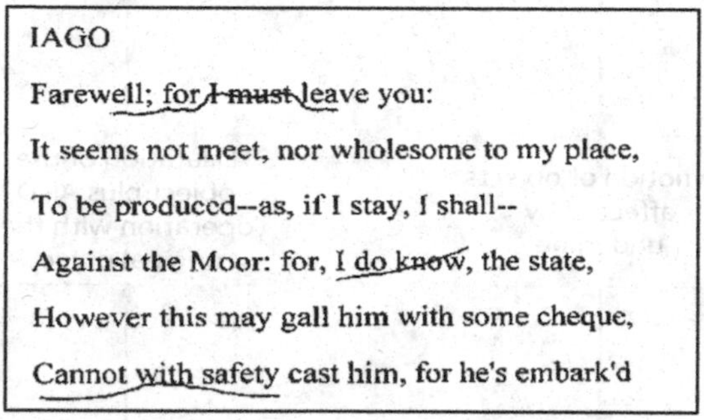

IAGO

Farewell; for, I must leave you:

It seems not meet, nor wholesome to my place,

To be produced--as, if I stay, I shall--

Against the Moor: for, I do know, the state,

However this may gall him with some cheque,

Cannot with safety cast him, for he's embark'd

Fig. 2. Monochromatic image with underline noises that touch and cross text areas.

The graph recognition and removal of readers' underline is performed taking into account the geometry of the line drawn by the reader in respect to the other textual or graphical elements in the image. This paper assumes that the underline is a noise that may or not intersept text characters.

The first processing phase is image segmentation by scanning the image and at each pixel identified as text a depth-first search is performed, as described by Shapiro [8]. Each boxed element is analyzed and those that have a height smaller than 15 % in relation to its base and occupy more than 20 % of the total area of the bounding box one considers as being affected by the underlining. This procedure allows to find and segment from the original image the objects that are affected by the underline, and this consists the second step of the underline removal algorithm.

The third step performed is the skelotonization of the image of each box segmented area that corresponds to the part of the underline segment with or without text. The variation of the values in relation to the y-axis of each boxed skeletonitized segment indicates a high probability of finding a part of the underline segment. All one needs is to follow such path to erase it without erasing the remaining text area. In the case that the underline touches or crosses text areas it contains the smallest 8-path way between the leftmost and rightmost pixels of the object formed by the merging of the line and text characters intersepted. Thus, such line segment may be found by applying the steps in Algorithm 1, at the end of this paper.

The pixels visited and marked by Algorithm 1 are part of the underline segment, thus they may be removed from the image. The final step is to restore the size of the skeletonized image by performing a morphological dilatation having as limit the size of the original object. This operation restores almost all the original data, eliminating the hand drawn underline. In the next phase, mathematical morphology is used to perform the skeletization, as described by Soille [9].

The operations performed for filtering out the reader's underline noise in binary documents are summarized in the flowchart presented in Fig. 3.

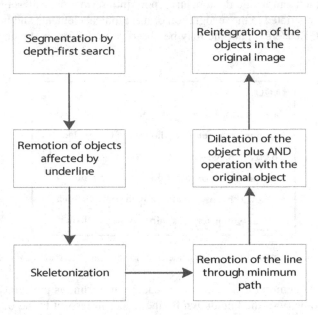

Fig. 3. Flowchart of the algorithm for underline removal for binary documents.

Now the whole process is explained in details with an example. The result of the segmentation phase performed in the image of Fig. 2 is shown in Fig. 4.

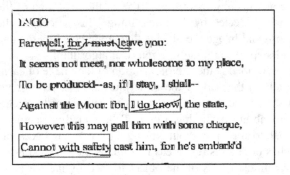

Fig. 4. Identification of the non-textual components by a depth-first search.

The topmost segmented area under analysis as presented in Fig. 4 is selected and part of it is shown in Fig. 5.

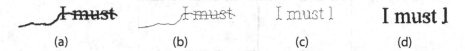

(a)   (b)   (c)   (d)

Fig. 5. (a) Segmented object from original image in Fig. 3. (b) Skeletonized version of the object in (a). (c) Line removal. (d) Dilated version of (c) assuming as limit the corresponding areas in image (a).

The extreme points of the bounding box that envelopes the segmented areas, shown in red in Fig. 5a, coincide with the extreme points of the "underline" noise one wants to filter out. Following the smallest path of black pixels between those points in the case of the skeletonized image and replacing them by white pixels one is able to remove the underline, as shown in Fig. 5c for the case of Fig. 5a.

Replacing the objects in the original image shown in Fig. 2 one obtains the underline removed image of Fig. 6, which may be considered satisfactory in quality.

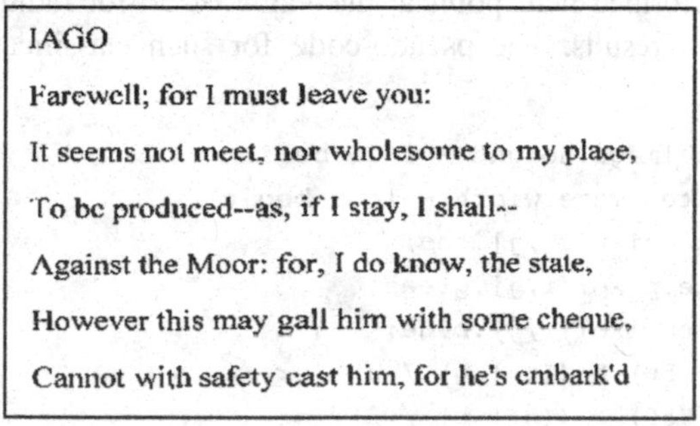

> IAGO
>
> Farewell; for I must leave you:
>
> It seems not meet, nor wholesome to my place,
>
> To be produced--as, if I stay, I shall--
>
> Against the Moor: for, I do know, the state,
>
> However this may gall him with some cheque,
>
> Cannot with safety cast him, for he's embark'd

Fig. 6. Processed image of Fig. 2 with underline noise removed.

3 Color Digitized Documents

The algorithm presented in the last section may be used in color documents also if a binarization pre-processinf phase is used to generate a mask to find the underline region to be removed. The algorithm presented in the last section is computationaly intensive. Color information may used directly to remove the underline in documents that the pen is in a different color from the paper background (white) and print (black) with good results and much less processing effort. Reference [7] presents a segmentation method in which non-grayscale pixels are identified based on the distance between the pixel color and the line segment in the diagonal of the RGB-cube $(0, 0, 0)$ and $(255, 255, 255)$ threshold is used, as depicted in Fig. 7.

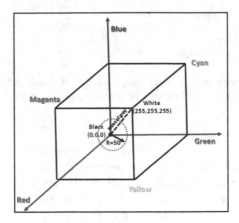

Fig. 7. The RGB-color cube showing the hues of gray diagonal and the basis of the threshold cylinder.

Experiments performed here point at the value of 50 for radius of the threshold cylinder for the best results. The pseudo-code for such classification is showed in Algorithm 2.

```
for j <- 0 to image.height - 1 do begin
    for i <- 0 to image.width - 1 do begin
        r <- image.pixel[i,j].red;
        g <- image.pixel[i,j].green;
        b <- image.pixel[i,j].blue;
        if (((b - 50) > ((r + g) / 2)) or
            ((r - 50) > ((g + b) / 2)) or
            ((g - 50) > ((r + b) / 2))) then
                set the pixel as noise;
    end for;
end for;
```
    Algorithm 2. Pseudo-code for initial image segmentation

The images shown in Fig. 1 were filtered with Algorithm 2. Figure 8(a) and (b) presents the resulting images (scaled down). One may observe that some non-underline pixels appear also in the image of Fig. 3. This is possibly due to digitalization noise introduced by the scanner [1] in the edges of letters due to discontinuity. After binarization and salt-and-pepper filtering one obtains the images shown in Fig. 8(c) and (d). Figure 9 presents the resulting image where the text underline noise has been completely removed.

Figure 10 shows that the application of the method proposed here works satis- factorily with other colors of pen used for text underlining.

3.1 Underline Removal in Aged Documents

This section addresses the problem of underline removal in documents with aged background, such as the one shown in Fig. 11.

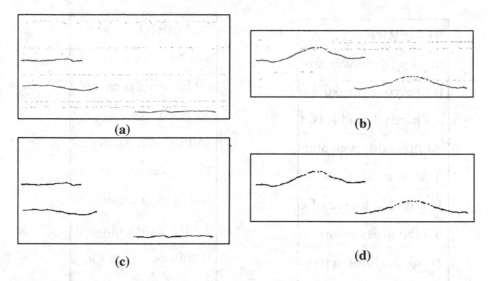

Fig. 8. (a) and (b) Scaled down Result of Processing Fig. 1 with Algorithm 1. (c) and (d) Segmentation masks.

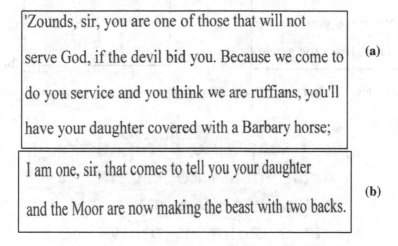

'Zounds, sir, you are one of those that will not serve God, if the devil bid you. Because we come to do you service and you think we are ruffians, you'll have your daughter covered with a Barbary horse;   **(a)**

I am one, sir, that comes to tell you your daughter and the Moor are now making the beast with two backs.   **(b)**

Fig. 9. Resulting images with underline removed.

Aged documents tend to have non-white background and exhibit a texture whose hues depend on a number of factors ranging from the quality of the original paper, its porosity, humidity and temperature of the environment where the document was kept, handling, fungi, etc.

Researching paper aging and color "decay" with documents from the last 100 years [11], the authors of this paper concluded that the blue component tends to fade first, followed by the green component, and the red is the last to fade. The mean value of the RGB-color component decay for documents written in a white sheet of paper ages (time span of 50 years) according to the plotting shown in Fig. 12.

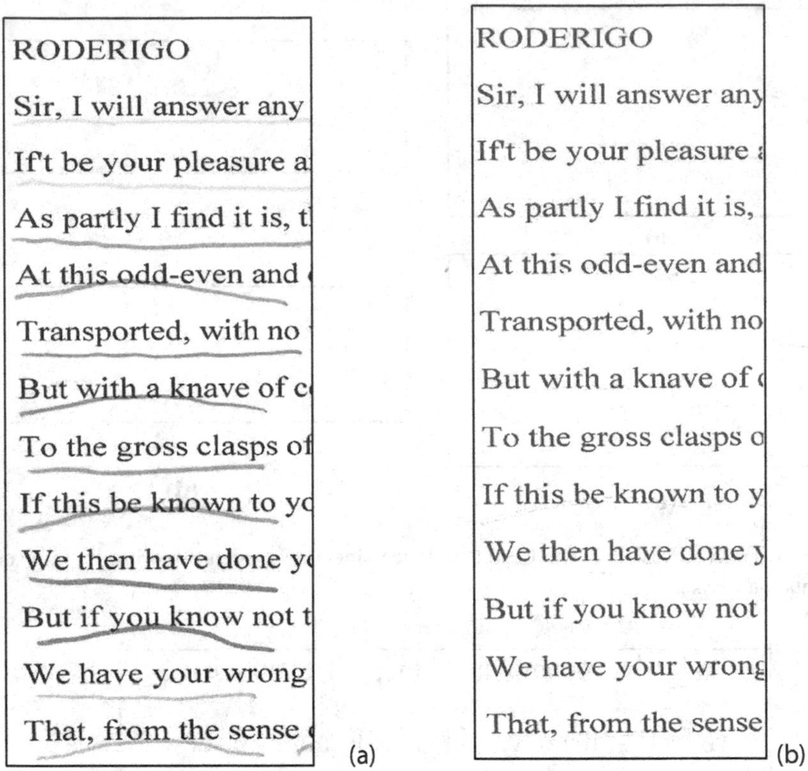

RODERIGO	RODERIGO
Sir, I will answer any	Sir, I will answer any
If't be your pleasure a	If't be your pleasure a
As partly I find it is, t	As partly I find it is,
At this odd-even and	At this odd-even and
Transported, with no	Transported, with no
But with a knave of c	But with a knave of
To the gross clasps of	To the gross clasps o
If this be known to yo	If this be known to y
We then have done yo	We then have done y
But if you know not t	But if you know not
We have your wrong	We have your wrong
That, from the sense	That, from the sense
(a)	(b)

Fig. 10. Text underline with different colors of pen and its removal.

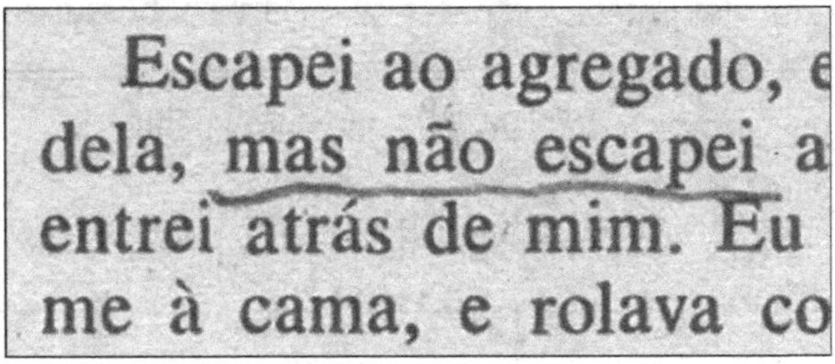

Escapei ao agregado, e
dela, mas não escapei a
entrei atrás de mim. Eu
me à cama, e rolava co

Fig. 11. Aged document with underlining noise.

Underlining alters the balance of such fading speed. In the case of the image shown in Fig. 7 the blue component presented an increase in intensity, making it higher than the red component, which became higher than the green one.

Using such knowledge one can tune the filter to the logic (blue > red and red > green) to obtain the image shown in Fig. 13.

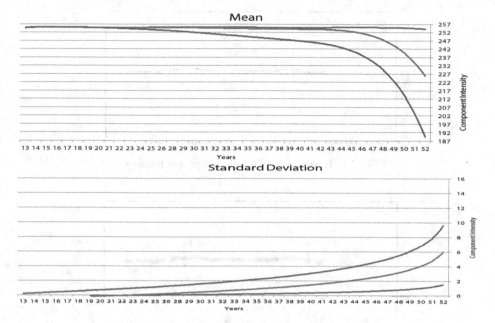

Fig. 12. Mean and standard deviation values of the decay of the normalized components of the RGB-histogram (color intensity) with age (years) of a white sheet of paper (Color figure online).

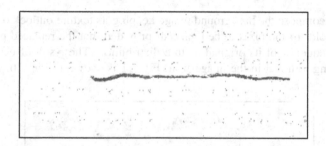

Fig. 13. Threshold filtered image from Fig. 11.

After binarization and salt-and-pepper filtering one obtains the binary mask shown in Fig. 14. To improve the quality of the removal of the text underline noise in aged documents the mask obtained should be dilated, yielding the mask shown in Fig. 15.

The aged paper has no uniform flat color. Document aging brings a texture effect to the background color. The experiments performed with over 6,000 historical documents about one century old showed that the texture of the aged background follows a Rayleigh distribution in the RGB-components. In the case of documents about half a century old the background texture is better represented by using normal distributions of RGB-components centered in the most frequent background color [11].

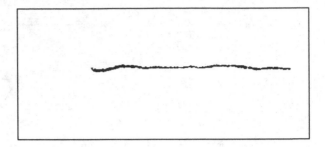

Fig. 14. Binary mask after salt-and-pepper filtering.

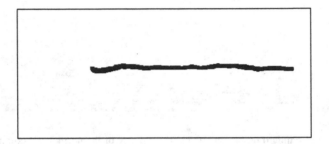

Fig. 15. Binary mask after dilatation.

Thus to recompose the background image keeping its texture outlook one randomly chooses the color of the pixel to be replaced, provided that the replaced pixel follows the relative frequency of its original texture distribution. The result of performing the text underlining removal in the image from Fig. 11 is shown in Fig. 16.

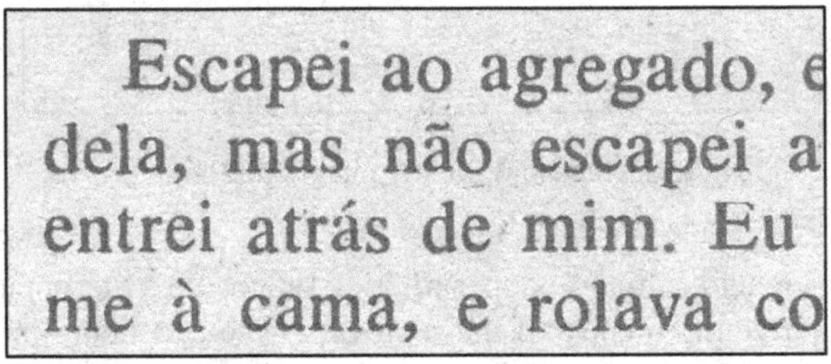

Escapei ao agregado, e
dela, mas não escapei a
entrei atrás de mim. Eu
me à cama, e rolava co

Fig. 16. Text underline removed from aged document image in Fig. 11.

In the case that the underline touches text areas the mask should not be dilated in those intercepting points.

4 Text Summarization

One can also see underlined or highlighted texts offer a summary of the most important parts of a document from a reader's perspective. The recent paper [10] presents a general algorithm for extracting the highlighted text and making summaries. It even allows generating different summaries for each color of marker used. A similar scheme for making summaries out of underlined text is presented here.

The proposed scheme is based on removing the text underline of monochromatic documents as presented in the last section. The bounding box that envelopes the segmented areas coincide with the extreme points of the "underline" noise one wants to filter out is often the area one wants to transcribe. Figure 17 shows an example of such underlined text for summarization.

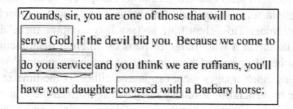

Fig. 17. Underlined text to be summarized.

The result of the summarization process having the reader's underline as the selection driver is obtained by copying the underlined block image and then removing the underline noise as already explained. The result of the underline-based text summarization of the image of Fig. 18 is shown in Fig. 19.

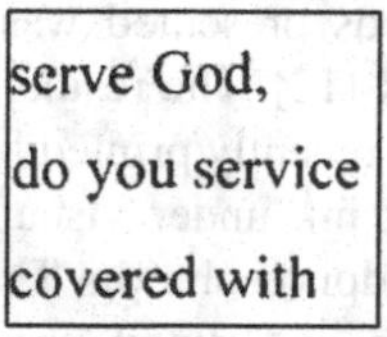

serve God,

do you service

covered with

Fig. 18. Result of summarization from image in Fig. 17.

Not always the underline bounding box coincides with the summarization area, however. Figure 20 zooms into the first line of the "careless" underline presented in Fig. 12, where one may observe that the underline starts almost at the end of the first word and stops in the middle of the word "leave".

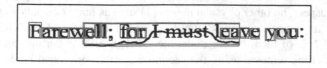

Fig. 19. Zoom into part of the text in Fig. 13.

In this case the bounding box for the summarization must envelope the whole words, "wrapping-up" the underline removal box.

5 Experimental Results and Conclusions

Two methods for removing reader's underline from textual documents are presented in this paper. The first one is suitable for images scanned in true-color. The second method applies to binary documents. The first method assumes that the original paper is plain white and the printed part is in black. It recognizes the graphical elements in the image by using a direct threshold in the image to find the users' underline, by generating a mask. Such a mask undergoes salt-and-pepper filtering and dilatation for enhancement. The pixels under such a mask correspond to the underline and are replaced by the color of pixels that are similar to the texture of the paper. This method is able to work satisfactorily in aged documents in which the paper background shows non-white darker color. This algorithm is fast in execution time, and efficient in removing the underline of a wide range of pens of different manufactures and colors.

The second scheme presented here targets at removing readers' underline marks from binary images. Such images were originated either by the binarization of a color scanned image or by generating a binary image straight from the scanning process. In this case, less information is present in the image, thus a more sophisticated technique is needed to be able to identify the graphical elements in the image and spot the readers' underline. In this case the whole image is swept to "box" the graphical elements. Statistical analysis is used on the size of such boxes. Readers' underlining have boxes of size that encompass several font or text cases, thus they are recognizable. Once found the boxes that envelope the readers' underline, some operations of mathematical morphology are used remove the noise. The process of this method for binary images is by far more processing intensive than the one presented for color images.

The effectiveness of the methods presented was tested using the ABBYY Finereader 12 Professional Edition OCR [12]. The results of two experiments are presented in Table 1. In the first experiment a recently printed book (in offset) with a background one may consider white and black ink under visual inspection was scanned using a commercial flatbed scanner in 300 dpi resolution. Then, 396 lines randomly chosen in different pages and positions were underlined using ballpoint pens totalling 5,235 words. The pages were re-scanned using the same equipment, parameters and saved in the same file format as before. The underlined text recognition dropped from 98.3 % to 69.2 % for the words before and after underlining.

The same pages were processed using the first algorithm presented here and then underwent OCR, yielding rising the correct recognition rate to 96.5 %. The second experiment was similar to the first one, but had as object a book printed 40 years ago which was kept under "normal" storage and use conditions and the paper presented the yellowish old aspect, no other physical noises [1] such as fungi or stains were observed, however. In this experiment 5,008 words were underlined and the OCR correctly transcribed 87.7 % of them before underline, 58.4 % after underline, and 83.9 % of them after underline removal using the second algorithm presented here.

Table 1. OCR Assessing the effectiveness of underline removal.

	White background	40 year-old background
Number of underlined words	5,235	5,008
OCR before underline	98.3 %	87.7 %
OCR with underline	69.2 %	58.4 %
OCR underline removed	96.5 %	83.9 %

The test images used here were more difficult than "real" ones, as in general readers' underline may touch the text areas, but tend not to cross extensive areas of the text as shown. Despite of that, the schemes presented have proved to be effective in text underline filtering out.

Current work targets to improve the underline removal scheme for binarized printed documents by using other untouched parts of the document to generate a font-set to replace the characters overwritten by the underlining. This post processing allows the complete character restoration.

Readers' annotations sometimes are not restricted to underlining. Often one finds other kinds of "noises" such as comments and vertical bars on the margins of documents. The vertical bars tend to stress the importance of the whole paragraph to the reader. In general, as these signs are in the margin, they are easily removed, but if one is interested in using them to guide summarization a new challenge, left for further work is set.

The source code and test images are freely available for non-commercial purposes by contacting one of the authors.

Algorithm 1. Pseudo-code of the algorithm for underline detection after segmentation and skeletonization:

```
// Find the leftmost point of the underline segment
    for i := 0 to Image1.Width - 1 do begin
      for j := 0 to image1.Height - 1 do begin
       if image1.Canvas.Pixels[i,j] = clBlack then begin
           x_ini := i;
           y_ini := j;
           break;
       end;
      end;
       if image1.Canvas.Pixels[i,j] = clBlack then begin
           break;
       end;
    end;
```

```
// Find the rightmost point of the underline segment
   for i := Image1.Width - 1 downto 0 do begin
     for j := image1.Height - 1 downto 0 do begin
       if image1.Canvas.Pixels[i,j] = clBlack then begin
         x_fim := i;
         y_fim := j;
         break;
       end;
     end;
       if image1.Canvas.Pixels[i,j] = clBlack then begin
         break;
       end;
   end;
// Remove all other segments with different left and rightmost points.
   removed := true;
   while removed do begin
     removed := false;
     for i := 1 to Image1.Width - 2 do begin
       for j := 1 to image1.Height - 2 do begin
         if ((neighbors(i,j) = 1) and
             (image1.Canvas.Pixels[i,j] = clBlack) and
             ((i <> x_ini) and (j <> y_ini))
             ((i <> x_fim)  and (j <> y_fim))) then begin
           remove_segment(i,j);
           removed := true;
         end;
       end;
     end;
   end;
// Load the remaining vertices.
   total_vertices := 0;
   for i := 1 to Image1.Width - 2 do begin
     for j := 1 to image1.Height - 2 do begin
       if ((vizinhos(i,j) > 2) and
           (image1.Canvas.Pixels[i,j] = clBlack)) then begin
         add_vertice(i,j);
         inc(total_vertice);
       end;
     end;
   end;
// Calculate the length between adjacent vertices.
   calc_lenth(Mvertices,Vvertices,total_vertices);

// Delete the paths that do not belong to the shortest path
   delete_path(Mvertices,total_vertices);

// At this point remains only the path that coeresponds to the readers
underline.
```

Acknowledgements. The research reported here was partly sponsored by CNPq – Conselho Nacional de Desenvolvimento Científico e Tecnológico – Brazilian Government.

References

1. Lins, R.D.: A taxonomy for noise in images of paper documents - the physical noises. In: Kamel, M., Campilho, A. (eds.) ICIAR 2009. LNCS, vol. 5627, pp. 844–854. Springer, Heidelberg (2009)
2. Cui, J., He, H., Wang, Y.: An adaptive staff line removal in music score images. In: IEEE 10th International Conference on Signal Processing (ICSP 2010), 24–28 October 2010

3. Khan, A.R., Kurniawan, F., Mohamad, D.: An automated approach to remove line from text bypassing restoration stage. In: The 2nd IEEE International Conference on Computer, Control and Communication (IEEE-IC4 2009)
4. Kumar, J., Doermann, D.: Fast Rule-line removal using integral images and support vector machines. In: ICDAR 2011, Beijing, China (2011)
5. Deivalakshmi, S., Harinivash, B., Palanisamy, P.: Line removal technique for document and non document images. In: 11th International Conference on Hybrid Intelligent Systems, HIS 2011, Melacca, Malaysia, 5–8 December 2011. IEEE (2011)
6. Pinto, J.R.C., Bandeira, L., Sousa, J.M.C., Pina, P.: Combining fuzzy clustering and morphological methods for old documents recovery. In: Marques, J.S., de la Blanca, N.P., Pina, P. (eds.) IbPRIA 2005. LNCS, vol. 3523, pp. 387–394. Springer, Heidelberg (2005)
7. Barboza, R., Lins, R.D., Mattos, V.S.: Removing highlighting in paper documents VII. In: IEEE International Telecommunications Symposium, ITS2010. Manaus-AM, Brazil, September 2010
8. Shapiro, L., Stockman, G.: Computer Vision, pp. 69–73. Prentice Hall, Englewood Cliffs (2002)
9. Soille, P.: Morphological Image Analysis: Principles and Applications, 2nd edn. Springer, Berlin, New York (2004). Corrected second printing of second edition
10. Barboza, R., Lins, R.D., Pereira, V.M.S.: Using readers' highlighting on monochromatic documents for automatic text transcription and summarization. In: ICDAR 2011, Beijing, September. IEEE Press (2011)
11. Barboza, R., Lins, R.D., de Jesus, D.M.: A color-based model to determine the age of documents for forensic purposes. In: ICDAR 2013 (2013)
12. ABBYY FineReader 12 Professional (2014), 12 July 2014. http://www.abbyy.com.br/finereader/
13. Shima, Y., et al.: One Method of underline extraction from business form image. In: FIT 2002 (Forum on Information Technology), I-85, pp. 169–170 (2002)
14. Bai, Z.-L., Huo, Q.: Underline detection and removal in a document image using multiple strategie. In: ICPR'04 —Vol. 2, pp. 578–581 (2004)
15. Patent: US8452133 B2 Underline Removal Appratus. Last visited 12 July 2014. http://www.google.com/patents/US8452133

Binarization with the Local Otsu Filter

Integral Histograms for Document Image Analysis

Anguelos Nicolaou[✉], Rolf Ingold, and Marcus Liwicki

Document, Image and Voice Analysis (DIVA) Group,
University of Fribourg, Bde des Perolles 90, Fribourg, Switzerland
anguelos.nicolaou@gmail.com,
{rolf.ingold,marcus.liwicki}@unifr.ch

Abstract. In this paper we introduce the use of integral histograms (IH) for document analysis. IH take advantage of the great increase of the memory size available on computers over time. By storing selected histogram features into each pixel position, several image filters can be calculated within constant complexity. In other words, time complexity is remarkably reduced by using more memory. While IH received much attention in the computer vision field, they have not been intensively investigated for document analysis so far. As a first step into this direction, we analyze IH for the toy problem of image binarization which is a prerequisite for many graphics and text recognition systems. The results of our participation in the HDIBCO2010 competition as well as our experiments with all DIBCO datasets show the capabilities of this novel method for Document Image analysis.

1 Introduction

Taking advantage of the great increase of available memory in the past decade, Porikli [1] introduced the integral histogram, (IH). As a generalization of the notion Integral Images (II), IH allow for real-time calculation of many popular image filters. While IH have quickly gained popularity in computer vision and image processing, they have not yet been popularized in document analysis. The aim of our research is to study the capabilities of IH for the field of Document Image Analysis (DIA) and to find out where they are most effective. Therefore we concentrate on a well-known problem in DIA, i.e., binarization. There is a trend to bypass this step [2] because some argue that its solved and, or is ill formed as a mathematical problem [3]. In the recent years a family of high-quality, manually annotated datasets and benchmarking, has made it possible to overcome such theoretical ambiguities. In a modern DIA pipeline, the binarized image should complement the gray-level data instead of replacing them. The need for fast and flawless binarization has a high impact on the output of the pipelines using it. While state of the art tends to revolve around complex binarization schemes and maybe over specialize for a specific domain, we introduce a more generic approach, which outperforms the well established methods and doesn't

© Springer-Verlag Berlin Heidelberg 2014
B. Lamiroy and J.-M. Ogier (Eds.): GREC 2013, LNCS 8746, pp. 176–190, 2014.
DOI: 10.1007/978-3-662-44854-0_14

Fig. 1. Input images (a) and (e), globally thresholded by Otsu's method (b) and (f), Sauvola's method (c) and (g), and our method (d) and (h). The input images are taken from the DIBCO datasets [4,5]. Sauvola's method had k = 0.5 and a 40 × 40 window

use preprocessing and post-processing. As we demonstrate in our experiments on the DIBCO datasets and with our participation to the DIBCO competitions, the results are very promising. Examples for the binarization performance of our IH-based method vs well established methods are illustrated in Fig. 1.

2   Related Work

2.1   Integral Images and Histograms

Integral Images where introduced for computer graphics by Crow [6] but gained high popularity in computer vision when used by Viola et al. [7]. Faisal et al. [8] used the integral of a squared image to compute the variance of any sub-image in $O(1)$ in the context of speeding up Niblack's binarization method. II have also been used very effectively for SURF feature extraction by Bay et al. [9].

Integral Histograms have been used in many applications in the recent years. Porikli when introducing them, applied them on object detection and texture detection [1]. In 2008, Porikli used IH to reduce the complexity of the bilateral filter to $O(1)$ [10] and in 2010 Kass et al. [11] used integral histograms to implement constant complexity anisotropic weighted median filter as well as highest mode and other histogram based filters. Zhang et al. extended integral histograms for stereo matching [12]. Out of all recently proposed methods, the method presented in [13] by Konya et al. stands out with respect to the method presented in this paper as it applies Otsu thresholding locally with a technique that could be perceived as a forerunner of integral histograms.

2.2   Binarization

Otsu's method is often taken for binarization as it is a powerful global thresholding algorithm. The localized and adaptive algorithms on the other hand perform better than global algorithms in most scenarios, especially when manually tuned. However, they have also introduced a lot ambiguity into performance assessment and optimal tuning. Two local methods that stand up to the test of time are Niblack's [14] (1) and Sauvola's [15] (2).

$$N_{w,k}(x,y) = m_w(x,y) + k * \sigma_w^2(x,y) \tag{1}$$

$$S_{w,k}(x,y) = m_w(x,y) * [1 + k * (\frac{\sigma_w^2(x,y)}{R} - 1)] \tag{2}$$

As can be seen in (1) and (2) these methods rely on local window average m_w, its variance $\sigma_{win}^2(x,y)$ and its dynamic range R to produce a threshold image $N_{w,k}(x,y)$ and $S_{w,k}(x,y)$ respectively. Both methods require the tuning of the window win and the k constant which is usually heuristically set to -0.2 and 0.5 respectively. State of the art tends to revolve around the fusion of adaptive methods [16,17] and even neural networks have [18] been used to optimally fuse the methods.

3   Integral Histograms for DIA

IH is a vast data-structure that is quite expensive to compute depending on the bit-depth we are interested to represent. Deep processing pipelines which is the main scenario in DIA could efficiently reuse IH in many stages of the pipeline. We suspect IH could be used to improve and speed-up various stages in a DIA pipeline such as shading correction, picture enhancement and binarization. In order to validate our belief we take on binarization as a popular problem that is part of most DIA pipelines.

3.1   Integral Images

Integral images (also referred to as summed area tables) as defined in (3) are an invertible transform which reduces to O(1) with respect to the kernel size, all box filters.

$$\forall x, y : x \in [1..width] \land y \in [1..height]$$

$$II(x,y) = \sum_{k=1}^{x} \sum_{l=1}^{y} I(k,l) \tag{3}$$

With integral images, we can obtain the sum of any sub-image with only 4 memory accesses. II are also ad-hoc image pyramids filtered by box filters.

3.2   Integral Histograms

The simplest way to describe integral histograms is as an evolution of integral images. An integral histogram $IH(x,y,g)$, is a transform of an input image

$I(x, y)$ as described by (4)

$$\forall x \in [1..width], y \in [1..height], g \in [1..2^{bitdepth}]$$

$$f(k, n) = \begin{cases} 1 : k = n \\ 0 : k \neq n \end{cases}$$

$$IH(x, y, g) = \sum_{h=1}^{x} \sum_{v=1}^{y} f(I(h, v), g)$$

(4)

where *width* and *height* are the input images dimensions and *bitdepth* is the number of relevant bits in our images, typically 8. We should consider *bitdepth* a constant with respect to an application domain. While Porikli [1] introduced IH for n-dimensional spaces, it is quite easier to demonstrate them in the context of 2D images. One can easily infer that the memory requirements of an integral histogram are $width * height * 2^{bitdepth}$ integers. Assuming that we use 32bit integers and 8bit images, the memory cost is 4*256 Bytes (1 KB per pixel). While IH have an $O(n)$ memory complexity with respect to number of pixels, they have an $O(2^n)$ memory complexity with respect to the bit-depth. Computer vision applications use IH among other things to speed up exhaustive object and texture detection in real time [1]. While [1] relies on keeping the bit-depth very low, 4 and 5 bits are used for real time processing. In the context of DIA where real time speed is not as crucial, but pixel-level precision is, the bit-depth could go quite higher.

3.3 Histogram of a Rectangle

Having an Integral Histogram Image $IH(x, y, b)$ with N bins, we can compute the histogram $H(g)$ of any rectangle as shown in (5)

$$\forall x, y, x', y', g : g \in [1..2^{bitdepth}] \wedge$$
$$x \in [1..width - 1] \wedge y \in [1..height - 1] \wedge$$
$$x' \in [x + 1..width] \wedge y' \in [y + 1..height]$$
$$H_{x,y,x',y'}(g) = IH(x, y, g) +$$
$$IH(x', y', g) - IH(x, y', g) - IH(x', y, g)$$

(5)

If we substitute N in for 256, we can easily infer that the cost of computing the Histogram is roughly 1024 asynchronous memory reads. If we add to that, the cost of thresholding by Otsu's method (256 sequential and 256 asynchronous memory reads), we get the cost of thresholding with respect to any rectangle in the image. Since the number of histogram-bins is a constant (usually) 256, any function on them should be considered to have a complexity of $O(1)$. There are many useful statistics that can be computed from the histogram with one or two passes. There are two internal representations of a histogram, the bin-count and the cumulative bin-count. Depending how we use them, a different representation might be computationally optimal. Among other uses, we can use IH's to efficiently compute image modes, local extrema and any specific percentile of a region in one pass (256 memory accesses). Having a pixel and its neighbourhoods histogram, we can also compute efficiently its rank within the neighbourhood. All of these operations can efficiently be applied on each pixel and its respective neighbourhood and can be seen as image filters. In our work, we briefly experimented with various filters provided by histograms, some of them are well established, but others are rather uncommon. Exploring thoroughly the properties and uses of such filters, exceeds the scope of our current work. Some of the filters (directly computable on integral histogram images, with respect to a local window) we found quite interesting are: percentile filters, statistical mode, rank, median and local extrema.

4   Integral Histograms for Binarization

Binarization of an image I(x,y) results in an image B(x,y) could be defined by (6).

$$\forall x \in [1..width], y \in [1..height]$$

$$B(I(x,y)) = \begin{cases} 1 : I(x,y) \in foreground \\ 0 : I(x,y) \in background \end{cases} \tag{6}$$

The real problem with the above definition is that foreground and background are very subjective terms that depend totally on the context of our goal. A pixel in an image can quite frequently be defined as either, foreground or background, depending on our perspective. A text pixel in a natural scene image, for example, can be deemed foreground in the context of text recognition but background in the context of face recognition. In document analysis and graphics recognition there is a consensus/convention that foreground pixels are the dark ones. This convention has allowed us to treat binarization as an image-processing problem instead of an image-understanding problem; thus avoiding the complications of properly defining the foreground and the background. Even so, the expression dark ones is quite vague; defining it in quantitative terms is the objective of any binarization method and ours. Our method was developed with text in mind, in both handwritten and printed documents. Our goal is to address and solve a range of very tough problems that are very frequent in historical documents such as bleed-through ink, stains in images, paper or papyrus degradation etc. At the same time we are also interested in maintaining the applicability of our method in other domains.

4.1   Otsu Threshold

Otsu's method provides the threshold that will separate a histogram into to two classes such that the intra-class variance is minimal [19]. The Otsu algorithm in its simple form has to iterate twice over a histogram, to calculate the maximal inter-class variances. Since the histogram bins of an image is constant (256 bins in standard grayscale images), the algorithm has a complexity of O(1). The shortcoming of Otsu's algorithm is that it disregards all geometry related information, which quite often is required in order to separate properly the pixels.

Fig. 2. A 5 layer LOF pyramid (b–f) and its input(a). The LOF window sizes are drawn as red boxes for scale. The input image is taken from the DIBCO2011 dataset [4] (color figure online)

4.2   Local Otsu Filter

We introduce an image filter called the Local Otsu Filter (LOF). This filter $LOF(I(x,y), l, t, b, r)$, depends on a grayscale image $I(x,y)$, an Integral Histogram $IH(x,y,g)$ and a rectangular neighbourhood defined by the left side l, the top side t, the bottom side b and the right side r. If we name as $fo(H(g))$ the function from a histogram H to its Otsu threshold, then formula (5) combined with Otsu's thresholding function, provides us with $LOF(I(x,y), l, t, b, r)$ as defined in (7).

$$\forall g, x, y, h, w :$$
$$g \in [1..2^{bitdepth}] \wedge$$
$$x \in [1..width] \wedge y \in [1..height] \wedge \qquad\qquad (7)$$
$$w \in [1..width] \wedge h \in [1..height]$$
$$LOF_{w,h}(x,y) = fo(H_{x-w/2,y-h/2,x+w/2,y+2/h}(g))$$

The LOF provides us with an image that contains the optimal threshold, for each pixel in the original image, estimated from the histogram of its neighbourhood. As we previously demonstrated, the complexity of computing the Otsu threshold of a rectangular area, is $O(1)$. Based on this, we can deduce that the complexity of computing the Local Otsu Filter for an image with n pixels is $O(n)$. Since a histogram, algorithm wise, should be considered having a constant size, all $H(g)$ to R^1 functions, have a complexity $O(1)$ therefore, all histogram derived filters, have a maximum complexity of $O(n)$. In Fig. 2 we can see the effects of LOF filter on an image for various window sizes.

4.3   Window Size

Having the Local Otsu Filter operation available, one has to address the troubling question of the ideal window size. Ideally we would like an area big enough to contain a statistically significant set of symbols/graphemes and small enough to be able to detect local of letters change in the background and treat it as such. Ideally, the window size should be tuned for a specific task, since both printed and handwritten texts have a finite and relatively small range of grapheme/symbol sizes as well a stroke thickness. The key factor in determining the window size should be resolution of scanning. Since we did not want to constrain our method to manual tuning, we improvised a way of compensating for the problem of the unknown resolution/scale. We worked under the assumption that most serious type of error is when the background is darker then it aught to be and especially when that happens with sharp gradients. Such situations as the stain in Fig. 2 tend to shift the threshold quite lower from where it should be and produce a large area of the image assigned to the foreground.

In order to address this type of problem, we considered that if a pixel is really a foreground pixel, it should stand out in any scale as long as the window contains a roughly representative ratio of background pixels. To state it differently, as long as our window size is big enough to always contain some background, Otsu's threshold should eliminate almost all false positives. It should be noted that Otsu's method is totally unbiased towards white or black. Thus background (white pixels) doesn't have to be a majority. The aforementioned rationale suggests image pyramids. After experimentation, we chose to produce a pyramid of five Local Otsu Filters. Although we might benefit more from other rectangular areas, this would require an a priori knowledge of the orientation of the text; we therefore preferred to use square windows. The pyramid base is set to have a window equal to the input image dimensions whichever was smaller. We computed our pyramid of filters such that each filter had a window size equal to half the size of the other previous image. Half was chosen as a compromise between having a pyramid that is dense enough and limiting computational time. The above constants add up to having five distinct window sizes: 100 %, 50 %, 25 %, 12.5 %, and 6.25 % of the width or height of the image whatever is smaller. In Fig. 2 such a pyramid can be seen. Although arbitrary, the rate of two allows us to avoid an exhaustive search through all the intermediary scales. At the same time, 6.25 % of the image size as the minimum window is practically guaranteed to avoid the serious problem of having a pixel whose neighbourhood contains only foreground. From a signal processing perspective, the limitation of avoiding windows that are too small to contain background can be simply described as avoiding sampling bellow the Nyquist frequency.

4.4   Foreground Area

While we discussed the problems related to an all foreground neighbourhood and the Niquist frequency, the invert problem, having a window where all pixels belong to the background, is far more frequent and harder to overcome. If those pixels are detected, they can directly be set to white (background), ignoring their local threshold. A way to detect these pixels is to search for abnormally low thresholds in the Local Otsu Filters. Otsu's method has no bias towards black or white sides of the histogram, it can partition a set of grey values no

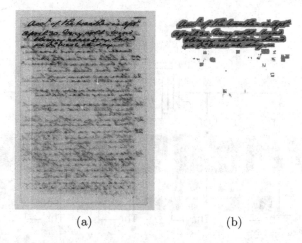

(a)   (b)

Fig. 3. Text areas, (a) is the input and in (b), grey is the foreground areas and black is the ground truth (superimposed) for reference.

matter how skewed the histogram is. We chose to threshold by Otsu's method the Local Otsu Filter itself. As can be seen in Fig. 3, the results are quite impressive.

4.5 The Algorithm

As demonstrated in Fig. 4, our algorithm consists of five major steps. First we obtain the integral histogram. Second, we compute local threshold images. Next, we get a foreground area estimation based on the high-frequency LOF and we threshold the input by each LOF. Finally, we perform a pixel-wise and operation on all intermediary binary images plus the foreground area image. Since we have a fixed height pyramid of five layers the number of image filters is predefined. Each of the filters we use, has a complexity of $O(n)$ with respect to the input pixel count.

5   Experimental Procedure

In the recent years a family of datasets have been presented by Pratikakis, Gatos and Ntirogiannis [4,5,20,21]. These datasets demonstrate a very broad range of problems related to document binarization. In 2010 we submitted an earlier version of our method to HDIBCO 2010 for independent evaluation on an unknown dataset. We also evaluated our method on all DIBCO datasets publicly available at the time of writing. Furthermore, we performed experiments related to the speed of our filters and our method.

5.1   DIBCO Participation

In 2010 the first author of this paper participated in the HDIBCO-2010 competition in the context of ICFHR 2010. The method presented was an earlier

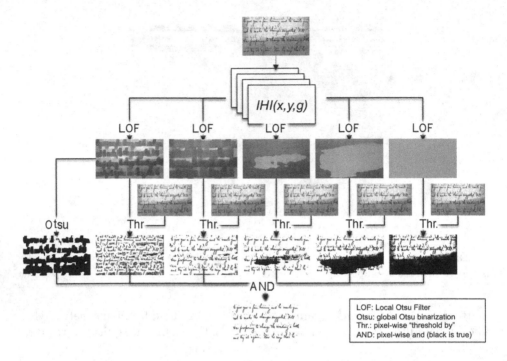

Fig. 4. A visual flowchart describing our algorithm. Filter window sizes increase from left to right

version of our method. Key differences are the pyramid steepness 11/20 instead of 0.5 the missing of the foreground areas step and that the submission had some minor post processing heuristics. The submitted method ranked 7th out of a total of 17. We also submitted an untuned version of a method similar to the method presented in this paper and it ranked 17th out of 23 methods.

5.2   Principal Experiment

Since there are many publicly available DIBCO datasets, the only way to evaluate our method without the temptation of choosing one, was to use them all. We therefore compiled a dataset which consists of all publicly available DIBCO datasets DIBCO2009, HDIBCO2010, DIBCO2011, and HDIBCO2012. The total dataset consists of 50 images, 37 handwritten and 13 printed. All images contain severe degradations of many sorts most typically encountered in historical documents. For a performance metric, we chose the F-Measure defined as the harmonic mean of precision and recall. We chose to test our method (LOF) at various bit-depths from 8 to 3. For reference we also used Sauvola's method and Wolf's method [22][1]. It should be mentioned that Wolf's method ranked 5th out of 35 in DIBCO2009. We tuned both Sauvola's and Wolf's methods

---

[1] As made available http://liris.cnrs.fr/christian.wolf/software/binarize/

Table 1. Experimental Results

Binarization Method	Average Precision	Average Recall	Average F-Measure	8bit LOF F-Measure T-Test
Foreground Area	13.36 %	96.67 %	23.12 %	0.0000‰
Global Otsu	77.09 %	88.18 %	78.28 %	2.0294‰
Sauvola	95.38 %	51.42 %	61.01 %	0.0001‰
Wolf et al.	91.85 %	77.38 %	82.25 %	13.2882‰
3bit LOF	52.72 %	90.03 %	62.27 %	0.0000‰
4bit LOF	74.64 %	89.96 %	79.45 %	0.0976‰
5bit LOF	84.35 %	88.07 %	85.14 %	107.7710‰
6bit LOF	87.72 %	85.65 %	85.83 %	439.9365‰
7bit LOF	88.90 %	84.42 %	85.80 %	467.4745‰
8bit LOF	89.54 %	83.81 %	**85.80 %**	NA

as where the default values $k = 0.5$ and a window size of $40 * 40$ pixels. We also measured global Otsu thresholding and our foreground area images on their own. In Table 1 we provide the average F-Measure each method scored against all images. We also provide the average recall and precision as well as a paired single tail T-test of each method against the 8 bit LOF. Precision recall and F-Measure, were rounded to two decimal digits and the paired T-test to 4 decimal digits. The F-Measure provides with a balance against both major errors false positives false negatives and we believe it to be good indicator of a methods valour. Precision and recall on the other hand, provide us with a good indication of the shortcomings of a method. Based on the result seen in Table 1 we can draw several conclusions. Assuming a 5 % alpha threshold we can see that our method (LOF8) performs significantly better than global Otsu thresholding and local Sauvola thresholding. We can also see that our method outperforms Wolf's method but not very far from the 5 % limit. In what concerns the bit depth, LOF8, LOF7 and LOF6 versions are practically indistinguishable. LOF5 performs worse than LOF8,7,6 but without statistical significance. LOF4 and LOF3 perform much worst than their counter parts. Based on these observations depending on whether we favour computational resources or accurate results the choice should be between 5 and 6 bits. Note that investigating whether the apparent insignificance of the 7th and 8th bit, would apply to other datasets as well exceeds the scope of this paper. Interestingly the Foreground Area method would be a good candidate for method fusion as it presents a very high recall rate. Another observation would be that Otsu's method has a recall rate that is quite higher than its precision rate while the local methods Sauvola's and Wolf's have higher precision rates over low recall rates. Our method on high bit-rates (8,7,6) has a higher precision than recall while in the low bit-depths (3,4,5) recall is higher than precision.

5.3   Benchmark

We considered that it was very important to evaluate our binarization method as well the LOF and our median filter implementation for performance. We wanted to see if performance will be consistent with our theoretical model of O(1) complexity. We also decided to use Matlab's binary implementation of the median filter as a reference. The benchmark was executed on the worst-case scenario of 8bit data. The memory consumption halves for every bit of precision we remove. It is a safe assumption that since the CPU iterates over half the memory, the exact same amount of time, execution time will follow memory consumption. All filters where executed on an image of 1414×1414 pixels. Our binarization method was also measured and is plotted a constant line for reference. As can be seen in Fig. 5, our filters have a totally constant complexity and outperform the standard median filter algorithm as soon as the window gets greater than 20 pixels. We believe that as technology progresses and image resolutions become higher and higher, the integral histograms methods will replace their counterparts which are faster in small windows in high

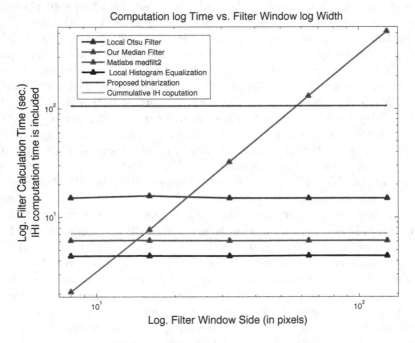

Fig. 5. Execution benchmark logtime vs window width. LOF filter computation times are blue, Our median filter computation times are green, matlab medfilt2 computation times are red. Localised histogram equalisation is light blue (assuming a cumulative IH is already computed). For reference our full method appears as a constant grey line and the computation of a cumulative integral histogram as a magenta purple line. All computations were measured on a 2MP image containing white noise (color figure online).

bit-depths, but have worst complexities. Benchmarking was performed by our demo software under wine 1.4 on a13 inch macbook pro with 8 GB of RAM and a 2.4 GHz core 2 duo CPU. Time counting starts after the images are loaded and stops before they are stored thus IO is not part of the benchmark. It should be noted that the benchmark run in multiuser mode and there is no guaranty of 100 % CPU availability.

5.4 Demo

In order to transparently support our claims in this paper, and provide the means for comparison to our method we have made publicly available[2] a demo of our method. The same program is the program we used in the experimental procedure as well as the benchmarks.

6 Local Histogram Equalization

As a simple indication of the reusability of IH, we also implemented a Local Histogram Equalization method and assessed some of its properties in a qualitative maner. From a DIA perspective, histogram equalization becomes very useful

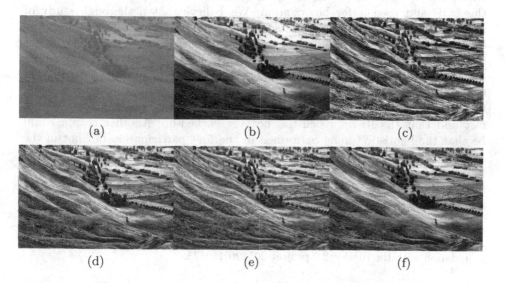

Fig. 6. A image with a low dynamic range and a resolution of 1024×683 pixels is restored using various histogram equalization scenarios. (a) is the input image, (b) is the global histogram equalization, (c) histogram equalization using only the local histogram for a window of 101×101. (d) Is a histogram equalization of the sum of the global and local histograms of a 101×101 window, while (e) is the result when using a 51×51 window for the local window and (f) when using a window of 201×201

---

[2] A binary version of our benchmarking program http://nicolaou.homouniversalis.org/demos/2013/05/15/Binarization-Demo.html

when documents contain non binary objects such as photos or drawings specifically if one thinks of acquisition under non uniform illumination. In traditional implementations local histogram equalization has a high computational cost. In our implementation it runs faster our median filter assuming a cumulative integral histogram is already computed. In Fig. 6(b) the inability of the global equalization method to reveal the details on the rivers surface or on the trees that lie near the center of the image can be clearly demonstrated. On the other hand, in Fig. 6(c) we can also observe that a pure local equalization is to rough and highlights JPEG artifacts near the sheep on the lower part of the image. As can be seen in Fig. 6(f) a large window of 201×201 enhances desired detail without amplifying any noise in an apparent manner.

7   Conclusion and Future Work

In this paper we have demonstrated the feasibility of using IH for DIA. Our initial experiments on binarization data have shown that our generic method performs better than typical broadly accepted generic methods like Sauvola and the more recent improvement by Wolf et al. We believe that the more generic nature of our method makes it better suited for applications such as graphics binarization which will be part of our future investigations. In this paper we introduced the LOF and used it for binarization. We believe that a thorough study of its properties as an image processing filter could produce interesting insights. We would like to incorporate other histogram based filters in our document analysis pipelines, such as the highest mode filter, the rank filter, percentile filters, etc., because IH make them very cheap. The results from the participation to competitions are a bit puzzling. The method got a significantly lower ranking in 2013 than in 2010. The reason could be that the state of the art is evolving fast and that the IH approach has not yet cached-up. Another reason could be that the heuristic tuning performed in the first participation but not in the second proved to be an important factor. The constant complexity allows for filter window sizes unthought of in the past. Our brief experimentation with histogram equalisation indicated that the best results are when a large windows are used and local histograms become more representative.

Acknowledgment. This work has been supported by the Swiss National Science Foundation with the HisDoc 2.0 project 205120 150173.

References

1. Porikli, F.: Integral histogram: a fast way to extract histograms in cartesian spaces. In: IEEE Computer Society Conference on Computer Vision and Pattern Recognition, CVPR 2005, vol. 1, pp. 829–836. IEEE (2005)
2. Garz, A., Fischer, A., Sablatnig, R., Bunke, H.: Binarization-free text line segmentation for historical documents based on interest point clustering. In: 2012 10th IAPR International Workshop on Document Analysis Systems (DAS), pp. 95–99. IEEE (2012)

3. Lopresti, D., Nagy, G.: When is a problem solved? In: 2011 International Conference on Document Analysis and Recognition (ICDAR), pp. 32–36. IEEE (2011)
4. Pratikakis, I., Gatos, B., Ntirogiannis, K.: Icdar 2011 document image binarization contest (dibco 2011). In: 2011 International Conference on Document Analysis and Recognition (ICDAR), pp. 1506–1510. IEEE (2011)
5. Pratikakis, I., Gatos, B., Ntirogiannis, K.: Icfhr 2012 competition on handwritten document image binarization (h-dibco 2012). In: 2012 International Conference on Frontiers in Handwriting Recognition (ICFHR), pp. 817–822. IEEE (2012)
6. Crow, F.C.: Summed-area tables for texture mapping. In: ACM SIGGRAPH Computer Graphics, vol. 18, pp. 207–212. ACM (1984)
7. Viola, P., Jones, M.: Rapid object detection using a boosted cascade of simple features. In: Proceedings of the 2001 IEEE Computer Society Conference on Computer Vision and Pattern Recognition, CVPR 2001, vol. 1, pp. I-511–I-518. IEEE (2001)
8. Shafait, F., Keysers, D., Breuel, T.M.: Efficient implementation of local adaptive thresholding techniques using integral images. Doc. Recogn. Retrieval XV 6815(1), 681510 (2008)
9. Bay, H., Tuytelaars, T., Van Gool, L.: SURF: speeded up robust features. In: Leonardis, A., Bischof, H., Pinz, A. (eds.) ECCV 2006, Part I. LNCS, vol. 3951, pp. 404–417. Springer, Heidelberg (2006)
10. Porikli, F.: Constant time o (1) bilateral filtering. In: IEEE Conference on Computer Vision and Pattern Recognition, CVPR 2008, pp. 1–8. IEEE (2008)
11. Kass, M., Solomon, J.: Smoothed local histogram filters. ACM Trans. Graph. (TOG) 29(4), 100 (2010)
12. Zhang, K., Lafruit, G., Lauwereins, R., Van Gool, L.: Joint integral histograms and its application in stereo matching. In: 2010 17th IEEE International Conference on Image Processing (ICIP), pp. 817–820. IEEE (2010)
13. Konya, I., Seibert, C., Eickeler, S., Glahn, S.: Constant-time locally optimal adaptive binarization. In: 10th International Conference on Document Analysis and Recognition, ICDAR'09, pp. 738–742. IEEE (2009)
14. Niblack, W.: An Introduction to Digital Image Processing. Prentice Hall, Englewood Cliffs (1986)
15. Sauvola, J., Pietikäinen, M.: Adaptive document image binarization. Pattern Recogn. 33(2), 225–236 (2000)
16. Ntirogiannis, K., Gatos, B., Pratikakis, I.: A combined approach for the binarization of handwritten document images. Pattern Recognit. Lett. 33(12), 1601–1613 (2012)
17. Su, B., Lu, S., Tan, C.L.: Combination of document image binarization techniques. In: 2011 International Conference on Document Analysis and Recognition (ICDAR), pp. 22–26. IEEE (2011)
18. Badekas, E., Papamarkos, N.: Optimal combination of document binarization techniques using a self-organizing map neural network. Eng. Appl. Artif. Intell. 20(1), 11–24 (2007)
19. Otsu, N.: A threshold selection method from gray-level histograms. Automatica 11(285–296), 23–27 (1975)
20. Gatos, B., Ntirogiannis, K., Pratikakis, I.: Icdar 2009 document image binarization contest (dibco 2009). In: 10th International Conference on Document Analysis and Recognition, ICDAR'09, pp. 1375–1382. IEEE (2009)

21. Pratikakis, I., Gatos, B., Ntirogiannis, K.: H-dibco 2010-handwritten document image binarization competition. In: 2010 International Conference on Frontiers in Handwriting Recognition (ICFHR), pp. 727–732. IEEE (2010)
22. Wolf, C., Jolion, J.M., Chassaing, F.: Text localization, enhancement and binarization in multimedia documents. In: Proceedings of the International Conference on Pattern Recognition, vol. 2, pp. 1037–1040 (2002)

Improved Contour-Based Corner Detection for Architectural Floor Plans

Max Feltes[1], Sheraz Ahmed[1,2](✉), Andreas Dengel[1,2], and Marcus Liwicki[2,3]

[1] University of Kaiserslautern, Kaiserslautern, Germany
[2] German Research Center for Artificial Intelligence (DFKI),
Kaiserslautern, Germany
{max.feltes,sheraz.ahmed,andreas.dengel}@dfki.de
[3] University of Fribourg, Fribourg, Switzerland
marcus.liwicki@unifr.ch

Abstract. A new rotation invariant corner detection method for architectural line drawing images is proposed in this paper. The proposed method is capable of finding corners of objects in line drawing images by filtering out unnecessary points without changing the overall structure. Especially, in case of diagonal lines and corners, our method is capable of removing repetitive points. The proposed method is applied to corner detection of walls in floor plans which in turn are used for detection of wall edges. To evaluate the effectiveness of detected corners, gap closing and wall edge detection is performed on a publicly available dataset of 90 floor plans, where we achieved a recognition and detection accuracy of 95 %.

1 Introduction

Even in our modern world it is very hard to find architectural floor plans fulfilling specific criteria. Most of the time, after a client specifies how he imagines his new home, the architect will go through his archive to find similar floor plans matching these criteria. As a next step, he will modify them to fulfill further constraints. However, this manual search takes a long time, and even though it might have a high precision rate, the recall rate is very low. In order to be able to automate the search, the archive has to be scanned and automatically analyzed.

Automated floor plan analysis is the task of extracting information about a building's structure that is embedded inside an image. It is composed of several subtasks, such as, segmenting the text and the graphics from the document, detecting the walls and doors, and finally recognizing the different rooms. Automated floor plan analysis is an ongoing topic of research in pattern recognition and machine learning. Several attempts with varying goals have been made to solve this problem: [1–3] try to reconstruct a 3D model from the 2D floor plans, whereas [4] tries to extract the rooms and their connections. References [5,6] focus on the understanding of hand-drawn and sketched floor plans.

Recently, we have introduced a method for automatic floor plan analysis [7]. An analysis of the results in [7] lead to the conclusion that the room retrieval

© Springer-Verlag Berlin Heidelberg 2014
B. Lamiroy and J.-M. Ogier (Eds.): GREC 2013, LNCS 8746, pp. 191–203, 2014.
DOI: 10.1007/978-3-662-44854-0_15

works quite good on rooms with walls going horizontally and vertically in the plan but fails on floor plans with diagonal walls. The main reason for these failures were problems while finding the borders of the rooms. The algorithm of [7] closes the gaps occurring at doors and windows and these gaps were not correctly found.

It is to be noted that corner/feature detectors like SIFT [8], FAST [9], etc. cannot be used in context of line drawing images. It is because they are based on blob detection, and the points where a blob is detected is considered as a corner/feature/key point. However, in case of line drawings the goal is to detect corners, which can be used to approximate objects in the image, with high precision and without excessive points.

In this paper, a novel method for corner detection in line drawing images is presented. This method is based on the algorithm introduced in [10] and improves it at different points. The proposed method solves the problem of over-segmentation, especially on diagonal lines. To show the impact of proposed method, detected corners are used for detection of wall edges and gap closing in architectural floor plans as done in [7]. Note, while the method of [10] is already quite old, it is considered as the standard method and being used in different toolkits, e.g. in OpenCV this is a standard method for contour extraction.

The rest of the paper is organized as follows. Section 2 summarizes different methods available for corner detection which can be used in architectural floor plans. Section 3 provides the insight about proposed corner detection method. Section 4 provides an application of detected corners in floor plan analysis. Experimental details and analysis of results are presented in Sect. 5. Finally, Sect. 6 concludes the paper with possible future directions.

2   Related Work

In literature mostly corner detection, vectorization, and key point detection are used alternatively. However, in context of line drawing images corner detection and key point detection are different. This section summarizes different approaches for corner detection/vectorization, which can be used in context of architectural floor plans. An overview of typical selection process of vectorization methods is given in [11].

A corner detection method based on self-similarity is presented in [12]. A pixel is referred to as corner, if similarity between the patch centered at the pixel and neighboring patches, is low. Similarity is computed using sum of square differences between patches. In [13] Harris et al. further improved the method presented in [12] by incorporating directionality into the similarity score. To refer to a pixel as corner it looks for significant changes in all directions.

An approach for contour detection is presented in [10]. It can be used as corner detector/vectorization method, because it simplifies contours points by approximating them as a polygon. These simplified points serve as detected corners. It is based on a simple border following algorithm, with the option to either detect only outer contours or to include inner borders.

In [14], an algorithm is proposed to approximate a digital line by recursively including points based on a distance measure. It finds the point farthest away from the approximated line, and includes it if the distance exceeds a given threshold. The segments formed by this are then recursively approximated. These approximated points are referred to as detected corners.

In [15] a method is presented to detect dominant/corner points on closed digital curves. It is a parameter free approach that first determines the region of support for each point based on its local properties. Using these regions relative significance (e.g. curvature) of each point is computed. To finally detect dominant/corner points non maximum suppression is applied.

A method for segmentation of edges into lines and arcs is presented in [16]. The main idea is to extract corners based on edges of object. It uses a recursive algorithm that analyzes lists of connected edge points and convert them into polygons. These polygonal descriptions are analyzed to groups of connected lines. Finally circular arcs and lines are obtained as image description, which are representing the corners of objects in the image.

Reference [17] approached the task of edge detection by finding points in the binary image and combining several vectors to form more complex forms. As this approach only return bars and poly-lines, it could lead to problems with some walls in floor plan analysis, as some walls are curved, e.g., corner towers. Similarly, [18] proposed an approach for corner detection based on the Chord-to-Point distance accumulation.

Another corner detection/vectorization approach was introduced by [19], which works on skeletonized shapes. The drawback is that the thickness of the lines are only approximated. This thickness however is used for the gap closing algorithm and should reflect the thickness of the line at the extremities. Reference [20] extracts local interest points as junctions by creating a skeleton connective graph and using a wavelet transform. Similarly, [21] proposed a contour based corner detector method. It is based on magnitude of imaginary part of Gabor filters response on contours.

All of the above-mentioned methods try to approximate objects in given image. However, there is another class of corner/feature detector where the goal is not to approximate the object but to locate important points (referred to as key points) in the image. For example, LoG [22], DoG [23], SIFT [8], SURF [9], FAST [24], BRISK [25], SUSAN [26], etc. These methods try to locate blobs using different masks and other information. All the points where blob is detected are referred as keypoint. This class of corner/key point detection is not suitable for line drawing images, where goal is to approximate objects with precision and as less points as possible.

3   Proposed Corner Detection

Most of the systems for analysis of line drawings/technical drawings/architectural floor plans are based on vectorization. The vectorization results are considered as corners of objects in these images. These corners are further processed to extract different structural information in these drawing images. If the corner detection/vectorization has errors, these errors are propagated to the next steps

(a) Detected points on a diagonal wall   (b) Detected points near an indentation

Fig. 1. Two cases which lead to over-segmentation using [10]

in the analysis, as next steps are based on processing these points. In order to explain our method in terms of real application, we applied it on architectural floor plans and compared our results with the method used in [7].

In [7] corners for wall image in architectural floor plans are detected using the method in [10]. However, using the method in [10] for corner detection from wall image inherits different drawbacks. As shown in Fig. 1a, the method in [10] worked correctly only for perfectly horizontal and vertical walls. However, if the walls were diagonal, many excess points would be detected along those walls, thus splitting a long edge on wall into several smaller ones and leading to over-segmentation. This over-segmentation will lead to errors in next steps, where each wall edge is processed for closing the gaps on the probable locations of doors and windows.

A second case which could lead to over-segmentation is when the walls don't have clean lines, but have some noise added to the edges. The most notable causes were binarization and removal of doors/windows, where small indentations were left on some of the wall segments, as shown in Fig. 1b.

The proposed corner detection improves the method in [10] by filtering out the points that appeared through over-segmentation on diagonal lines. To filter every point, it calculates the distance to the line connecting the previous and the next point. This distance indicates whether the point was necessary or if it appeared because of an over-segmentation of a horizontal edge.

The equation of the line passing through $P_1(x_1, y_1)$ and $P_3(x_3, y_3)$ has the general form:

$$l \equiv a * x + b * y + c = 0 \tag{1}$$

The distance of a given point $P(x, y)$ to l is defined as:

$$distance(P, l) = \frac{a * x + b * y + c}{\sqrt{a^2 + b^2}} \tag{2}$$

Points can now be filtered out using the following formula:

$$discard(P_2, l) = \begin{cases} True & \text{if } distance(P_2, l) < \Theta_d \\ False & \text{else} \end{cases} \text{with } \Theta_d = theshold_{distance}$$

$$\tag{3}$$

The proposed method needs as an input only the ordered list of detected points, as well as the threshold Θ_d mentioned above. The order list of corner points is created by traversing and arranging all the detected points in clock wise direction.

Algorithm 1. filter_cornerpoints

Input: A threshold *threshold*
An ordered list containing the detected points *Ordered_points_list*
Output: A filtered ordered list of points

```
point_list ← Ordered_point_list
i ← 0
while i + 3 < len(point_list) do
    P1 ← point_list[i]
    P2 ← point_list[i + 1]
    P3 ← point_list[i + 2]
    line ← get_line(P1, P3)
    d ← distance(P52, line)
    if d < threshold then
        del point_list[i + 1]
    else
        i ← i + 1
    end if
end while
return point_list
```

In Fig. 3 there is an over-segmentation of the two diagonal lines because of the detected points P_2 and P_7/P_8. The proposed method will consecutively check the detected points if they meet the distance threshold (Fig. 2).

It is important to note that if consecutive points are close together, only the last one will be kept. In rare cases however, each point is needed to retain the shape of the wall, most notably in corner towers. This can be solved by not only considering the three consecutive points, but increasing the index of the right delimiter as long as all the points between the two corners defining the line lie within the defined distance threshold. However, as these are very rare, the very small increase in the detection rate did not outweight the decrease in recognition accuracy of the gap closing evaluated in Sect. 4. In the example in Fig. 3, it is not clear which point should be kept (P_7 or P_8). As these are very rare, it is acceptable to lose some information in this case. In another rare case, a small indentations indicates that a door closes as this position. This information is unfortunately lost (see Fig. 4).

Another important point to note is that this proposed method is different from [14] in the way that it is more robust against over-segmentation by calculating the distances of the points to different segments than the method proposed by [14]. This can lead to different results, as seen in Fig. 5. Figure 7 shows an

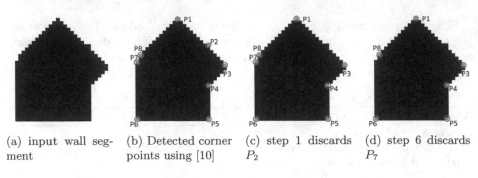

(a) input wall seg- (b) Detected corner (c) step 1 discards (d) step 6 discards
ment points using [10] P_2 P_7

Fig. 2. Different stages of the proposed method with $\Theta_d = 1.5$

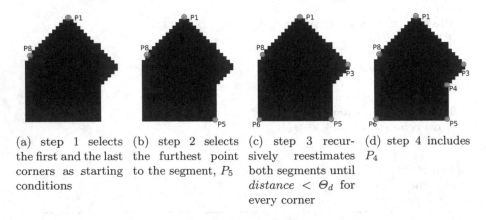

(a) step 1 selects (b) step 2 selects (c) step 3 recur- (d) step 4 includes
the first and the last the furthest point sively reestimates P_4
corners as starting to the segment, P_5 both segments until
conditions   *distance* $< \Theta_d$ for
    every corner

Fig. 3. Different stages of [14]

undersegmentation that happens when applying [14]. Our proposed approach works locally, meaning it only needs to calculate the distance of a single corner, whereas [14] needs to compute the distances of every corner on the segment.

The detected corner points can be used for different purposes. In [7] these detected corner points are used for extraction of parallel wall edges, which in turn are used to close the gaps on the probable location of door and windows. To show the effectiveness of our improved corner detection method, we have applied our and several different corner detection methods on architectural floor plans and evaluated the gap closing (See Sect. 4).

4   Gap Closing: An Application of Corner Detection

Gap closing is a process in architectural floor plan analysis which is performed to find the closed regions of rooms in the floor plan. It is performed on the edges which correspond to the parallel walls, as these are the probable locations of door and/or windows. Wall edges are constructed using detected corner points (for more details on wall edges see [7]). Therefore, if there is an error in corner point

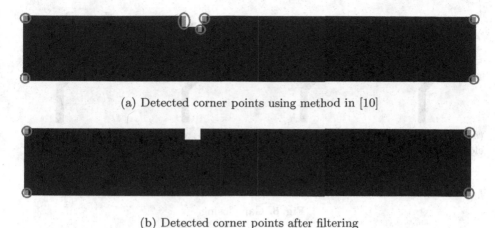

(a) Detected corner points using method in [10]

(b) Detected corner points after filtering

Fig. 4. Failure case: a small indentation is lost where a door might possibly connect

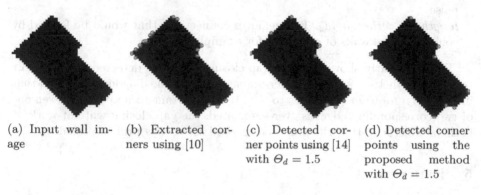

(a) Input wall image

(b) Extracted corners using [10]

(c) Detected corner points using [14] with $\Theta_d = 1.5$

(d) Detected corner points using the proposed method with $\Theta_d = 1.5$

Fig. 5. Comparison of the proposed method and [14], both with $\Theta_d = 1.5$ Note that [14] was not able to filter 2 noisy points on diagonal lines.

detection (over/under segmentation) it would propagate to wall edge detection and then to gap closing.

Here gap closing is presented to show that our method has improved detection and recognition accuracy remarkably by resolving errors in corner point detection in [10] which was used in [7]. Gaps are closed by connecting pairs of previously detected edges, which fulfilled several conditions:

- The angles of the rectangle created by connecting the two edges should be ∼ 90°. This ensures that the edges are aligned.
- The area between the two edge candidates should be empty. This ensures that two edges will not be connected if they are separated by another wall.
- $length_{edge1} <= 2 * length_{edge2}$. This ensures that edges are only connected if they have approximately the same length (as is almost always the case in architectural floor plans).

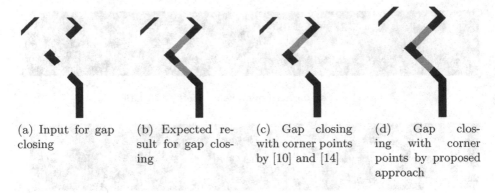

(a) Input for gap closing

(b) Expected result for gap closing

(c) Gap closing with corner points by [10] and [14]

(d) Gap closing with corner points by proposed approach

Fig. 6. Gap closing

- $length_{edge} > threshold_1$. This removes some edges which exist because of noise.
- $length_{edge} < threshold_2$. This removes connections that would be formed by connecting the walls of a hallway for example.

Figure 6 clearly shows that the gap closing using the detected corner points by proposed method solves the over-segmentation of the diagonal lines, and thus introduces a rotation invariance to [10]. It is important to note that if even one of two corresponding edges is over-segmented, the gap closing will not work. It is therefore crucial that the proposed method solves this problem reliably.

5   Experiments

5.1   Evaluation Method

The evaluation method introduced by [27] is used to evaluate the proposed methods. It is able to evaluate exact matches as well as partial matches.

The detected regions are compared to the ground-truth regions by calculating the overlap between them and determining several parameters:

one_to_one is the number of detected regions which overlap with exactly one ground-truth region

$g\_one\_to\_many$ is the number of ground-truth regions that overlap with more than one detected region

$g\_many\_to\_one$ is the number of detected regions where more than one detected region overlaps with a single ground-truth region

$d\_one\_to\_many$ is the number of detected regions that overlap with more than one ground-truth region

$d\_many\_to\_one$ is the number of ground-truth region where more than one ground-truth region overlaps with a single detected region

To determine these parameters, the overlap between each pair of detected regions and ground-truth regions is detected using the following formula:
Let d[i] be the ith detected region, g[j] be the jth ground-truth region:

$$match\_score(i, j) = \frac{area(d[i] \bigcap g[j])}{max(area(d[i]), area(g[j]))} \qquad (4)$$

If $match\_score(i, j) > acceptance\_threshold$, the overlap is kept. By building a table containing every possible combination of detected regions and ground-truth regions (called *match score table*), the aforementioned parameters can easily be deduced. These parameters are then used to calculate the detection rate and recognition accuracy of the evaluated method:

$$DetectionRate = \frac{one\_to\_one}{N} + \frac{g\_one\_to\_many}{N} + \frac{g\_many\_to\_one}{N} \qquad (5)$$

$$RecognitionAccuracy = \frac{one\_to\_one}{M} + \frac{d\_one\_to\_many}{M} + \frac{d\_many\_to\_one}{M} \qquad (6)$$

with N = number of ground-truth regions
M = number of detected regions

5.2 Results

Gap closing has been evaluated for the original system presented by [7]. It is compared to the gap closing using the corner point detected in this paper. The results for gap closing with the different types of corner point detection are summarized in Table 1.

The data set consists of 90 architectural floor plans[1], which are rescaled to a smaller size. This ensures that all the walls have the same thickness, and the same thresholds can be used on all images for edges that are to small/big. If the images had not been resized to the same size, a different threshold would possibly have to be chosen for different sizes of the images. An example of the floor plans can be seen in Fig. 7.

5.3 Performance Analysis

The proposed algorithm needs to calculate the distance from every point to the line connecting its neighbouring points exactly once. To compute this, it needs to first compute the parameters a, b, c of the line, and subsequently the distance. It runs in $O(n)$.

In comparison, the method proposed by [14] needs the same computation steps to calculate the distance. However, as it needs to calculate all distances of the given segment in every iteration, it runs in $O(n \, log(n))$, with a worst case scenario of $O(n^2)$. The algorithm proposed in this paper works more efficiently, while still conserving the original shape of the contour.

---

[1] The actual image size is 2479 * 3508. For making the analysis process more efficient, isotropic down scaling to 1413 * 2000 has been applied.

Table 1. Results for gap closing

	Detection rate	Recognition accuracy
Original system	54.5 %	51.27 %
[15] with L curvature	95.88 %	92.46 %
[15] with K curvature	95.77 %	92.34 %
[14] with $\Theta_d = 1.5$	93.39 %	93.46 %
Proposed method ($\Theta_d = 1.5$)	94.99 %	94.40 %
Proposed method with multiple corners ($\Theta_d = 1.5$)	95.01 %	94.14 %

5.4   Analysis

First, it should be mentioned that the threshold has been determined manually. The idea behind the value of this threshold is that over-segmentation happens because of binarization on not perfectly horizontally aligned lines. Therefore, our proposed value is small enough to correct small errors that lead to the over-segmentation, but not too high that it would lead to cutting of actual corners.

The gap closing criteria using the proposed corner points clearly performed very well. Unclosed gaps are mostly edge cases, where gaps have to be closed on curved walls (i.e. corner towers) or the walls don't align (i.e. windows or doors on corners). The proposed corner point detection improved mostly diagonal edges, even if noise is added due to binarization.

The wall edge detection using the corner points detected by the proposed approach performed very well on the evaluation data. It was able to solve the over-segmentation problem of the previous method. Also, this method of edge detection is rotation invariant, which is a big advantage for analysing scanned floor plans.

It is important to note that the data set consists of floor plans that are all perfectly aligned with the frame of the image. Thus, only diagonal walls really profit from the improvements of the edge detection. If the data set had featured scanned floor plans, the difference would have been a lot more noticeable, as the horizontal and vertical lines would have been subject to the over-segmentation problem mentioned earlier.

The disadvantages of the proposed method are that fine details on the walls (i.e. small indentations) can be lost during the filtering process. This effect can be seen in Fig. 4. A second noteworthy point is that if wrong corners have been detected close to a real corner, it is possible that the real corner will be filtered out, and one of the other wrong corners will be kept. This can lead to the effect that the corner appear to drift a small amount from the expected position. However, as this method is used as a preprocessing step to perform gap closing to delimit the rooms from outside, both of these drawbacks have little or no impact on the final performance due to the use of information from other steps, e.g. door detection.

Plan du Rez de Chaussée

(a) Floor plan from the data set

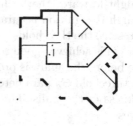

(b) Extracted walls

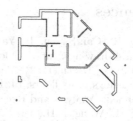

(c) Walls redrawn after extracting the corners with[15] (n.b. the walls are heavily over-segmented)

(d) Walls redrawn after filtering the corners with the proposed method (the walls are no longer over-segmented)

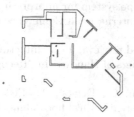

(e) Walls redrawn after filtering the corners with [14]

Fig. 7. A floorplan from the dataset

6   Conclusion and Future Work

In this paper, an improved corner point detection method based on border following algorithm is presented by improving the method in [10]. This method rendered the algorithm rotation invariant, as the diagonal edges are no longer over-segmented into smaller ones.

Afterwards, several criteria for gap closing based on the distance measure are used in order to close the outer walls of a building. Although they seem simple and straight-forward, they achieved a very high detection rate, as well as an equally high recognition accuracy.

At present, the thresholds used during the evaluation were estimated by trial and error. This achieved good results, as the analysed floor plans are rescaled to a fixed size before the analysis process. To further improve wall edge detection, the distance threshold Θ_d parameter could be dynamically calculated by estimating the thickness of the walls. This would render the process less prone to varying input sizes.

The gap closing could also benefit from dynamically calculated edge length thresholds, as well as the error tolerance that they are granted when deciding whether to connect the edges or not.

References

1. Yang, R., Cai, S., Lu, T., Yang, H.: Automatic analysis and integration of architectural drawings. Int. J. Doc. Anal. Recogn. (IJDAR) **9**(1), 31–47 (2007)
2. Masini, G., Dosch, P.: Reconstruction of the 3d structure of a building from the 2d drawings of its floors. In: Proceedings of the Fifth International Conference on Document Analysis and Recognition, pp. 487–490 (1999)
3. Or, S.H., Wong, K.H., Yu, Y.K., Chang, M.M.Y.: Abstract highly automatic approach to architectural floorplan image understanding & model generation (2005)
4. Valveny, E., Tabbone, S., Macé, S., Locteau, H.: A system to detect rooms in architectural floor plan images. In: Proceedings of the 9th IAPR International Workshop on Document Analysis Systems, DAS '10, pp. 167–174 (2010)
5. Arai, H., Aoki, Y., Shio, A., Odaka, K.: A prototype system for interpreting hand-sketched floor plans. In: Proceedings of the 13th International Conference on Pattern Recognition, vol. 3, pp. 747–751 (1996)
6. Liwicki, M., Weber, M., Dengel, A.: A sketch-based retrieval for architectural floor plans. In: 12th International Conference on Frontiers of Handwriting Recognition, pp. 289–294 (2010)
7. Ahmed, S., Weber, M., Liwicki, M., Langenhan, C., Dengel, A., Petzold, F.: Automatic analysis and sketch-based retrieval of architectural floor plans. Pattern Recogn. Lett. **35**, 91–100 (2014). (Frontiers in Handwriting Processing)
8. Lowe, D.G.: Object recognition from local scale-invariant features. In: The Proceedings of the Seventh IEEE International Conference on Computer Vision, vol. 2, pp. 1150–1157 (1999)
9. Bay, H., Ess, A., Tuytelaars, T., Van Gool, L.: Speeded-up robust features (surf). Comput. Vis. Image Underst. **110**(3), 346–359 (2008)
10. Suzuki, S., Abe, K.: Topological structural analysis of digitized binary images by border following. Comput. Vis. Graph. Image Process. **30**(1), 32–46 (1985)
11. Tombre, K., Ah-Soon, C., Dosch, P., Masini, G., Tabbone, S.: Stable and robust vectorization: how to make the right choices. In: Chhabra, A.K., Dori, D. (eds.) GREC 1999. LNCS, vol. 1941, pp. 3–16. Springer, Heidelberg (2000)
12. Moravec, H.: Obstacle avoidance and navigation in the real world by a seeing robot rover. Technical report CMU-RI-TR-80-03, Robotics Institute, Carnegie Mellon University and doctoral dissertation, Stanford University, number CMU-RI-TR-80-03, September 1980
13. Harris, C., Stephens, M.: A combined corner and edge detector. In: Proceedings of Fourth Alvey Vision Conference, pp. 147–151 (1988)

14. Peuker, T.K., Douglas, D.H.: Algorithms for the reduction of the number of points required to represent a digitized line or its caricature. Cartographica: The Int. J. Geogr. Inf. Geovisualization **10**(2), 113–122 (1973)

15. Teh, C.H., Chin, R.T.: On the detection of dominant points on digital curves. IEEE Trans. Pattern Anal. Mach. Intell. **11**(8), 859–872 (1989)

16. Rosin, P.L., West, G.A.W.: Segmentation of edges into lines and arcs. Image Vis. Comput. **7**(2), 109–114 (1989)

17. Dori, D., Liu, W.: Sparse pixel vectorization: an algorithm and its performance evaluation. IEEE Trans. Pattern Anal. Mach. Intell. **21**(3), 202–215 (1999)

18. Awrangjeb, M., Lu, G.: Robust image corner detection based on the chord-to-point distance accumulation technique. IEEE Trans. Multimedia **10**(6), 1059–1072 (2008)

19. Hilaire, X., Tombre, K.: Robust and accurate vectorization of line drawings. IEEE Trans. Pattern Anal. Mach. Intell. **28**(6), 890–904 (2006)

20. Barrat, S., Ramel, J., Pham, T.-A.; Delalandre, M.: A robust approach for local interest point detection in line-drawing images. In: 2012 10th IAPR International Workshop on Document Analysis Systems (DAS), pp. 79–84 (2012)

21. Zhang, W.-C., Wang, F.-P., Zhu, L., Zhou, Z.-F.: Corner detection using gabor filters. IET Image Processing, May 2014

22. Lindeberg, T.: Feature detection with automatic scale selection. Int. J. Comput. Vision **30**(2), 79–116 (1998)

23. Lowe, D.G.: Distinctive image features from scale-invariant keypoints. Int. J. Comput. Vision **60**(2), 91–110 (2004)

24. Rosten, E., Drummond, T.: Fusing points and lines for high performance tracking. In: IEEE International Conference on Computer Vision, vol. 2, pp. 1508–1511, Oct 2005

25. Leutenegger, S., Chli, M., Siegwart, R.: Brisk: binary robust invariant scalable keypoints. In: ICCV, pp. 2548–2555 (2011)

26. Smith, S.M., Michael Brady, J.: Susana new approach to low level image processing. Int. J. Comput. Vision **23**(1), 45–78 (1997)

27. Phillips, I.T., Chhabra, A.K.: Empirical performance evaluation of graphics recognition systems. IEEE Trans. Pattern Anal. Mach. Intell. **21**, 849–870 (1999)

Performance Evaluation
and Ground Truthing

The ICDAR/GREC 2013 Music Scores Competition: Staff Removal

Alicia Fornés[1]([✉]), Van Cuong Kieu[2,3], Muriel Visani[2], Nicholas Journet[3], and Anjan Dutta[1]

[1] Computer Vision Center - Department of Computer Science,
Universitat Autònoma de Barcelona, Ed.O, 08193 Bellaterra, Spain
afornes@cvc.uab.es
[2] Laboratoire Informatique, Image Et Interaction - L3i,
University of La Rochelle, La Rochelle, France
muriel.visani@univ-lr.fr
[3] Laboratoire Bordelais de Recherche En Informatique LaBRI,
University of Bordeaux I, Bordeaux, France
{vkieu,journet}@labri.fr

Abstract. The first competition on music scores that was organized at ICDAR and GREC in 2011 awoke the interest of researchers, who participated in both staff removal and writer identification tasks. In this second edition, we focus on the staff removal task and simulate a real case scenario concerning old and degraded music scores. For this purpose, we have generated a new set of semi-synthetic images using two degradation models that we previously introduced: local noise and 3D distortions. In this extended paper we provide an extended description of the dataset, degradation models, evaluation metrics, the participant's methods and the obtained results that could not be presented at ICDAR and GREC proceedings due to page limitations.

Keywords: Competition · Graphics recognition · Music scores · Writer identification · Staff removal

1 Introduction

The recognition of music scores has been an active research field for decades [1,2]. Many researchers in Optical Music Recognition have proposed staff removal algorithms in order to make easier the segmentation and enhance the accuracy of music symbol recognition [3,4]. However, the staff removal task cannot be considered as a solved problem, especially when dealing with degraded handwritten music scores. This task is even defined as one of the "three challenges that should be addressed in future work on OMR as applied to manuscript scores" in the 2012 survey of Rebelo et al. [2].

At ICDAR /GREC 2011, we organized the first edition of the music scores competition [5]. For the staff removal task, we created several sets of distorted images in order to test the robustness of the staff removal algorithms. Each set

© Springer-Verlag Berlin Heidelberg 2014
B. Lamiroy and J.-M. Ogier (Eds.): GREC 2013, LNCS 8746, pp. 207–220, 2014.
DOI: 10.1007/978-3-662-44854-0_16

corresponded to a different kind of distortion (e.g. Kanungo noise, rotation, curvature, staffline interruption, typeset emulation, staffline y-variation, staffline thickness ratio, staffline thickness variation and white speckles). The staff removal task woke up the interest of researchers, with eight participant methods. Most staff removal methods showed good performance in front of severe distortions, although the detection of the staff lines still needed improvement.

After GREC 2011, we extended the staff removal competition [6]. The goal was to simulate a real scenario, in which music scores usually contain more than one single kind of distortion. For this purpose, we combined some of the ICDAR 2011 distortions at different levels to create new sets of degraded images. We then asked the participants to run their algorithms on this new set of images. Unsurprisingly, the new results demonstrated that the performances of most methods were significantly decreased because of the combination of distortions.

By organizing a second edition of this competition, we aim at fostering the interest of researchers and focusing on the challenging problem of old document image analysis and recognition. For this second edition, we have generated realistic semi-synthetic images that emulate typical degradations appearing in old handwritten documents such as local noise and 3D distortions.

The rest of the paper is organized as follows. Firstly, we will describe the original dataset, the degradation models, and the generated training and test sets. Then, we will present the participants' methods. Finally, we will detail the evaluation metrics, the results analysis, and conclude the paper.

2   Database

In this section we describe the original database, the degradation methods, and the semi-synthetic database for the competition.

2.1   Original CVC-MUSCIMA Database

The original CVC-MUSCIMA[1] database [7] consists of 1,000 handwritten music score images, written by 50 different musicians. The 50 writers are adult musicians, in order to ensure that they have their own characteristic handwriting music style. Each writer has transcribed exactly the same 20 music pages, using the same pen and kind of music paper. The 20 selected music sheets contain music scores for solo instruments, choir or orchestra. For more information on the database (e.g. resolution, kind of music compositions, presence of text, etc.), the reader is referred to [7].

2.2   Degradation Models

3D Degradation Model. Since the geometric distortions such as skews and curvatures are challenging for detecting staffs, we used them for the 2011 staff

---

[1] Available at http://www.cvc.uab.es/cvcmuscima/

removal competition [5, 6]. However, these distortion models were only 2D models which are unable to reproduce the geometric distortions commonly encountered in real old documents such as dents, small folds, and torns... (see Fig. 1). Therefore, in this 2013 edition, we use the 3D degradation [8] that can generate more realistic and more challenging distortions of the staff lines, making their detection and removal more difficult. This 3D degradation model is based on 3D meshes and texture coordinate generation. It can wrap any 2D (flat) image of a document on a 3D mesh acquired by scanning a non-flat old document using a 3D scanner. The wrapping functions we use are specifically adapted to document images. In our case, we wrap the original music score images on different 3D meshes. For more details, please refer to [8].

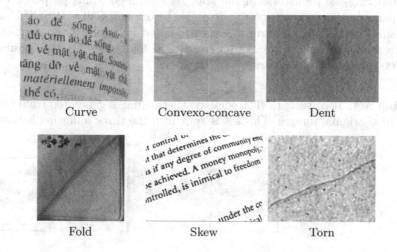

Fig. 1. Geometric distortions in real document images

Local Noise Model. This model, introduced in [9], can mimic old documents' defects due to document aging and to the old printing/writing processes. Examples of these defects include ink splotches and white specks or streaks (see Fig. 2). Such defects might break the connectivity of strokes or add a connection between separate strokes. For staff line removal algorithms, local noise can lead to many types of challenging degradations. Indeed, it can lead to disconnections of the staff lines or to the addition of dark specks connected to a staff line. In the latter case, for instance, the dark specks might be confused with musical symbols.

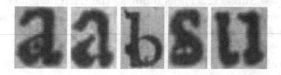

Fig. 2. Examples of local noise in real old documents

As detailed in [9], the local noise is generated in three main steps. Firstly, the "seed-points" (i.e. the centres of local noise regions) are selected in the neighborhood of connected components' borders (obtained by binarizing the input grayscale image). Then, we define an arbitrary noise region at each seed-point (in our case, its shape is an ellipse). Finallly, the grey-level values of the pixels inside the noise regions are modified so as to obtain realistic looking bright and dark specks, and mimic defects due to the age of the document (ink fading, paper degradation...) and writing process (ink drops).

2.3   Degraded Database

For comparing the robustness of the staff removal algorithms proposed by the participants to this competition, we degrade the original CVC-MUSCIMA database using the two degradation models presented in Sect. 2.2. As a result, we obtain a semi-synthetic database that consists of 4000 images in the training set and 2000 images in the test set.

Training Set. It consists in 4000 semi-synthetic images generated from 667 out of the 1000 original images. This set is split into the three following subsets:

Fig. 3. TrainingSubset1 samples. From left to right: original image and two semi-synthetic images generated from two different meshes.

- *TrainingSubset1* (see Fig. 3) contains 1000 images generated using the 3D distortion model and two different meshes. The first mesh consists in a perspective distortion due to the scanning of a thick and bound volume, while the second one contains many small curves, folds and concavities. We wrap the 667 original images on two meshes to produce $2 \times 667 = 1334$ semi-synthetic images. Then, 500 images per mesh are randomly selected so as to obtain a total of 1000 images.
- *TrainingSubset2* (see Fig. 4) contains 1000 images generated with three levels of local noise (see Subsect. 2.2), as follows (the flattening factor of the elliptic noise region is fixed as $g=0.6$ for the three levels, whereas the noise region size a_0 increases after each level):
  - *Low level*: 333 images, 500 seed-points, a_0: 7;
  - *Medium level*: 334 images, 1000 seed-points, a_0: 8.5;
  - *High level*: 333 images, 1300 seed-points, a_0: 10.

Fig. 4. TrainingSubset2 samples. From left to right and top to bottom: original image and semi-synthetic images generated from the original image using the low, middle and high levels of local noise.

- *TrainingSubset3* (see Fig. 5) contains 2000 images generated using both the 3D distortion and the local noise models. We obtain six different levels of degradation (the two meshes used for TrainingSubset1 × the three levels of distortion used for TrainingSubset2).

  For each image in the training set, we provide its grey and binary versions. The associated ground-truth are the binary staff-less version (binary images without staff lines), as illustrated in Fig. 6.

Test Set. It consists of 2000 semi-synthetic images generated from the 333 original images that differ from the ones for the training set.

- *TestSubset1* contains 500 images generated using the 3D distortion (see Subsect. 2.2). Two meshes - distinct from the ones used in the training set - are applied to the 333 original images and then only 500 images (250 for each mesh) are randomly selected among the $2 \times 333 = 666$ degraded images.
- *TestSubset2* contains 500 images generated using three levels of local noise, using the same values of the parameters as in TrainingSubset2, under the proportions $\frac{1}{3} / \frac{1}{3} / \frac{1}{3}$.
- *TestSubset3* contains 1000 images equally distributed between six different levels of degradation. These six levels of degradation come from the combination of the same two meshes as in TestSubset1 with the same three different levels of local noise as in TrainingSubset2.

  For each image in the test set, we provide its grey and binary versions. The test set was provided to the participants 46 days after the training set (containing 4000 degraded images together with their ground-truth). The participants were asked to send to the organizers the outputs of their algorithms as binary staff-less images (such images containing only binarized music symbols but no staff lines) 23 days after the test set was provided to them.

Fig. 5. TrainingSubset3 samples. First row, from left to right: images generated using mesh 1 and the low and high levels of local noise. Second row, from left to right: images generated using mesh 2 and the low and high levels of local noise.

Fig. 6. From left to right: an image from TrainingSubset3, its binary version and its binary staff-less version (ground-truth).

3 Participants Information

In this section we will briefly describe the eight submitted methods of five participants for the ICDAR/GREC2013 competition. Methods 1–3 work on binary images (in that case the participants used the binary versions we provided for the competition), while methods 4–5 can handle both binary and grayscale images.

3.1 TAU-bin

This method was submitted by Oleg Dobkin from the Tel-Aviv University, Israel. It is based in the Fujinaga's method [10]. First, the *staffline_height* and *staffspace_height* are estimated using vertical scans. Then, the vertical black runs which are longer than the *staffspace_height* are removed. Afterwards, the music page is globally deskewed, and the staff lines are located using a projection on the y-axis. Finally, the staff lines are removed using masks.

3.2   NUS-bin

This method was submitted by Bolan Su (National University of Singapore), Umapada Pal (Indian Statistical Institute, Kolkata, India) and Chew-Lim Tan (National University of Singapore). The method, detailed in [11], first estimates the *staffline_height* and *staffspace_height* using the vertical run length histogram. These estimated values are used to predict the lines' direction and fit an approximate staff line curve for each line. Then, the fitted staff line curve is used to identify the exact location of staff lines in the image. Finally, those pixels belonging to these staff lines are removed.

3.3   NUASi

Christoph Dalitz and Andreas Kitzig, from the Niederrhein University of Applied Sciences (iPattern Institute), Krefeld, Germany, submitted the following two different methods:

- NUASi-bin-lin: This method is described in Sect. 2 of [3]. First, the staffs are detected, and the *staffline_height* is estimated as the most frequent black vertical run length. Then, the skeleton of the staff lines is extracted, and all vertical foreground runs shorter than 2* *staffline_height* are removed. The function *chordlength*(φ) (where φ is the angle of the chord at the intersection region) is used to filter staff-line pixels belonging to a crossing music symbol. The source code is available at http://music-staves.sourceforge.net/ (classMusicStaves_linetracking).
- NUASi-bin-skel: This method, detailed in the Sect. 3.D of [3], first splits the skeleton of the staff lines at branching and corner points. Each segment is considered as a staff line segment if it satisfies some heuristic rules. Then, two staff segments are horizontally linked if their extrapolations from the end points with the least square fitted angle are closer than *staffline_height*/2. The staff segment results may contain false positive staff segments (*e.g.* in the case where a staff line is tangent with the curve of a music symbol or it overlaps with the music symbol at a staff segment). Then, to check for the false positives, non-staff segments which have the same splitting point as a staff segment are extrapolated by a parametric parabola. If the staff segment is tangent with the parabola, it is a non-staff segment. Finally, vertical black runs around the detected staff skeleton are removed when they are shorter than 2* *staffline_height*. The source code is available at http://music-staves. sourceforge.net/(classMusicStaves_skeleton).

3.4   LRDE

Thierry Géraud, from the EPITA Research and Development Laboratory (LRDE), Paris, France, submitted two methods. For more details, the reader is referred to http://www.lrde.epita.fr/cgi-bin/twiki/view/Olena/Icdar2013Score.

- LRDE-bin: This method relies on mathematical morphological operators. First, a permissive hit-or-miss with a horizontal line pattern as structuring element extracts some horizontal chunks. Second, a horizontal median filter cleans up the result, and a dilation operation is applied using a horizontal neighbourhood in order to enlarge the connected components. A binary mask is obtained thanks to a morphological closing with a rectangular structuring element. Last, a vertical median filter, applied inside the largest components of this mask, removes the staff lines.
- LRDE-gray: After removing the image border, Sauvola's binarization and a dilation using a horizontal neighbourhood are applied. The resulting image serves as a mask in which a two-level thresholding with hysteresis of the original image is applied. Finally, some spurious horizontal parts of the staff-lines are erased in a post-processing step.

3.5   INESC

Ana Rebelo and Jaime S. Cardoso (INESC Porto and Universidade do Porto) submitted the following two methods (more details are given in [4]) based on graphs of Strong Staff-Pixels (SSP: pixels with a high probability of belonging to a staff line):

- INESC-bin: First, the *staffline_height* and *staffspace_height* are estimated by the method presented in [12]. Then, all the pixels of the black runs of *staffline_height* pixels followed or preceded by a white run of *staffspace_height* pixels are set as the SSPs. To decide if a SSP belongs to a staff line, the image grid is considered as a graph with pixels as nodes, and arcs connecting neighbouring pixels. Then, SSPs are classified as staff line pixels according to some heuristic rules. Then, the groups of 5 staff lines are located among the shortest paths by using a global optimization process on the graph.
- INESC-gray: For grayscale images, the weight function is generalized by using a sigmoid function. The parameters of the sigmoid function are chosen to favor the luminance levels of the stafflines. A state-of-the-art binarization technique is used in order to assign the cost for each pixel in the graph (pixels binarized to white have a high cost; pixels binarized to black have a low cost). Once the image is binarized, the previous method is applied.

4   Results

In this section we compare the participant's output images with the ground-truth (binary staff-less images) of the test set using the measures presented in the next Section. The ground-truth associated to the test set was made public after the competition.

4.1   Measures Used for Performance Comparison

The staff removal problem is considered as a two-class classification problem at the pixel level. For each test subset and each level of noise, we compare the output images provided by the participants to their corresponding ground-truth. For this purpose, we compute the number of True Positive pixels (TP, pixels correctly classified as staff lines), True Negative pixels (TN, pixels correctly classified as non-staff lines) False Positive pixels (FP, pixels wrongly classified as staff lines) and False Negative pixels (FN, pixels wrongly classified as non-staff lines). Then, from these measures, we compute the accuracy (also called Classification Rate), precision (also called Positive Predictive Value), recall (also called True Positive Rate or sensitivity), F-measure and specificity (or True Negative Rate) as follows:

$$accuracy = \frac{TP + TN}{TP + TN + FP + FN} \tag{1}$$

$$precision = \frac{TP}{TP + FP} \tag{2}$$

$$recall = \frac{TP}{TP + FN} \tag{3}$$

$$F - Measure = 2 \times \frac{precision \times recall}{precision + recall} \tag{4}$$

$$specificity = \frac{TN}{TN + FP} \tag{5}$$

Since the first step of a staff removal system is usually the detection of the staff lines, the overall performance highly depends on the accuracy of this preliminary staff detection. Indeed, if the staff line is undetected, it is unable to be removed. For example, a staff removal system may obtain very good results (when the staff is correctly detected) while rejecting many music scores images (if no staff line is detected in the image, it is discarded). Therefore, for each participant's method, we provide the number of rejected pages for each of the three test subsets, and for each level of degradation inside each test subset. Furthermore, we compute the evaluation measures (1–5) in two ways:

- Without rejection: the five average values of the five measures (1–5) are computed inside each test subset and for each level of degradation, taking into account only the images that the system pre-classified as music score. Thus, the rejected images are not taken into account for these measures.
- With rejection: the five average values of the five measures (1–5) are computed inside each test subset and for each level of degradation, taking into account every image in the test set, no matter if it was rejected by the system or not. Thus, for a rejected image, every staff line pixel is considered as a False Negative and every non-staff line pixel is considered as a False Positive.

Table 1. Competition results for each test subset and each degradation level. We give the number # of rejected images, and the values of the measures computed with and without rejection. The measures (M.), showed in %, are: P=Precision, R=Recall, F-M=F-Measure, S=Specificity, A=Accuracy.

Deform.	Level	M.	TAU-bin	NUS-bin	NUASi-bin-lin	NUASi-bin-skel	LRDE bin	LRDE gray	INESC bin	INESC gray	Baseline
Set1: 3D dist.	Mesh 1 (M1)	P	75.51	98.75	99.05	98.58	98.89	87.26	99.76	32.50	98.62
		R	96.32	52.80	89.90(89.77) #2	90.26(90.03) #3	96.19	98.41	85.41	50.91	79.86
		F-M	84.65	68.81	94.25(94.18)	94.24(94.11)	97.52	92.50	92.03	39.67	88.26
		S	98.81	99.97	99.96(99.96)	99.95(99.95)	97.52	99.45	99.99	95.97	99.95
		A	98.721	98.25	99.60(99.60)	99.60(99.60)	99.82	99.42	99.46	94.32	99.22
	Mesh 2 (M2)	P	82.22	99.50	99.70	99.39	99.52	86.59	99.90	34.36	99.29
		R	91.90	55.05	92.07(91.38) #4	89.63(89.36) #2	96.39	97.76	76.33	40.85	75.47
		F-M	86.79	70.88	95.73(95.36)	94.26(94.11)	97.93	91.83	86.54	37.33	85.76
		S	99.26	99.99	99.98(99.99)	99.97(99.97)	99.98	99.44	99.99	97.12	99.98
		A	99.01	98.39	99.71(99.68)	99.61(99.60)	99.86	99.38	99.16	95.12	99.10
Set2: Local Noise	High (H)	P	65.71	95.37	98.41	97.28	95.54	53.22	97.63	38.81	95.65
		R	97.01	92.27	90.81	89.35	96.65	98.58	96.62	79.35	96.53
		F-M	78.35	93.79	94.46	93.15	96.09	69.12	97.13	52.13	96.09
		S	98.59	99.87	99.95	99.93	99.87	97.58	99.93	96.51	99.87
		A	98.55	99.67	99.71	99.64	99.79	97.61	99.85	96.05	99.78
	Medium (M)	P	69.30	97.82	99.24	98.38	97.50	68.10	98.95	39.61	97.26
		R	97.34	96.97	91.94(91.41) #3	90.56(89.80) #4	97.13	98.77	97.19	74.83	97.10
		F-M	80.96	97.39	95.45(95.16)	94.31(93.90)	97.32	80.62	98.07	51.81	97.18
		S	98.71	99.93	99.97(99.97)	99.95(99.95)	99.92	98.61	99.96	96.58	99.91
		A	98.67	99.85	99.75(99.73)	99.68(99.66)	99.84	98.62	99.89	95.96	99.83
	Low (L)	P	77.07	98.56	99.25	98.07	97.89	80.65	99.42	40.13	98.52
		R	96.88	96.58	90.48	90.17	96.47	98.47	96.52	75.48	96.45
		F-M	85.85	97.56	94.66	93.95	97.17	88.67	97.95	52.40	97.47
		S	99.12	99.95	99.97	99.94	99.93	99.28	99.98	96.59	99.95
		A	99.06	99.86	99.70	99.66	99.84	99.26	99.88	95.98	99.85
Set3: 3D dist. + Local Noise	H + M1	P	66.01	94.31	96.88	96.37	96.14	56.19	97.63	31.70	96.41
		R	96.35	50.00	88.03	87.93	96.13	98.59	85.79	55.21(50.48) #17	85.98
		F-M	78.34	65.35	92.25	91.96	96.14	71.58	91.33	40.27(38.94)	90.90
		S	98.30	99.89	99.90	99.88	99.86	97.37	99.92	95.93(96.27)	99.89
		A	98.24	98.25	99.51	99.49	99.74	97.41	99.46	94.58(94.76)	99.43
	H + M2	P	73.40	97.50	98.55	98.07	97.61	57.18	98.35	33.11	97.62
		R	92.42	53.56	90.99(90.32) #4	89.15(88.68) #3	96.66	98.00	75.17	42.15(39.19) #12	81.26
		F-M	81.82	69.14	94.62(94.25)	93.40(93.14)	97.13	72.22	85.22	37.09(35.90)	88.69
		S	98.86	99.95	99.95(99.95)	99.94(99.94)	99.92	97.51	99.95	97.11(97.31)	99.93
		A	98.65	98.43	99.66(99.64)	99.59(99.54)	99.81	97.53	99.14	95.31(95.41)	99.32
	M + M1	P	69.26	95.45	97.52	96.93	97.11	67.44	98.51	32.34	97.29
		R	96.44	49.07	89.15	87.98	95.98	98.46	85.63	53.52(48.76) #16	85.96
		F-M	80.62	64.81	93.15	92.24	96.54	80.05	91.62	40.31(38.88)	91.27
		S	98.47	99.91	99.91	99.90	99.89	98.30	99.95	96.01(96.36)	99.91
		A	98.406	98.168	99.549	99.491	99.763	98.312	99.461	94.556(94.730)	99.43
	M + M2	P	77.50	98.39	99.02	98.53	98.42	68.09	99.06	33.76	98.35
		R	91.83	53.47	91.57(90.85) #4	88.43(87.94) #3	96.52	97.92	75.21	41.64(39.13) #10	81.08
		F-M	84.05	69.29	95.15(94.76)	93.20(92.93)	97.46	80.27	85.50	37.29(36.25)	88.88
		S	99.06	99.96	99.96(99.96)	99.95(99.95)	99.94	98.38	99.97	97.12(97.30)	99.95
		A	98.87	98.39	99.68(99.66)	99.56(99.54)	99.83	98.37	99.13	95.24(95.32)	99.31
	L + M1	P	73.28	96.75	98.06	97.50	97.92	79.32	99.14	32.77	97.96
		R	96.38	50.22	88.96	88.74	95.92	98.38	85.48	53.83(48.83) #17	85.23
		F-M	83.26	66.12	93.29	92.92	96.91	87.83	91.80	40.74(39.22)	91.15
		S	98.70	99.93	99.93	99.91	99.92	99.05	99.97	95.93(96.30)	99.93
		A	98.62	98.17	99.55	99.52	99.78	99.03	99.46	94.44(94.62)	99.41
	L + M2	P	80.17	99.00	99.39	98.94	99.02	78.81	99.53	34.31	98.84
		R	91.98	54.01	91.97(91.22) #4	89.14(88.63) #3	96.46	97.85	75.18	41.34(39.08) #8	80.14
		F-M	85.67	69.89	95.54(95.13)	93.78(93.50)	97.72	87.30	85.66	37.50(36.54)	88.52
		S	99.17	99.98	99.97(99.98)	99.96(99.96)	99.96	99.04	99.98	97.13(97.28)	99.96
		A	98.92	98.37	99.70(99.67)	99.59(99.57)	99.84	99.01	99.12	95.18(95.25)	99.27
Total rejected images			#0	#0	#21	#18	#0	#0	#0	#80	#0

4.2 Baseline

For comparison purposes, we have computed some baseline results using the existing staff removal method proposed by Dutta et al. [13]. This method is based on the analysis of neighboring components. Basically, it assumes that a staff-line candidate segment is a horizontal linkage of vertical black runs with uniform height. Then, some neighboring properties are used to validate or discard these segments.

4.3 Performance Comparison

Table 1 and Fig. 7 present staff removal results obtained by the eight participant methods (three out of the five participants presented two different algorithms). We have also tested the baseline method presented in [13]. Each of the nine columns indicates the name of the participant and the staff removal method category. All the metrics used for performance comparison (presented in Sect. 4.1) are presented according to the type of degradation (3D distortion, local noise

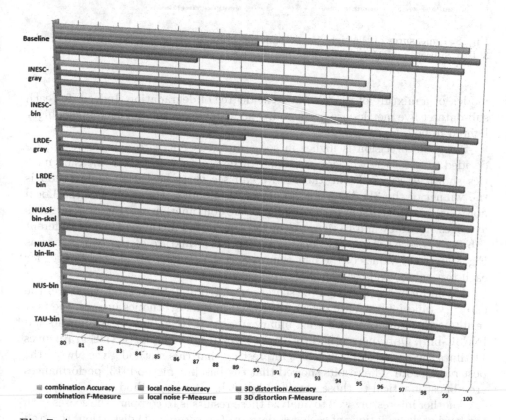

Fig. 7. Average music score competition results. The figure presents, for each participant method, the Average Accuracy and F-Measure of their method on the different sets.

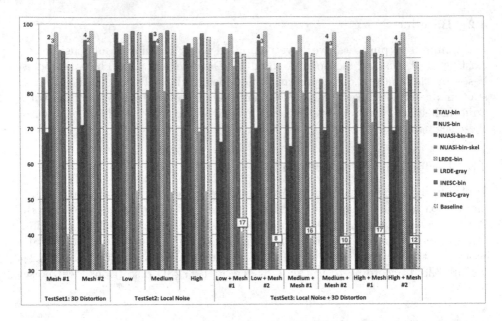

Fig. 8. F-measures of the eight participant methods (plus the baseline method) on the 3 Test Subsets and 11 levels of degradation.

model, or a mixture of the two) and the degree of degradation. Indeed, for each sub-dataset five metrics are presented. The winner's method of each line is high-lighted in bold.

Since the precision is higher in some methods but with a lower recall, we decided to select the winners according to the accuracy and the F-measure metrics shown in Fig. 7. From Table 1, we can see that the LRDE-bin method is the winner of the 3D distortion set, the INESC-bin is the winner of the Local noise set, and LRDE-bin is the winner of the combination set. Figure 7 presents averages Accuracy and F-Measures of the nine tested methods on three different sub-datasets (3D distortion, local noise model, a mixture of the two), whereas Fig. 8 gives the values of the F-measures and the number of rejected images for each test subset and each level of degradation.

Much can be learned from the scores presented in Table 1. First, whatever the category (and intensity) of defect integrated in semi-synthetics images, the best results are mainly obtained with binary images (LRDE-bin, NUAS-bin-lin and INESC-bin). Only one method with grey-level image as input (LRDE-gray) gives 11 times the best results. It is also interesting that this method gives always the best recall score. The results showed that the baseline method [13] performances are almost identical to those obtained by each winning method.

Another interesting way to analyze these results is to compare the scores with the level of degradations of each sub dataset. Concerning 3D distortion, the staff lines images mapped on Mesh 1 (M1) were a bit more difficult to analyze for all the participants (except LRDE-gray and INESC-bin). On average the precision scores drop by 1 point. One method drops its precision by 7 points. We can conclude that these methods seems less robust to perspective deformation defects (Mesh 1) than to the presence of small curves and folds (Mesh 2). The precision scores of each participant decrease when the local noise is getting higher. On average, the precision scores decrease from 13 %. In the best case it dropped by less than 1 %. In the worst case the precision is dropped by 33 %. These results clearly show that all these methods are sensitive to the local noise deformation. The tests carried out with images generated by combining local noise and 3D distortions confirm that the results decrease when the level of degradation is important.

5   Conclusion

The second music scores competition on staff removal held in ICDAR2013 has raised a great interest from the research community, with eight participants' methods in the competition. For this competition, we generated a database of semi-synthetic images using the 1000 images from the CVC-MUSCIMA database and two models of degradation specifically designed to mimic the defects that can be seen in historical documents. This database contains three subsets both for training and testing: one subset containing only 3D distorsions at two different levels; one subset containing three levels of local noise and one subset with a combination of both sources of noises, with six different levels of degradation. We evaluated the performances of the eight methods proposed by the participants and compared it towards a baseline method based on the analysis of neighbouring connected components.

The eight submitted methods have obtained very satisfying performances, even though the degradations in the proposed images were quite severe. The results of the participants have demonstrated that the performance of most methods significantly decreases when dealing with a higher level of degradation, especially in the presence of both sources of degradation (3D distortion model + local noise model). We hope that our semi-synthetic database, which is now available on the internet and labelled with different types and levels of degradation for both the training set and the test set, will become a benchmark for the research on handwritten music scores in the near future.

Acknowledgements. This research was partially funded by the French National Research Agency (ANR) via the DIGIDOC project, and the spanish projects TIN2011-24631 and TIN2012-37475-C02-02.

References

1. Blostein, D., Baird, H.S.: A critical survey of music image analysis. In: Baird, H.S., Bunke, H., Yamamoto, K. (eds.) Structured Document Image Analysis, pp. 405–434. Springer, Heidelberg (1992)

2. Rebelo, A., Fujinaga, I., Paszkiewicz, F., Marcal, A., Guedes, C., Cardoso, J.: Optical music recognition: state-of-the-art and open issues. Int. J. Multimedia Inf. Retrieval 1(3), 173–190 (2012)
3. Dalitz, C., Droettboom, M., Pranzas, B., Fujinaga, I.: A comparative study of staff removal algorithms. IEEE Trans. Pattern Anal. Mach. Intell. 30(5), 753–766 (2008)
4. dos Santos Cardoso, J., Capela, A., Rebelo, A., Guedes, C., Pinto da Costa, J.: Staff detection with stable paths. IEEE Trans. Pattern Anal. Mach. Intell. 31(6), 1134–1139 (2009)
5. Fornés, A., Dutta, A., Gordo, A., Lladós, J.: The icdar 2011 music scores competition: Staff removal and writer identification. In: International Conference on Document Analysis and Recognition (ICDAR), pp. 1511–1515 (2011)
6. Fornés, Alicia, Dutta, Anjan, Gordo, Albert, Lladós, Josep: The 2012 music scores competitions: staff removal and writer identification. In: Kwon, Young-Bin, Ogier, Jean-Marc (eds.) GREC 2011. LNCS, vol. 7423, pp. 173–186. Springer, Heidelberg (2013)
7. Fornés, A., Dutta, A., Gordo, A., Lladós, J.: Cvc-muscima: a ground truth of handwritten music score images for writer identification and staff removal. Int. J. Doc. Anal. Recogn. (IJDAR) 15(3), 243–251 (2012)
8. Kieu, V., Journet, N., Visani, M., Mullot, R., Domenger, J.: Semi-synthetic document image generation using texture mapping on scanned 3d document shapes. In: 12th International Conference on Document Analysis and Recognition (ICDAR), pp. 489–493 (2013)
9. Kieu, V., Visani, M., Journet, N., Domenger, J.P., Mullot, R.: A character degradation model for grayscale ancient document images. In: International Conference on Pattern Recognition (ICPR), Tsukuba Science City, Japan, pp. 685–688, November 2012
10. Fujinaga, I., Adviser-Pennycook, B.: Adaptive Optical Music Recognition. McGill University, Montreal (1997)
11. Su, B., Lu, S., Pal, U., Tan, C.L.: An effective staff detection and removal technique for musical documents. In: IAPR International Workshop on Document Analysis Systems (DAS), pp. 160–164 (2012)
12. Cardoso, J., Rebelo, A.: Robust staffline thickness and distance estimation in binary and gray-level music scores. In: 20th International Conference on Pattern Recognition (ICPR), pp. 1856–1859 (2010)
13. Dutta, A., Pal, U., Fornés, A., Lladós, J.: An efficient staff removal approach from printed musical documents. In: International Conference on Pattern Recognition (ICPR), pp. 1965–1968 (2010)

Interpretation, Evaluation and the Semantic Gap ... What if We Were on a Side-Track?

Bart Lamiroy[✉]

LORIA (UMR 7503), Campus Scientifique, Université de Lorraine, BP 239, 54506
Vandoeuvre-lès-Nancy CEDEX, France
Bart.Lamiroy@loria.fr

Abstract. A significant amount of research in Document Image Analysis, and Machine Perception in general, relies on the extraction and analysis of signal cues with the goal of interpreting them into higher level information. This paper gives an overview on how this interpretation process is usually considered, and how the research communities proceed in evaluating existing approaches and methods developed for realizing these processes. Evaluation being an essential part to measuring the quality of research and assessing the progress of the state-of-the art, our work aims at showing that classical evaluation methods are not necessarily well suited for interpretation problems, or, at least, that they introduce a strong bias, not necessarily visible at first sight, and that new ways of comparing methods and measuring performance are necessary. It also shows that the infamous *Semantic Gap* seems to be an inherent and unavoidable part of the general interpretation process, especially when considered within the framework of traditional evaluation. The use of Formal Concept Analysis is put forward to leverage these limitations into a new tool to the analysis and comparison of interpretation contexts.

1   Introduction

One of the very basic aspects of experimental research is the level of *"verifiability"* and traceability of claims an results published by their authors. In [1] we already wrote that the basics of reproducible research, set by Popper [2], notably

1. reporting of clearly set goals and defined interpretation framework,
2. full access to all experimental data,
3. reporting of the experimental apparatus, setup and protocol, in such a way that it becomes fully reproducible,
4. all parameters defining the data (if applicable) and those related to the experimental process.

are difficult to achieve in real life; especially when related to document analysis. We reported in [3] that:

> The goal of document image analysis is to achieve *performance* using automated tools that is *comparable* to what a *careful* human expert

© Springer-Verlag Berlin Heidelberg 2014
B. Lamiroy and J.-M. Ogier (Eds.): GREC 2013, LNCS 8746, pp. 221–233, 2014.
DOI: 10.1007/978-3-662-44854-0_17

would achieve, or at least to do *better* than *existing algorithms* on the same *task*.

Our use of terms like "performance," "comparable," and "better" indicate that there is an underlying notion of *quality* and therefore *measurement*. It suggests a controlled process that continually improves toward perfection. However, we also make mention of "careful" humans, "tasks," and "existing algorithms." While humans may believe themselves to be expert and careful when performing a task, there are situations where they unavoidably disagree [4–7], meaning that, at best, quality and improvement are subjective notions. It also strongly suggests that, depending on the task, measurements will differ, advocating again for multiple ways of measuring overall performance. [...] It is important to note, however, that shared datasets are only a part of what is needed for performance evaluation, and since research in document analysis is often task-driven, specific interpretations of a dataset may exist. [...] This most certainly does not affect the intrinsic quality of the underlying research, but it does tend to generate isolated clusters of extremely focused problem definitions and experimental requirements. [...] It is generally assumed that there is a single, unambiguous annotation in every case and that it is recorded correctly in the ground-truth. [...] Existing tools allow the user to indicate how he/she believes a document should be interpreted, but do little to help users understand differences in interpretations. Such differences might be called "errors" when there is a strong consensus about what constitutes the right answer. In many cases, however, there are legitimate differences of opinion [4, 8] by various "readers" of the document, and these may differ from the *intention* of the author (which is usually hard or impossible to determine, although sometimes we can get access to it [9]).

The bottom line is that although standard document collections exist, their annotations or "ground truth" may be specific, recorded in predetermined representations, incomplete or partially erroneous, while, on the other hand, there is a need to collect and manage annotations in ways that make it possible to construct more robust and general document analysis solutions.

These excerpts, although taken from publications considering the problem initially from the angle of document image analysis easily apply to broader machine perception research. They raise the following fundamental questions:

1. How can individual contributions to the state-of-the-art, solving machine perception problems, be objectively evaluated? Can they be compared to previous work? Can there be a set of measurable criteria establishing that it actually contributes to improving the state-of-the-art?
2. In how far are these contributions constrained to a specific context of use? What is a context of use? Can it be described, formalized or measured?

3. Is it actually possible to evaluate a contribution with respect to human perception performance? Does it make sense? What would be required to be able
to do so?

While these questions seem to be naively simple and common sense, there
does not seem to be any thoroughly established framework addressing them.
They actually seem to be taken for granted and *"obvious"*. We shall prove in
what follows that they are far from being so, and that considering them lightly
actually leads to severely distorted perceptions of the quality of research in many
ways.

In what follows we shall develop the following reasoning: first we analyze the
way current machine perception research considers the definition and evaluation
of interpretation problems and how it establishes the so called *Semantic Gap* [10]
(Sect. 2); we conclude that uncertainty and ambiguity in ground truth is intrinsic
to interpretation problems, and cannot be avoided in all but in the most trivial
cases. Section 3 proposes a paradigm shift in the ways of measuring and modeling performance differences, by incorporating this intrinsic level of *difference
of opinion* (rather than talking about *errors*) in interpretation by using Formal
Concept Analysis.

2   Evaluation and the Semantic Gap

In this section we are taking a look into how the global research community
is considering evaluation of interpretation problems. Many quite advanced and
interesting benchmarking and evaluation initiatives exist, aimed at measuring
the performance of machine perception methods (*cf.* all competitions at ICDAR
2013[1] as well as other initiatives like Pascal VOC [11], LSVRC[2], TREC [12],
IMAGECLEF [13]) They all adopt the same meta-framework:

- Provide annotated training data (ground truth or golden standard)
- Develop perceptive interpretation algorithms that fit these training data
- Compare algorithms and rank them with respect to their performance on
  annotated test data, different from the training data.

The overall consensus is that, if the training data sufficiently covers all examples to be handled in a particular perception problem, this approach provides
sufficient support for developing and evaluating appropriate solutions. The significant progress of artificial perception methods and applications in the last few
decades seems to support this viewpoint. We partially reject these assumptions
and claim that they are too rigidly biased toward the interpretation context fixed
by the annotated data, that, consequently, the evaluation and ranking process
is intrinsically flawed because of this, and that, eventually, this way of proceeding hinders the discovery and development of objectively quantifiable perception

---

[1] http://www.icdar2013.org/program/competitions
[2] http://www.image-net.org/challenges/LSVRC/2012/

approaches. It should be clear that this does not invalidate nor intends to disqualify current research methods. However, it tries to introduce complementary and theoretically supported metrics and methodology that lift the mentioned biases and shortcomings.

2.1   Analysis of the Performance Metrics

In general, the performance of methods is expressed with respect to their level of agreement to the *ground truth*. Often precision-recall based metrics are used to express this, but this does not need to be. Often, approaches also give a more detailed, multi-dimensional measure of performance [14].

The *ground truth* itself, and, subsequently, the coverage of the training data, is considered to be flawlessly representative of a well defined interpretation problem for which the state-of-the-art research is expected to provide an algorithm. It is interesting to take a look at what would happen if we accepted less than perfect ground truth. Let us assume that the ground truth were tainted with errors, and that $\varepsilon\%$ of it were annotated with wrong interpretations. This would mean that a method, achieving a 100% agreement with the ground truth, would actually be off the initial interpretation problem with $\varepsilon\%$, and that there is a non-null probability that any method within the $]100\%, 100 - \varepsilon\%]$ agreement range actually outperforms the one with the highest score. This is actually a well known problem, and has been studied before [15]. The only apparent solutions to this problem seem to be to either resort to very strict, but essentially human, verification and cross-verification of ground truth, to either use synthetically generated ground truth data, or to do away with classical metrics, altogether [16, 17].

In the next section, we shall show that these apparent solutions are not sufficient, and that difference in interpretation is a core component of the overall interpretation problem.

2.2   Expressing the Interpretation Context

Independently of what was enunciated in the previous section, evaluating and comparing interpretation approaches fundamentally rely on *interpretation context*. The context is what defines the interpretation domain $\mathcal{I}$ as the set of possible interpretations, the application or input domain Δ of the data to be interpreted, and an oracle function $\mathcal{O}$ assigning the assumed-to-be correct interpretations to the input data:

$$\mathcal{O}\left(\Delta\right) = \mathcal{I}_{\mathcal{O}} = \{(\delta, \mathcal{O}\left(\delta\right))\}_{\delta \in \Delta}$$

It is generally assumed that *ground truth* is a sampling of $\mathcal{I}_{\mathcal{O}}$. Furthermore, it is often implicitly assumed (although rarely, if ever, actually formalized or factually established) that Δ is a manifold of some sorts and that some local continuity properties exist (generally related to tolerance to noise and small deformations of the input) such that it is likely that $\Delta\vert_i$ (*i.e.* the class of all data for which the oracle returns i) constitutes a sub-manifold of some kind. If sufficient sampling points are chosen from $\Delta|_i$, the consensus is that appropriate techniques can provide a fairly accurate approximation of it. This is what underpins a large part of current Machine Perception research performance evaluation.

In this paper, we are not going to consider the question of whether the ground truth sampling (especially the training data) is representative and sufficient, and if it captures the complete scope of the interpretation context it is supposed to cover from an information theory, Shannon-Nyquist or linear algebra point of view, to name a few. While this is an essential and fundamental question, it obviously requires a much larger and elaborate study than what can be reported here. From here on, and for argument's sake, we are going to assume that the ground truth used in Machine Perception, is generally a sufficiently representative sampling for the intended interpretation context.

But what is this *interpretation context*? It is the set of rules, conditions and constraints that define whether a given interpretation $i \in \mathcal{I}$ applies to some given input data $\delta \in \Delta$. We previously associated this set to an oracle $\mathcal{O}$. We can reasonably assume there exists no known algorithm for $\mathcal{O}$, otherwise the corresponding Machine Perception problem would be solved (except, perhaps, for some performance issues). Although this sounds trivial, it actually leads to a very interesting paradox we are going to make explicit, here.

The Case of Human Annotated Ground Truth. The most common approach to generating ground truth is to use human annotators. In this configuration, the annotators serve as instances of the oracle $\mathcal{O}$ and are provided with input data, for which they are to produce the corresponding interpretations, following clear instructions. These instructions correspond to the interpretation context and are defined as precisely as possible using both natural language and mathematically formalized criteria. The paradox arises immediately: either the instructions are totally unambiguous, and identically interpreted by all human annotators; either the instructions are ambiguous at some point, and may create legitimate different interpretations, depending on the annotators' viewpoints. Yet, totally unambiguous, fully formalized and totally reproducible instruction sets bear a name: algorithms. Hence, if the interpretation context can be formalized, the Machine Perception problem is solved. Consequently, in the case of human annotated ground truth, it is impossible to avoid a certain level (may it be minimal) of ambiguity, and therefore legitimate differences of interpretation will persist.

This is actually supported by many findings. [6] reports an experiment of pixel-level human annotation for document binarization, for instance. [18], reporting on the Pascal Visual Object Classes (VOC) Challenge, spends a significant part of the paper on an account of the various conditions to acquiring, annotating and validating the data and refers to explicit annotation guidelines [19]. The annotation guidelines contain descriptions of the data like *"Bounding box should contain all visible pixels, except where the bounding box would have to be made excessively large to include a few additional pixels (<5 %)"*, *"Images which* *are poor quality (e.g. excessive motion blur) should be marked bad. However, poor illumination (e.g. objects in silhouette) should not count as poor quality unless objects cannot be recognised.*" ... as for the categories, "Bus" includes minibus, and "Car" includes cars, vans, people carriers *etc.* but should not be labeled when only the vehicle interior is shown. Obviously, images like the one in Fig. 1 fall in an ambiguous category both whether they should be labeled as "Car" (as van) or "Bus" (as minibus) on the one hand, and whether they *only* depict the interior of the vehicle.

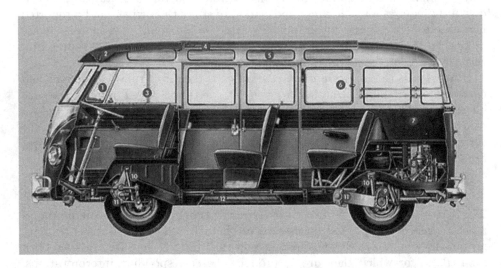

Fig. 1. Example of an ambiguous image category. Source: http://www.doobybrain. com/2008/01/30/car-cut-away-gallery/

The Case of Synthetic Data. Synthetically generated ground truth is the dual configuration of human annotated ground truth, with respect to interpretation context. Indeed, in this case, there exists and algorithm $\mathcal{S}$ that is capable of generating data that is conforming to a given interpretation context. Formally speaking,

$$\mathcal{S} : \mathcal{I} \times \mathbf{P} \to \Delta$$
$$i, p \ \mapsto \delta \qquad (1)$$

where $\mathbf{P}$ is the parameter space of $\mathcal{S}$. Under those conditions, trying to determine an algorithm for $\mathcal{O}$ becomes an *Inverse Problem*, which is class of reputably hard, ill-posed problems, introducing a high level of ambiguity [20] in the general case.

It is interesting to consider the cases where $\mathcal{S}$ either is injective, surjective or bijective (other situations can, without loss of generality, be reduced to these three).

1. $\mathcal{S}$ is injective (and not bijective): this means that the generated ground truth does not cover the entire set of possible interpretation configurations, and therefore is not an appropriate, nor a representative tool for performance evaluation[3].
   Given that $\mathcal{S}$ can still be used for addressing a sub-part of the interpretation problem by restricting $\mathcal{O}$ to $\Delta' = \mathcal{S}(\mathcal{I}, \mathbf{P})$, the derived use comes down to considering the surjective or bijective case.
2. $\mathcal{S}$ surjective (and not bijective): this means that the interpretation problem is potentially ambiguous. If

$$\exists (i, p), (i', p') \in \mathcal{I} \times \mathbf{P} : i \neq i' \wedge \mathcal{S}(i, p) = \mathcal{S}(i', p')$$

then there is a δ for which both interpretation i and i' hold[4]. However if, independently of any p, p'

$$\forall i \neq i' \in \mathcal{I} : \mathcal{S}(i, p) \neq \mathcal{S}(i', p')$$

then the subjectivity is only due to an over-parametrization of the generative function, and has no impact on interpretation ambiguity. In that case the problem can be reduced, using an alternative $\mathcal{S}'(\mathcal{I}, \mathbf{P}')$, to the bijective case.
3. $\mathcal{S}$ is bijective: in that case $\mathcal{O} = \mathcal{S}^{-1}$.

Besides the fact that most of the synthetic ground truth generating methods have not been categorized into one of the above classes, and that, consequently, performance evaluation based on their use cannot be considered totally reliable (if not seriously flawed) they introduce a similar paradox as in the previous case: either the problem is well posed ($\mathcal{S}$ is bijective) but then it should be theoretically possible compute $\mathcal{O}$ as $\mathcal{S}^{-1}$ and the problem is solved by posing it; either the problem is ill-posed and any proposed solution will either be irrelevant ($\mathcal{S}$ is injective) or non-unique or ambiguous ($\mathcal{S}$ is surjective).

2.3   Standoff

The infamous Semantic Gap is here to stay, and seems to be a fundamentally intrinsic part of interpretation: either one is capable of very precisely state an interpretation problem, in which case the mere fact of stating it lifts any possible ambiguity and consists in solving it; either the problem is open to interpretation, and multiple contradictory solutions may fit the problem.

This is not really surprising, and is in line with post-modernist philosophic considerations on truth and interpretation [21, 22]. While this does not mean that

---

[3] This is a somewhat strong statement, and in many cases it can be helpful to use these functions anyway, as an instance of common practice in experimental research: "If we cannot immediately solve the global problem, let's try and solve a more manageable sub-problem."

[4] We are making the implicit assumption that interpretations are mutually exclusive. Although this may seem restrictive, it is not. In cases where multiple interpretations are acceptable, one can simply replace $\mathcal{I}$ by $\{0, 1\}^{|\mathcal{I}|}$.

interpretation is impossible, it does conclude that multiple possible interpretations coexist and cannot be compared to one another. In the following section we shall be developing a set of computational tools to accommodate to this paradigm shift, very much in line with Eco's idea that only a limited number of all possible interpretations are worthwhile to consider [23,24].

3 Comparing and Modelling Differences in Interpretation Contexts

An extreme example of the previously mentioned standoff can be seen below. By considering for $\mathcal{I}$ set of allowable concepts $\{circle, triangle, square\}$, and for Δ the following input $\{\bigcirc, \triangle, \square\}$, Peirce's *unlimited semiosis* [22] would perfectly well admit the following interpretation

$$\bigcirc \models triangle$$
$$\triangle \models square$$
$$\square \models circle$$

Most of us would agree, however, that this interpretation is, at the least, unconventional, although one could imagine contexts where it actually makes sense (*e.g.* for obfuscation and cryptography[5]). The mere fact that conventional, self-imposing, interpretations exist (although they may not be unique) [23], hints that there may be common characteristics that can be extracted from them. In what follows, and in the light of the reasoning in the previous section, the term "algorithm" should be taken as equivalent to "interpretation context", and may therefore also refer to humans.

The main idea is to try and capture the possible structure underpinning the consensus and differentiation areas of a set of competing algorithms on the same data. By using Formal Concept Analysis [26,27] on the one hand, and possibly statistical clustering techniques on the other hand, we expect to be able to characterise their differences in interpretation.

The general idea is developed below.

We are assuming that the task at hand can be expressed as a discrete set of expected results $\mathcal{I} = \{i_1 \dots i_n\}$. If not, discretisation techniques like those developed in [28] can be used or adapted to fit the specific kind of descriptors used.

In that case, as in [17], we consider m algorithms $\{\mathcal{A}_k\}_{1\dots m}$ and a data set $\Delta = \{\delta_1 \dots \delta_d\}$. This allows us to construct a family of m $d \times n$ matrices M_k such that

$$M_k(s,t) = \begin{cases} 1 \ iff \ \mathcal{A}_k(\delta_s) = i_t \\ 0 \ \text{otherwise} \end{cases}$$

Let the final matrix $\overline{M}$ be the concatenation of the matrices M_k such that $\overline{M} = [M_1 \dots M_m]$ as represented in Table 1.

---

[5] This fuzzy distinction between syntax, semiosis and semantics is actually what troubled interpretation of hieroglyphs [25].

Table 1. Representation matrix $\overline{M}$ for FCA-based ground-truth interpretation and performance evaluation

	M_1			M_2			...	M_m		
	$\mathcal{A}_1$			$\mathcal{A}_2$			...	$\mathcal{A}_m$		
	i_1	i_2 ...	i_n	i_1	i_2 ...	i_n		i_1	i_2 ...	i_n
δ_1	0	1	0	1	0	0		0	1	0
δ_2	1	0	0	0	0	1		0	1	0
$\vdots$										
δ_d	0	1	0	1	0	0		0	0	0

By conducting a Formal Concept Analysis on these data, the appropriate clusters of coherent interpretations can be uncovered and compared with the "natural" concepts underpinning them. This will eventually result in a better understanding of how Machine Perception methods compare to one another in a more semantic sense, since the result of the FCA is a lattice structure, capturing the partial order (or hierarchy) of data/algorithm clusters sharing the same interpretation/agreeing. The interesting side-effect associated to this approach, which we also already discovered in [17], is that it contains a duality between data and methods, in the sense that it cannot only be seen as a tool for comparing and studying different algorithms, but that it can also be considered as a way to assess the appropriateness of data with respect to the methods.

The outputs we can use from the FCA are:

- For a given set of algorithms $\{\mathcal{A}_i\}$, which are the δ_k on which they share the same interpretation?
- Dually, for a given set of $\{\delta_k\}$, which interpretations i_j are observed and by which algorithms?
- Given a set of algorithms $\{\mathcal{A}_i\}$, what sets of disagreement of $\bar{\delta}_k$ exist, and how are they structured?
- What items $\bar{\delta}_k$ offer the largest level of disagreement (highest scattering between different observed interpretations)?

This last point is particularly interesting, since it offers a mathematically formalised metric for ambiguous data (in the case of [6], for instance, it allows to precisely identify the pixels for which the notion of binarisation does not seem to make much sense, or, at least, for which very legitimate differences of opinion exist). By extension, it offers a clearly defined bootstrap to extend the formalisation of existing interpretation contexts by precisely highlighting those input data on which it seems ambiguous. Combining this with current statistical classification methods may actually provide very interesting learning approaches, since they would focus on pertinent data.

Example

The ideas expressed in the previous section will require a profound paradigm shift with respect to comparing results from various sources. As an example,

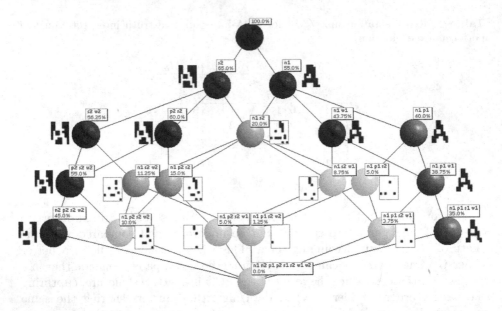

Fig. 2. Preliminary results on the use of FCA for binarisation algorithm comparison. Otsu (p) [29], Niblack (n) [30], Sauvola (s) [31] and Wolf (w) [32]. Suffix 1 to the algorithm names signifies foreground categorisation, suffix 2 means background categorisation.

Fig. 2 shows some preliminary results we obtained[6] by taking 4 off-the-shelf binarisation algorithms (Otsu [29], Niblack [30], Sauvola [31] and Wolf [32]) and by considering each pixel of a grey level image of an 'A' and feed their classification results to *Lattice Miner*[7] [33]. It needs to be noted that, unlike what is usually done in FCA, both attributes (here foreground pixels) and their complements (background pixels) have been used for concept construction. This creates a left-right symmetry in the concept lattice: the left side concerns concepts based on background information, the right side concerns foreground information. Our concept lattice that expresses the following knowledge.

1. Each concept node lists three elements: an image of the pixels belonging to the concept, the list of binarisation algorithms that *agree* on the categorisation of these pixels, the percentage of the whole image these pixels present.
2. The lattice hierarchy (top-down) goes in increasing order of combination of algorithms, and in decreasing order of categorised pixels. This means that a child node shows the pixels categorised by the parent node's algorithms that are also categorised by a another algorithm, which is added to the list of algorithms. In other terms, if a parent node shows the agreement of a set of algorithms, a child node shows the agreement of an extended set of these algorithms.

---

[6] Results by Z. Jiang, M.Eng. student at Mines Nancy, France.

[7] http://sourceforge.net/projects/lattice-miner/

Some of the immediate conclusions that can be drawn from the output is that Niblack is consistently more optimistic than the others in classifying foreground pixels (to the point that any foreground pixel classified by the other approaches is also classified as such by Niblack), and conversely, that Sauvola is consistently more pessimistic than the others (all foreground pixels classified by Sauvola are also classified as such by the others). This is confirmed by the lattice structure on the left hand side, expressing the dual configuration on background pixels. Other interesting findings are in the center of the lattice, where it can be seen that consensus on foreground pixels between Niblack and Otsu on the one hand and the consensus on background pixels between Sauvola and Wolf on the other hand, are consistent with each-other, to the exception of a single pixel.

4 Conclusion

We have shown that ground truth is the instance of a very specific and unique interpretation context that is either immediately transposable into an algorithm (and therefore addressing an already solved problem) or otherwise fundamentally ambiguous. Not taking into account this intrinsic ambiguity has an impact on traditional performance evaluation consisting in measuring agreement/disagreement with ground truth, since there is no way of establishing whether disagreements are due to incorrect implementations or caused by an alternative, legitimate interpretation due to this ambiguity.

In order to formally establish and measure differences in interpretation context, we propose to rely on Formal Concept Analysis, which is capable of computing a lattice structure that links, in a dual way, interpreted data and the interpreting algorithms (or humans) such that clusters of agreement and disagreement can be clearly established. Analysis of these clusters can then further determine to what extent algorithms are comparable on the one hand, and what categories of data are to be considered as ambiguous for a given set of contexts, on the other. Some preliminary results were shown on binarisation algorithms, but those can be extended to any other kind of interpretation problem.

References

1. Lamiroy, B., Lopresti, D.: An open architecture for end-to-end document analysis benchmarking. In: 11th International Conference on Document Analysis and Recognition - ICDAR 2011, Beijing, China, pp. 42–47. IEEE Computer Society (2011)
2. Popper, K.R.: The Logic of Scientific Discovery, Reprint edn. Routledge, New York (1992) (Original edition, 1934 "Logik der Forschung")
3. Lamiroy, B., Lopresti, D.: A platform for storing, visualizing, and interpreting collections of noisy documents. In: Fourth Workshop on Analytics for Noisy Unstructured Text Data - AND'10, Toronto, Canada. ACM International Conference Proceeding Series. ACM (2010)

4. Hu, J., Kashi, R., Lopresti, D., Nagy, G., Wilfong, G.: Why table ground-truthing is hard. In: Proceedings of the Sixth International Conference on Document Analysis and Recognition, Seattle, WA, pp. 129–133, September 2001
5. Lopresti, D., Nagy, G., Smith, E.B.: Document analysis issues in reading optical scan ballots. In: Proceedings of the 8th IAPR International Workshop on Document Analysis Systems, Boston, MA, USA, pp. 105–112. ACM (2010)
6. Smith, E.H.B.: An analysis of binarization ground truthing. In: Proceedings of the 8th IAPR International Workshop on Document Analysis Systems, Boston, MA, USA, pp. 27–34. ACM (2010)
7. Clavelli, A., Karatzas, D., Lladós, J.: A framework for the assessment of text extraction algorithms on complex colour images. In: Proceedings of the 8th IAPR International Workshop on Document Analysis Systems, Boston, MA, USA, pp. 19–26. ACM (2010)
8. Lopresti, D., Nagy, G.: Issues in ground-truthing graphic documents. In: Proceedings of the Fourth IAPR International Workshop on Graphics Recognition, Kingston, Ontario, Canada, pp. 59–72, September 2001
9. Eco, U.: The Limits of Interpretation. Indiana University Press, Bloomington (1990)
10. Smeulders, A.W., Worring, M., Santini, S., Gupta, A., Jain, R.: Content-based image retrieval at the end of the early years. IEEE Trans. Pattern Anal. Mach. Intell. 22(12), 1349–1380 (2000)
11. Everingham, M., Van Gool, L., Williams, C.K.I., Winn, J., Zisserman, A.: The PASCAL Visual Object Classes Challenge 2011 (VOC2011) Results (2011). http://www.pascal-network.org/challenges/VOC/voc2011/workshop/index.html
12. Voorhees, E., Harman, D., et al.: TREC: Experiment and Evaluation in Information Retrieval, vol. 63. MIT press, Cambridge (2005)
13. Mller, H., Clough, P., Deselaers, T., Caputo, B.: ImageCLEF: Experimental Evaluation in Visual Information Retrieval, 1st edn. Springer, Heidelberg (2010)
14. Valveny, E., Dosch, P., Fornés, A., Escalera, S.: Report on the third contest on symbol recognition. In: Liu, W., Lladós, J., Ogier, J.-M. (eds.) GREC 2007. LNCS, vol. 5046, pp. 321–328. Springer, Heidelberg (2008). (French Techno-Vision program (Ministry of Research) Spanish project TIN2006-15694-C02-02 Spanish research program Consolider Ingenio 2010:MIPRCV (CSD2007-00018))
15. Carlotto, M.J.: Effect of errors in ground truth on classification accuracy. Int. J. Remote Sens. 30(18), 4831–4849 (2009)
16. Lopresti, D.P., Nagy, G.: Adapting the turing test for declaring document analysis problems solved. In: Blumenstein, M., Pal, U., Uchida, S., eds.: Document Analysis Systems, pp. 1–5. IEEE, New York (2012)
17. Lamiroy, B., Sun, T.: Computing precision and recall with missing or uncertain ground truth. In: Kwon, Y.-B., Ogier, J.-M. (eds.) GREC 2011. LNCS, vol. 7423, pp. 149–162. Springer, Heidelberg (2013)
18. Everingham, M., Van Gool, L., Williams, C.K.I., Winn, J., Zisserman, A.: The PASCAL visual object classes (VOC) challenge. Int. J. Comput. Vis. 88(2), 303–338 (2010)
19. Winn, J., Everingham, M.: The PASCAL visual object classes challenge 2007 (VOC2007) annotation guidelines (2007). http://PASCALlin.ecs.soton.ac.uk/challenges/VOC/VOC2007/guidelines.html
20. Tarantola, A.: Inverse Problem Theory and Methods for Model Parameter Estimation. Society for Industrial Mathematics, Philadelphia (2005)
21. Heidegger, M.: Being and Time. Library of Philosophy and Theology. Blackwell, Oxford (1967)

22. Peirce, C.S.: Syllabus: Nomenclature and Division of Triadic Relations, as far as they are determined. MS [R] 540 (1903)
23. Eco, U., Collini, S., Culler, J., Rorty, R., Brooke-Rose, C.: Interpretation and Over-interpretation. Tanner Lectures in Human Values. Cambridge University Press, Cambridge (1992)
24. Eco, U.: Dall'albero al labirinto: studi storici sul segno e l'interpretazione. Bompiani (2007)
25. Champollion, J.: Précis du système hiéroglyphique des anciens égyptiens, ou recherches sur les élémens premiers de cette écriture sacrée, sur leurs diverses combinaisons, et sur les rapports de ce système avec les autres méthodes graphiques égyptiennes. Imprimerie royale (1828)
26. Ganter, B., Wille, R.: Formal Concept Analysis - Mathematical Foundations. Springer, Heidelberg (1999)
27. Ganter, B., Stumme, G., Wille, R. (eds.): Formal Concept Analysis. LNCS (LNAI), vol. 3626. Springer, Heidelberg (2005)
28. Coustaty, M., Bertet, K., Visani, M., Ogier, J.M.: A new adaptive structural signature for symbol recognition by using a Galois lattice as a classifier. IEEE Trans. Syst. Man Cybern. B 41(4), 1136–1148 (2011)
29. Otsu, N.: A threshold selection method from gray-level histograms. IEEE Trans. Syst. Man Cybern. 9(1), 62–66 (1979)
30. Niblack, W.: An Introduction to Digital Image Processing. Strandberg Publishing Company, Birkeroed (1985)
31. Sauvola, J., Pietikäinen, M.: Adaptive document image binarization. Pattern Recogn. 33(2), 225–236 (2000)
32. Wolf, C., Jolion, J.M., Chassaing, F.: Text localization, enhancement and binarization in multimedia documents. In: Proceedings of the International Conference on Pattern Recognition, vol. 2, pp. 1037–1040 (2002)
33. Lahcen, B., Kwudia, L.K.: Lattice miner: a tool for concept lattice construction and exploration. In: Supplementary Proceeding of International Conference on Formal concept analysis (ICFCA'10) (2010)

Final Report of GREC'13 Arc and Line Segmentation Contest

Syed Saqib Bukhari[1], Hasan S.M. Al-Khaffaf[2($\boxtimes$)], Faisal Shafait[3],
Mohd Azam Osman[4], Abdullah Zawawi Talib[4], and Thomas M. Breuel[1]

[1] Technical University of Kaiserslautern, Kaiserslautern, Germany
{bukhari,tmb}@informatik.uni-kl.de
[2] University of Duhok, Kurdistan Region, Iraq
hasan.salim@uod.ac
[3] The University of Western Australia, Perth, Australia
faisal.shafait@uwa.edu.au
[4] Universiti Sains Malaysia, Georgetown, Malaysia
{azam,azht}@cs.usm.my

Abstract. Recognition of geometric primitives such as line and arc helps in automatic conversion of line drawing document images into electronic form. A large number of raster to vector methods can be found in the literature. A line and arc segmentation contest was held in conjunction with the tenth IAPR International Workshop on Graphics Recognition (GREC 2013) for comparing performance of different methods on a uniform platform. The contest was broken down into two challenges: arc segmentation and line segmentation. The dataset includes engineering drawings (for arc segmentation challenge) and cadastral maps (for line segmentation challenge). Jianping Wu's method got the highest score (0.541), hence the winner of the Arc Segmentation Contest. Liu Wenyin's method, the only method participated in the line segmentation contest achieved 66 % segmentation accuracy.

Keywords: Graphics recognition · Line drawing · Arc and line segmentation contest · Performance evaluation

1 Introduction

This paper summarizes the outcomes of the Arc and Line Segmentation contest 2013 that was held in conjunction with the Tenth IAPR International Workshop on Graphics RECognition (GREC) held in Lehigh University, Bethlehem, PA, in August 2013. In this edition of the contest, two challenges were available for the contestants: arc segmentation and line segmentation of engineering drawings and cadastral maps respectively. The images were selected from a text book and from Internet. The output of research prototypes as well as commercial software were acceptable.

© Springer-Verlag Berlin Heidelberg 2014
B. Lamiroy and J.-M. Ogier (Eds.): GREC 2013, LNCS 8746, pp. 234–239, 2014.
DOI: 10.1007/978-3-662-44854-0_18

Final Report of GREC'13 Arc and Line Segmentation Contest   235

2   Test Images, Ground Truthing, and Expected Vectors

For the arc segmentation contest challenge, eight binary images were selected from a text book and the Internet (Fig. 1). Manual editing using a raster image editor is used to remove all text annotations from the drawings leaving only graphical elements. A vector editor was manually used to recreate the mechanical parts by drawing the vectors on the top of the raster image. Contextual knowledge was used to align the graphical elements with each other such as co-centered arcs/circles. Line width information is not supported in this dataset. The width field of the graphical elements is set to the value of 1.

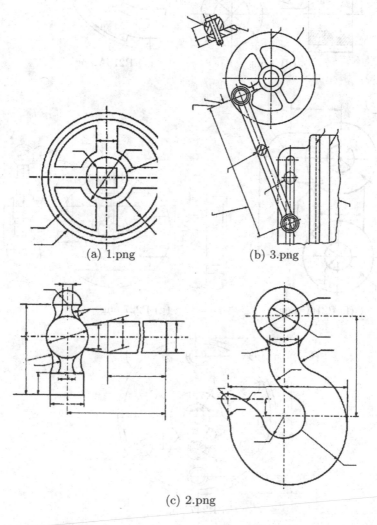

(a) 1.png   (b) 3.png

(c) 2.png

Fig. 1. Test images for the arc segmentation challenge

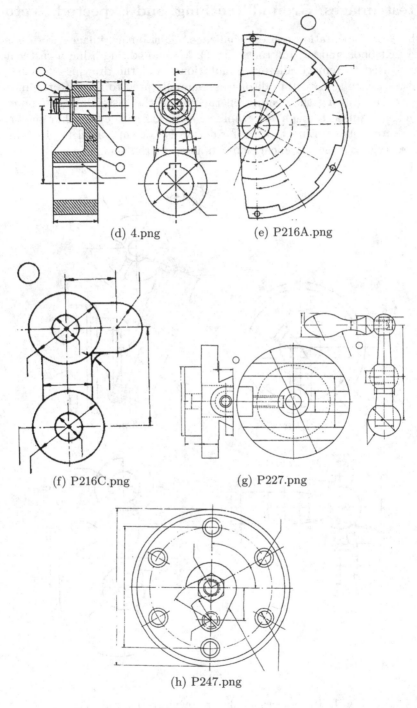

(d) 4.png

(e) P216A.png

(f) P216C.png

(g) P227.png

(h) P247.png

Fig. 1. (*continued*)

As its name implied, the arc segmentation challenge involve only arcs and circles. Other graphical elements such as straight lines and text were ignored. Dashed circles/arcs entities were vectorised in a different way. Each part of the dashed arc/circle was vectorized as a standalone arc with its own center, radius, starting and ending angles.

For the line segmentation contest challenge, four cadastral maps, that are captured from record rooms and gathered from the Internet, were used. The sample images are shown in Fig. 2. Altogether, these images contain both non-broken and broken types of lines, where broken lines occur due to image degradations. The annotations/texts were removed from the sample images. The ground-truth was marked using pixel-accurate color-coding of page segmentation as presented in [1] and was also used in GREC 2007 Arc Segmentation Contest [2]. The ground-truthed images are shown in Fig. 2 These sample images were used for both training and testing.

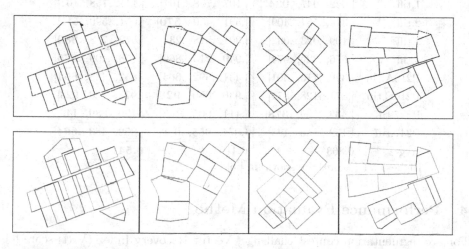

Fig. 2. [Top-Row] Training and testing (cadastral map) images for line segmentation contest challenge. [Bottom-Row] Pixel-accurate color-coding ground-truthed.

A webpage[1] holding the test/train images is available for interested parties.

3 Participated Methods

Three participants (Table 1) for Arc Segmentation Contest provided the output of their research methods. One of the participants, Liu [3], also submitted the results for line segmentation contest challenge.

---

[1] https://sites.google.com/a/iupr.com/grec2013_arc_and_line_seg_contest/

Table 1. Participated methods for arc and line segmentation contest

Vectorizer	Author(s)	Affiliation
Liu's method$^{A\&L}$ [3]	Liu Wenyin	Department of Computer Science, City University of Hong Kong, Hong Kong, China
Qgar-Lamiroy^A [4]	Bart Lamiroy	Université de Lorraine, LORIA, Nancy, France
FACILE^A V2.1 [5]	Jianping Wu	School of Computer Engineering, Suzhou Vocational University, Suzhou, China

$^{A\&L}$ participation in arc and line challenges, ^{A} arc challenge only

Table 2. Arc challenge performance scores $[D_v, F_v, VRI]$ for the participated methods

Image	Liu's	Qgar-Lamiroy	FACILE
1.tiff	[.022, .947, **.034**^{a}]	[.107, .758, .161]	[.111, .758, .164]
2.tiff	[.375, .554, .409]	[.591, .450, **.570**]	[.651, .599, .511]
3.tiff	[.109, .923, .092]	[.301, .818, .234]	[.512, .718, **.380**]
4.tiff	[.676, .329, .674]	[.940, .213, .860]	[.858, .109, **.875**]
P216A.tiff	[.320, .716, .301]	[.431, .692, .364]	[.852, .483, **.664**]
P216C.tiff	[.871, .128, .871]	[.936, .080, **.928**]	[.977, .128, .923]
P227.tiff	[.432, .669, **.378**]	[.111, .905, .103]	[.199, .889, .149]
P247.tiff	[.152, .866, .143]	[.074, .955, .058]	[.852, .483, **.664**]
Avg	0.363	0.410	**0.541**

^{a}Highest VRI scores are shown in bold

4   Performance Evaluation Method

For arc segmentation contest challenge, Vector Recovery Index (VRI) score [6] was used in this contest as performance criterion for the three contested methods.

$$VRI = \sqrt{D_v * (1 - F_v)} \qquad (1)$$

where D_v is the detection rate and F_v is the false alarm rate. The VRI in the range [0..1] is the overall score used to select the winner of arc segmentation contest. The higher VRI value, the better recognition we have.

For line segmentation contest challenge, the vectorial score proposed in [1] is used for the performance evaluation. Together with one-to-one segmentation accuracy, the vectorial score also reports over-segmentation, under-segmentation, and missed-segment failures. The ground-truthed images are marked here in more details where we consider two or more collinear adjacent line segments as different lines. However, the challenge is line segmentation contest, not line segment detection. Therefore we consider under-segmentations also as correct detection, and the line segmentation accuracy is the summation of one-to-one accuracy and under-segmentations.

5   Results and Discussion

FACILE method gets the highest VRI scores on 4 out of 8 test images (Table 2) and an average VRI score of 0.541, hence the winner of the this edition of the arc segmentation challenge.

For line segmentation challenge, the test dataset contains total 244 lines. Liu's method reported 585 lines, out of which 161 are correctly detected lines, 112 over-segmentation failures, and 1 missed-segment failure. Liu's method achieved 66 % of line segmentation accuracy.

Acknowledgment. The authors would like to thank Abdul Halim Ghazali for his efforts in preparing the ground truth images for the arc segmentation challenge.

References

1. Shafait, F., Keysers, D., Breuel, T.M.: Pixel-accurate representation and evaluation of page segmentation in document images. In: Proceedings of the 18th International Conference on Pattern Recognition, Hong Kong, China, vol. 1, pp. 872–875 (2006)
2. Shafait, F., Keysers, D., Breuel, T.M.: GREC 2007 arc segmentation contest: evaluation of four participating algorithms. In: Liu, W., Lladós, J., Ogier, J.-M. (eds.) GREC 2007. LNCS, vol. 5046, pp. 310–320. Springer, Heidelberg (2008)
3. Liu, W.Y., Dori, D.: Incremental arc segmentation algorithm and its evaluation. IEEE Trans. Pattern Anal. Mach. Intell. **20**(4), 424–431 (1998)
4. Lamiroy, B., Guebbas, Y.: Robust and precise circular arc detection. In: Ogier, J.-M., Liu, W., Lladós, J. (eds.) GREC 2009. LNCS, vol. 6020, pp. 49–60. Springer, Heidelberg (2010)
5. Wu, J., Chen, K., Gao, X.: Fast and accurate circle detection using gradient-direction-based segmentation. J. Opt. Soc. Am. A **30**(6), 1184–1192 (2013)
6. Liu, W.Y., Dori, D.: A protocol for performance evaluation of line detection algorithms. Mach. Vis. Appl. **9**(5–6), 240–250 (1997)

Datasets for the Evaluation
of Substitution-Tolerant Subgraph Isomorphism

Pierre Héroux[1]($\boxtimes$), Pierre Le Bodic[2], and Sébastien Adam[1]

[1] UFR des Sciences et Techniques, Université de Rouen – LITIS EA 4108,
76800 Saint-Etienne du Rouvray, France
{Pierre.Heroux,Sebastien.Adam}@univ-rouen.fr
[2] School of Industrial and Systems Engineering, Georgia Tech, Atlanta, USA
lebodic@gatech.edu

Abstract. Due to their representative power, structural descriptions have gained a great interest in the community working on graphics recognition. Indeed, graph based representations have successful been used for isolated symbol recognition. New challenges in this research field have focused on symbol recognition, symbol spotting or symbol based indexing of technical drawing.

When they are based on structural descriptions, these tasks can be expressed by means of a subgraph isomorphism search. Indeed, it consists in locating the instance of a pattern graph representing a symbol in a target graph representing the whole document image. However, there is a lack of publicly available datasets allowing to evaluate the performance of subgraph isomorphism approaches in presence of noisy data.

In this paper, we present five datasets that can be used to evaluate the performance of algorithms on several tasks involving subgraph isomorphism. Four of these datasets have been synthetically generated and allow to evaluate the search of a single instance of the pattern with or without perturbed labels. The fifth dataset corresponds to the structural description of architectural plans and allows to evaluate the search of multiple occurrences of the pattern. These datasets are made available for download. We also propose several measures to qualify each of the tasks.

1 Introduction

Graphs are data structures which have gain a great interest in the document analysis community during the last decade thanks to the computation power of nowadays computers. Indeed, the high computational complexity of algorithms which process graphs is now compensated by computer capacities. It is now possible to leverage the flexibility and the description power of this kind of data structure.

Many approaches in the literature on technical documents use region adjacency graphs in which vertices describe regions while edges express an attributed adjacency relationship [1]. In other representations, vertices is associated to primitive shapes (segments, arcs...) while edges carry information on the relative position of these shapes [2,3].

© Springer-Verlag Berlin Heidelberg 2014
B. Lamiroy and J.-M. Ogier (Eds.): GREC 2013, LNCS 8746, pp. 240–251, 2014.
DOI: 10.1007/978-3-662-44854-0_19

In the mean time, research on technical documents has shifted from recognition of isolated symbols to recognition in context, symbol spotting or indexing through visual words.

When using structural representations, recognize, locate or count the occurrences of a pattern symbol in an image turns into a subgraph isomorphism problem. Indeed, these tasks need to identify, locate or count the occurrences of the structural representation of the searched pattern in the structural representation of the whole document image.

As often in pattern recognition applications, noise may affect the structural representation, that is to say that there exist differences between the pattern graph and each of its searched occurrences. This implies that the subgraph isomorphism must tolerate these differences. This problem is known as error-tolerant subgraph isomorphism.

The differences between the pattern and its occurrences in the target graph can be separated in two categories:

1. differences between labels may occur because the features which label vertices or edges are extracted with non sufficiently robust methods.
2. topological differences occur because of a non robust segmentation, that is to say that a region or a shape may be splitted or merged with an other one, resulting in splitted or merged vertices.

Consequently, the error-tolerant subgraph isomorphism problem may result from two distinct sources: a difference in the labeling or a difference in the topology. The substitution-tolerant subgraph isomorphism refers to the search of a subgraph isomorphism in the only presence of differences on label values, whereas topological differences are tackled by inexact subgraph isomorphism.

The communities working on graphics recognition or structural pattern analysis have always had concerns to propose databases that can be references for benchmarking or performance evaluation of an individual processing or a complete system. For example, the IAPR TC-10 and TC-15 provide several datasets among which we can cite the GREC symbol recognition contests [4], the IAM Graph dataset [5]. However, there is very few data that can be used to test error-tolerant subgraph isomorphism. Moreover, to the best of our knowledge, those existing only contain unlabeled graphs or graphs with nominal labels [6]. The upcoming contest on graph matching algorithms for pattern search in biological databases which will be held in conjunction with the 22nd International Conference on Pattern Recognition is another initiative which illustrates the need to benchmark algorithms for graph/subgraph isomorphism. Unfortunately, this contest only addresses graphs labeled with nominal values. Hence, there is a need for datasets for the evaluation of error-tolerant subgraph isomorphism methods which process graphs labeled with continuous values.

In this paper, we present several ground-truthed databases that we make available. These datasets are intended to evaluate methods for substitution-tolerant subgraph isomorphism when graphs are labeled with continuous values. We also propose the definition of performance measures to numerically qualify the detection of subgraphs.

This paper is structured as follows. The problem statement and main definitions are presented in Sect. 2. Section 3 presents three datasets which are made available and the way the ground-truth is defined. Section 4 proposes measures to evaluate the performance of subgraph isomorphism in the context of spotting and counting occurrences of pattern graphs. Finally, Sect. 5 concludes the paper and draws some perspectives to continue this initiative.

2   Substitution-Tolerant Subgraph Isomorphism

Definition 1. A directed attributed multigraph[1] $\mathcal{G}$ is a *4-tuple* $(V_{\mathcal{G}}, E_{\mathcal{G}}, \mu_{\mathcal{G}}, \xi_{\mathcal{G}})$ where $V_{\mathcal{G}}$ is the set of vertices of $\mathcal{G}$, $E_{\mathcal{G}}$ is a multiset of ordered pairs $e = (v_1, v_2)$ with $v_1 \in V_{\mathcal{G}}$ and $v_2 \in V_{\mathcal{G}}$, i.e. edges of $\mathcal{G}$. $\mu_{\mathcal{G}} : V_{\mathcal{G}} \to L_V$ is a function assigning a *label* to a vertex, L_V being the set of possible labels for vertices. $\xi_{\mathcal{G}} : E_{\mathcal{G}} \to L_E$ is a function assigning a *label* to an edge, L_E being the set of possible labels for edges.

Definition 2. Given a graph $\mathcal{G} = (V_{\mathcal{G}}, E_{\mathcal{G}}, \mu_{\mathcal{G}}, \xi_{\mathcal{G}})$, a subgraph of $\mathcal{G}$ is a graph $\mathcal{G}' = (V_{\mathcal{G}'}, E_{\mathcal{G}'}, \mu_{\mathcal{G}'}, \xi_{\mathcal{G}'})$ such that $V_{\mathcal{G}'} \subseteq V$, $E_{\mathcal{G}'} \subseteq E$, $\forall e = (v_1, v_2) \in E_{\mathcal{G}'}, v_1 \in V_{\mathcal{G}'}, v_2 \in V_{\mathcal{G}'}$ and $\mu_{\mathcal{G}'}$ and $\xi_{\mathcal{G}'}$ are the restrictions of $\mu_{\mathcal{G}}$ and $\xi_{\mathcal{G}}$ to $V_{\mathcal{G}'}$ and $E_{\mathcal{G}'}$, i.e. $\mu_{\mathcal{G}'}(v) = \mu_{\mathcal{G}}(v)$ and $\xi_{\mathcal{G}'}(e) = \xi_{\mathcal{G}}(e)$.

Definition 3. An injective function $f : V_{\mathcal{S}} \to V_{\mathcal{G}}$ is a subgraph isomorphism from a graph $\mathcal{S} = (V_{\mathcal{S}}, E_{\mathcal{S}}, \mu_{\mathcal{S}}, \xi_{\mathcal{S}})$ to a graph $\mathcal{G} = (V_{\mathcal{G}}, E_{\mathcal{G}}, \mu_{\mathcal{G}}, \xi_{\mathcal{G}})$ if there exists a subgraph $\mathcal{G}'$ of $\mathcal{G}$ such that f is a graph isomorphism from $\mathcal{S}$ to $\mathcal{G}'$:

- $\forall v \in V_{\mathcal{G}}, f(v) = v' \in V_{\mathcal{G}'}, f^{-1}(v') = v$
- for all $e = (v_1, v_2) \in E_{\mathcal{G}}$, there exists a distinct edge $e' = (f(v_1), f(v_2)) \in E_{\mathcal{G}'}$.

Note that extra edges may exist in $\mathcal{G}'$ between mapped vertices, *i.e.* a subgraph does not need to be induced.

In its exact formulation, the subgraph isomorphism must preserve the labeling, *i.e.* $\mu(v) = \mu'(v')$ and $\xi(e) = \xi'(e')$. In pattern recognition applications, where vertices and edges are labeled with measures which may be affected by noise, a substitution-tolerant formulation which allows differences between labels of mapped vertices and edges is mandatory. However, in order to take into account these differences, they are penalized by a non decreasing cost function. Finally, the total cost associated to the mapping between a graph $\mathcal{S} = (V_{\mathcal{S}}, E_{\mathcal{S}}, \mu_{\mathcal{S}}, \xi_{\mathcal{S}})$ and a subgraph of $\mathcal{G} = (V_{\mathcal{G}}, E_{\mathcal{G}}, \mu_{\mathcal{G}}, \xi_{\mathcal{G}})$ is given by Eq. (1).

$$C_M(\mathcal{S}, \mathcal{G}) = \sum_{i \in V_S} \sum_{k \in V_{\mathcal{G}}} c_V(i, k) * x_{i,k} \\ + \sum_{ij \in E_S} \sum_{kl \in E_{\mathcal{G}}} c_E(ij, kl) * y_{ij,kl} \tag{1}$$

In this equation, $c_V(i, k)$ and $c_E(ij, kl)$ respectively denote the elementary cost for mapping a vertex $i \in V_S$ to a vertex $k \in V_{\mathcal{G}}$ and the cost for mapping an edge $ij \in E_S$ to an edge $kl \in E_{\mathcal{G}}$. M represents a possible isomorphism

---

[1] In the remaining of the paper, the term graph denotes a directed attributed multigraph.

f between $\mathcal{S} = (V_{\mathcal{S}}, E_{\mathcal{S}}, \mu_{\mathcal{S}}, \xi_{\mathcal{S}})$ and a subgraph of $\mathcal{G} = (V_{\mathcal{G}}, E_{\mathcal{G}}, \mu_{\mathcal{G}}, \xi_{\mathcal{G}})$ as a set of binary variables $x_{i,k}$ and $y_{ij,kl}$. $x_{i,k}$ is set to 1 if $f(i) = k$ and equals 0 otherwise. Similarly, $y_{ij,kl}$ is set to 1 if $ij \in V_{\mathcal{G}}$ is mapped to $kl \in V_{\mathcal{S}}$ and is set to 0 otherwise. Moreover, the binary variables in M must respect the following constraints in order to ensure that f is an isomorphism.

– Every vertex of $V_{\mathcal{S}}$ must be matched to a unique vertex of $V_{\mathcal{G}}$:

$$\sum_{k \in V_{\mathcal{G}}} x_{i,k} = 1 \quad \forall i \in V_{\mathcal{S}} \tag{2}$$

– Every edge of $E_{\mathcal{S}}$ must be matched to a unique edge of $E_{\mathcal{G}}$:

$$\sum_{kl \in E_{\mathcal{G}}} y_{ij,kl} = 1 \quad \forall ij \in E_{\mathcal{S}} \tag{3}$$

– Every vertex of $V_{\mathcal{G}}$ must be matched to at most a vertex of $E_{\mathcal{S}}$:

$$\sum_{i \in V_{\mathcal{S}}} x_{i,k} \leq 1 \quad \forall k \in V_{\mathcal{G}} \tag{4}$$

– If two vertices are matched together, an edge originating the vertex of $\mathcal{S}$ must be matched with an edge originating the vertex of $\mathcal{G}$:

$$\sum_{kl \in E_{\mathcal{G}}} y_{ij,kl} = x_{i,k} \quad \forall k \in V_{\mathcal{G}}, \forall ij \in E_{\mathcal{S}} \tag{5}$$

– If two vertices are matched together, an edge targeting the vertex of $\mathcal{S}$ must be matched with an edge targeting the vertex of $\mathcal{G}$:

$$\sum_{kl \in E_{\mathcal{G}}} y_{ij,kl} = x_{j,l} \quad \forall l \in V_{\mathcal{G}}, \forall ij \in E_{\mathcal{S}} \tag{6}$$

3   Datasets

In this section, we present the five datasets that are made available at http://litis-ilpiso.univ-rouen.fr[2]. Three of these datasets have been used to evaluate the substitution-tolerant subgraph isomorphism approach described in [7]. Two other ones were designed later.

3.1   Exact Synthetic Dataset

The `ILPIso_exact_synth` dataset is a synthetic dataset which provides 180 pattern-target graph couples. The graph couples have been synthetically generated according to the following procedure. First, a random graph $\mathcal{S}$ is generated according to the Erdös-Rényi model [8] whose parameters are $n_{\mathcal{S}}$, the number of

---

[2] This dataset is now listed on the website of the IAPR Technical Committee #15.

vertices and p which is the probability that a directed edge between two distinct vertices exists. Vertices and edges are labeled with a random numerical value according to a uniform probability distribution in $[-100, 100]$. Then, a graph $\mathcal{G}_0$ is created as an exact copy of $\mathcal{S}$. Finally, $\mathcal{G}_0$ is completed to form a graph $\mathcal{G}$ with vertex and edge insertions (with the same random model for labels) according to the Erdös-Rényi model until its size is $n_{\mathcal{G}}$.

The following parameters have been chosen:

- Size of $\mathcal{G}$: $|V_G| = n_{\mathcal{G}} \in \{50, 100, 250, 500\}$
- Size of $\mathcal{S}$: $|V_S| = n_{\mathcal{S}} \in \{10, 25, 50\}$
- Probability that an edge connects two vertices: $p \in \{0.01, 0.05, 0.1\}$.

The `ILPIso_exact_synth` dataset is composed of five instances of pattern-target graph couples for each combination of $(n_{\mathcal{G}}, n_{\mathcal{S}}, p)$.

During this procedure, the mapping between the vertices of $\mathcal{S}$ and $\mathcal{G}$ is tracked to finally constitute the ground-truth. Even if new non-tracked isomorphisms can be added during the completion of $\mathcal{G}_0$ to $\mathcal{G}$, their cost cannot be lower than the ground-truth one whose cost is 0. Moreover, it has been experimentally checked that the isomorphism in the ground-truth information is the only one whose cost is 0.

This dataset is mainly intended to check whether a unique instance of an exact subgraph isomorphism is successfully found with a tested algorithm.

3.2 Noisy Synthetic Dataset

The `ILPIso_noisy_synth` dataset is also a synthetic dataset. It also contains 180 pattern-target graph couples. It has been created in the same manner than the `ILPIso_exact_synth` dataset (with the same combination of values for $(n_{\mathcal{G}}, n_{\mathcal{S}}, p)$) but an additional step has been introduced. Before its completion to $\mathcal{G}$, $\mathcal{G}_0$ has been modified by editing vertices and edges labels. Each label has been added a random value according to a Gaussian distribution with $m = 0$ and $\sigma^2 = 5$.

This dataset is intended to evaluate the performance of a substitution-tolerant subgraph isomorphism search program where the mapping with the lower cost is searched. As for the `ILPIso_exact_synth` dataset, new non tracked isomorphisms are added when $\mathcal{G}_0$ is completed to $\mathcal{G}$, but it has been checked that the ground-truth corresponds to the isomorphism with the lowest cost.

Figure 1 illustrates an output produced by the synthetic data generation in the presence of noise.

3.3 Synthetic Datasets with Connected Graphs

The Erdös-Rényi model [8] used to create graphs in `ILPIso_exact_synth` and `ILPIso_noisy_synth` datasets does not guarantee that the generated graphs are connected. However, graphs (or at least pattern graphs) used in real structural pattern recognition problems are often connected e.g. region adjacency graphs.

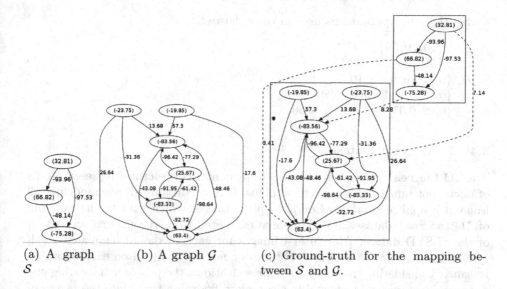

(a) A graph $\mathcal{S}$ (b) A graph $\mathcal{G}$ (c) Ground-truth for the mapping between $\mathcal{S}$ and $\mathcal{G}$.

Fig. 1. Illustration of the generation of synthetic data for the substitution-tolerant subgraph isomorphism search with the following parameters: $n_{\mathcal{S}} = 3$, $n_{\mathcal{G}} = 6$, $p = 0.3$, labels in $[-100, 100]$ and a Gaussian noise ($\sigma^2 = 5$). The mapping cost is 24.93

Some algorithms are only able to process connected graphs [9]. Some others may exploit this property to speed up the matching. In order to respond to the need of benchmarking these algorithms, we also provide an exact and a noisy version of the synthetic datasets in which graphs are connected. These datasets are called `ILPIso_exact_connected_synth` and `ILPIso_noisy_connected_synth`. The connectivity property induce some restrictions on the values that can be taken for the parameters $n_{\mathcal{S}}n_{\mathcal{S}}$, $n_{\mathcal{G}}$ and p. Indeed, if a graph contains n vertices, the minimum number of edges which can lead to a connected graph is $n - 1$, and a complete 1-graph without loop contains $n.(n - 1)$ edges. So, p, the probability that two vertices v_1 and v_2 are linked with a directed edge (v_1, v_2) is constraint by the following relation.

$$\frac{(n - 1)}{n.(n - 1)} \leq p \leq \frac{(n - 1)}{n.(n - 1)}$$

$$\frac{1}{n} \leq p \leq 1 \qquad (7)$$

or

$$n \geq \frac{1}{p} \qquad (8)$$

So, the set of parameters used in these dataset is[3]:

- $n_S \in \{10, 20, 50\}$
- $n_G \in \{50, 100, 250, 500\}$
- $p \in \{0.1\}$ for $n_S = 10$
- $p \in \{0.05, 0.1\}$ for $n_S = 20$
- $p \in \{0.02, 0.05, 0.1\}$ for $n_S = 50$.

3.4   ILPIso_real Dataset

The ILPIso_real dataset is a dataset that contains structural representations of document images of architectural plans. It also contains graphs modeling 16 isolated graphical symbols. Complete plan images which lead to the building of ILPIso_real dataset are 200 images extracted from the floorplan section of the SESYD dataset [10]: 20 first images for each of the 10 templates. Each symbol may occurs once or several times or not occur at all on each floorplan instance. Considering the structural representations, the problem of locating one or several instances of a symbol in a complete floorplan turns into the search of a subgraph isomorphism problem.

The structural representation for both complete plans and isolated symbol models are region adjacency graphs (RAG), which are extracted according to the following process. A vertex is created for each white connected component after a skeletonization process [11] which has reduced the width of black strokes to 1 pixel. Two directed edges are created between the vertices which describe adjacent white regions. Vertices are labeled with a feature vector corresponding to a set of the 24 first Zernike Moments (ZM) [12] and edges are labeled with *relative scale* and *relative distance*. The algorithm used for extracting such RAGs is fully described in [1]. The whole ILPIso_real dataset contains 5609 symbol instances, with an average of 28 instances per document image. The graphs corresponding to symbol instances contain 4 vertices and 7 edges on average, whereas the structural representations of the plans contain 121 vertices and 525 edges on average.

Figure 2 shows two examples of plans and the corresponding RAGs. Figure 3 represent the 16 symbol models.

Even if the document images have been synthetically generated, the graph dataset which has been produced can be considered as a real dataset. It can be used to evaluate the search of one or multiple instances of substitution-tolerant subgraph isomorphism. Indeed, since the images are synthetic there is not any problem with splitted or merged regions which would have generated topological differences between the pattern graph and its occurrences in the target graph. The only differences concern vertices and edges labels.

The ground-truth information associated to this dataset gives for each target graph, the number of occurrences for each of the 16 pattern graph. For each

---

[3] As $n_S \leq n_G$, if the constraint given by Eq. 8 is satisfied for n_S, it is also satisfied for n_G.

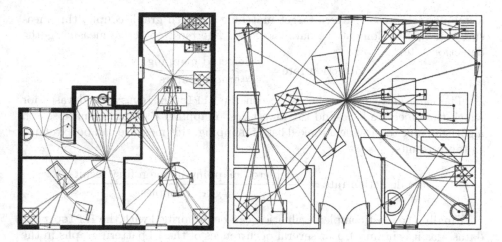

Fig. 2. Examples of plans from the `floorplan` dataset with the corresponding RAGs

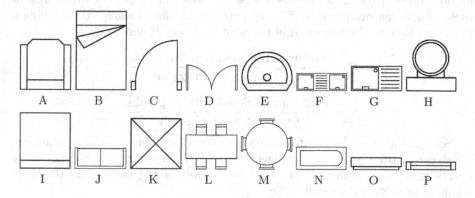

Fig. 3. Symbol models

occurrence, the vertices identifier from the target graph involved are listed. The induced subgraph represents the subgraph of the target graph which is isomorphic with the pattern graph. However, due to symmetry phenomenons, there can not be an exact vertex-to-vertex mapping between a pattern graph and its isomorphic subgraph in the target. This impacts the definition of performance measures which can only be done at a subgraph level and not at the vertex level.

4 Performance Measures

In this section, we propose some performance measures which can be used with the databases presented in Sect. 3 to evaluate substitution-tolerant subgraph method.

The `ILPIso_exact_synth` dataset can be used to evaluate the ability of an approximate algorithm to detect an exact subgraph isomorphism. As there is a unique instance of pattern-target matching for each graph couple, this measure can only be done at the database level. The most objective measure is the detection rate

$$\text{detection rate} = \frac{\#\text{detected mapping}}{\#\text{graph couples}}$$

The same measure can be used with the `ILPIso_noisy_synth` dataset for which the objective is to find the lowest cost mapping. For approximate search algorithm able to provide a ranked list of mapping, this measure can be extended to top n results.

$$\text{top n detection rate} = \frac{\#\text{detected mapping in the n first results}}{\#\text{graph couples}}$$

Finally, the most complex evaluation can be performed with the `ILPIso_real` dataset as it contains 0, 1 or several occurrences of the 16 pattern graphs in the 200 target graphs. This dataset can first be used to evaluate a structural information retrieval system where the objective is to select among the target graphs those containing occurrences of query patterns. As for classical IR techniques, the evaluation can be measured in terms of precision P and recall R.

$$P = \frac{\#\text{relevant retrieved pattern graphs}}{\#\text{retrieved pattern graphs}}$$

$$R = \frac{\#\text{relevant retrieved pattern graphs}}{\#\text{relevant pattern graphs}}$$

Some algorithms are able to compute a numerical value (cost or probability) which can be thresholded to decide whether there is an occurrence of the query or not. Several values of the P/R trade-off can be obtained by varying the threshold resulting in a precision-recall curve.

But this dataset can also be used to evaluate a subgraph isomorphism as a spotting system. Indeed, in each structural representation of a complete floorplan, several sets of vertices have been identified. The induced subgraph for each vertex set is considered as an instance of the structural representation of a symbol model.

For a single query, the system under evaluation should return its results as a set that contains the identifiers of the vertices in the target graph that are involved in the searched instance. It may also be the case that the system decides that no instance of the pattern graph occurs in the pattern. When comparing the result with the ground-truth information, several configurations can happen:

- There can be a perfect mapping between the detected set of identifiers and the set given in the ground-truth (good detection).
- There can also be a decision of reject when to instance of the searched pattern exists in the target graph (good reject).
- We consider a false reject decision, when the system decides a reject whereas an instance of the pattern graph exists in the ground-truth.

- On the other hand, we denote as a false alarm the event of detecting a pattern graph instance whereas the ground-truth indicates that it does not exist.

Moreover, besides these classical definitions, we also consider:

- an erroneous detection when a pattern instance is detected but the corresponding vertex identifier set has an empty intersection with the one defined in the ground-truth.
- a partial detection when a pattern instance is detected but the corresponding vertex identifier set has a non empty intersection with the one defined in the ground-truth.

The `ILPIso_real` dataset contains 16 pattern graphs and 200 target graphs allowing to test a system according to the criterion on 3200 single occurrence searches. As mentioned before, the reject decision may be taken according to a threshold on the cost of the mapping. As a consequence, several trade-offs between the measures can be achieved with different threshold values.

Finally, the `ILPIso_real` dataset can also be used to evaluate a system in its ability to find multiple occurrences of a pattern in the target graph. For this purpose, the measures detailed above can be used for the evaluation performance with some adjustments. Indeed, when a system tries to find the nth occurrence of a pattern graph, it should be considered that $n-1$ occurrences have already been, at least, partially found. So, the nth detected occurrence should be considered as a false alarm if and only if the real number of occurrences given by the ground-truth information is lower than n. Otherwise, it should be considered as a perfect, partial or erroneous detection. If the system returns a reject decision in the nth whereas not all occurrences have already been detected, it should be classified as a non detection. A good rejection decision is taken if the nth is a reject whereas all occurrences given in the ground-truth have been detected. For a complete evaluation, the number of searched instances should be greater than the maximum number of real instances of a pattern in target graph, which is 13.

5 Conclusion

In this paper, five datasets are presented that can be used for several tasks involving the search for subgraph isomorphisms. We have also proposed several measures allowing performance evaluation on different tasks.

Four synthetic datasets can be used to benchmark the search for a single instance of a pattern in a target graph. In two of them, no perturbation is brought to labels whereas the two other ones have numerical labels which have been modified with the add of a Gaussian noise. For each category, there is a version of the dataset in which the graphs are connected, whereas this constraint is not necessarily satisfied in the other version. The measure defined for this task quantify the detection rate for a subgraph isomorphism tool, and the noisy datasets serve at evaluating its robustness to noise on numerical labels.

The fifth dataset is a real dataset composed from the structural descriptions by means of attributed RAGs of architectural plans. These target graphs contain several instances of several pattern graph describing symbols occurring in the plans. Thanks to the associated measures, this dataset can be used to benchmark a retrieval system based on structural description or the search of multiple occurrences of pattern graph in a target in presence of perturbed numerical labels.

This work could be extended in several directions. First, in order to have a better review of the robustness to label perturbation, it could be considered to offer several noise models with several levels. Otherwise, the real dataset is currently composed of attributed RAGs. Despite the important labeling effort this would require, it could be interesting to propose alternative structural descriptions such as graphs of graphical primitives [2].

In the longer term, the scope of evaluated tasks could be extended by the integration of error-tolerant subgraph isomorphism, where topological differences are allowed between the pattern and its occurrences in the target graph. But, this extension is not manifest since it raises some issues on the ground-truth definition. Indeed, defining if a vertex in the target graph belongs or not to the pattern instance is questionable. Moreover, this may require to define one-to-one, many-to-one, one-to-many and many-to-many mappings between vertices.

The authors hope that the presented work could help the community. Any suggestion would be welcome and will be considered.

References

1. Le Bodic, P., Locteau, H., Adam, S., Héroux, P., Lecourtier, Y., Knippel, A.: Symbol detection using region adjacency graphs and integer linear programming. In: Proceedings of the International Conference on Document Analysis and Recognition (ICDAR'09), pp. 1320–1324 (2009)
2. Qureshi, R.J., Ramel, J.-Y., Barret, D., Cardot, H.: Spotting symbols in line drawing images using graph representations. In: Liu, W., Lladós, J., Ogier, J.-M. (eds.) GREC 2007. LNCS, vol. 5046, pp. 91–103. Springer, Heidelberg (2008)
3. Locteau, H., Adam, S., Trupin, E., Labiche, J., Héroux, P.: Symbol spotting using full visibility graph representation. In: Proceedings of the Seventh International Workshop on Graphics Recognition, pp. 49–50 (2007)
4. Valveny, E., Delalandre, M., Raveaux, R., Lamiroy, B.: Report on the symbol recognition and spotting contest. In: Kwon, Y.-B., Ogier, J.-M. (eds.) GREC 2011. LNCS, vol. 7423, pp. 198–207. Springer, Heidelberg (2013)
5. Riesen, K., Bunke, H.: IAM graph database repository for graph based pattern recognition and machine learning. In: da Vitoria Lobo, N., Kasparis, T., Roli, F., Kwok, J.T., Georgiopoulos, M., Anagnostopoulos, G.C., Loog, M. (eds.) SSPR&SPR 2008. LNCS, vol. 5342, pp. 287–297. Springer, Heidelberg (2008)
6. Foggia, P., Sansone, C., Vento, M.: A database of graphs for isomorphism and sub-graph isomorphism benchmarking. In: CoRR, pp. 176–187 (2001)
7. Le Bodic, P., Héroux, P., Adam, S., Lecourtier, Y.: An integer linear program for substitution-tolerant subgraph isomorphism and its use for symbol spotting in technical drawings. Pattern Recogn. **45**(12), 4214–4224 (2012)
8. Erdös, P., Rényi, A.: On random graphs. Publicationes Math. **6**, 290–297 (1959)

9. Dutta, A., Lladós, J., Bunke, H., Pal, U.: A product graph based method for dual subgraph matching applied to symbol spotting. In: Proceedings of the 10th IAPR Workshop on Graphics Recognition, pp. 7–11 (2013)
10. Delalandre, M., Valveny, E., Pridmore, T., Karatzas, D.: Generation of synthetic documents for performance evaluation of symbol recognition; spotting systems. Int. J. Doc. Anal. Recogn. **13**, 187–207 (2010)
11. di Baja, G.S., Thiel, E.: Skeltonization algorithm running on path-based distance maps. Image Vis. Comput. **14**, 47–57 (1996)
12. Teague, M.: Image analysis via the general theory of moments. Journal of the Optical Society of America **70**(8), 920–930 (1980)

Evaluation of Diagrams Produced
by Text-to-Graphic Conversion Systems

Anirban Mukherjee[1], Utpal Garain[2(✉)], and Arindam Biswas[3]

[1] RCC Institute of Information Technology, Kolkata, India
anirbanm.rcciit@gmail.com
[2] Indian Statistical Institute, Kolkata, India
utpal@isical.ac.in
[3] Indian Institute of Engineering Science and Technology,
Shibpur, Howrah, India
barindam@gmail.com

Abstract. A piece of text that basically describes a graphic (or diagram) often appears in many branches of science and engineering. Researchers have attempted to involve machine in drawing the underlying graphics after automatically understanding the text but automatic evaluation of the accuracy of such drawing remained unexplored. This paper aims at measuring the accuracy of the graphic which comes from a text-to-graphic conversion process. Experiments show that this evaluation problem poses several challenges which have not been addressed before and hence calls for new initiatives. School level geometry problems have been taken as reference to demonstrate the underlying challenges and related issues.

Keywords: Text-to-graphic conversion · Evaluation · Geometry problems · Graphs

1 Introduction

Consider this geometry statement: *'AB is a line and C is the midpoint of AB. CD is perpendicular to AB'*. This simple text basically describes a graphical item. Now if we assume that we can configure machine which is able to draw the underlying graphical diagram after automatically understanding the text, a pertinent question would be how correct the machine is. Such diagram describing text appears in many branches of science like mechanics, chemistry, geometry, engineering drawing, etc. and so far many researchers have tried to develop algorithms so that automatic text-to-graphic conversion becomes possible [1]. Earlier we have reported our system that does this conversion job for geometry word problems [2, 3]. The system takes a geometry text as input and generates the underlying graphic as output. However, measuring accuracy of such a system has not been explored before.

The major challenge behind evaluating such a system arises from the fact that the scale and orientation of many entities in the resultant graphic may vary without any bound and hence, the comparison between the machine output and the groundtruth graphic becomes extremely difficult. For example, for the above geometry problem, the line AB could be drawn of any length and in any direction. Similarly CD could be

© Springer-Verlag Berlin Heidelberg 2014
B. Lamiroy and J.-M. Ogier (Eds.): GREC 2013, LNCS 8746, pp. 252–265, 2014.
DOI: 10.1007/978-3-662-44854-0_20

drawn of any length, D could be placed in either side of AB and the direction of CD is determined relative to that of AB so that they are perpendicular. These variations can result in infinite number of correct output representations but the determination of their correctness against the groundtruth representation is a non-trivial task.

Some other issues are there that make the evaluation task more complicated. For example, the graphical representation of a text can have several graphic items and some of them are correctly drawn whereas others are missing. This paper illustrates the difficulties of this evaluation problem, explains why the existing (and apparently workable) techniques are not sufficient for the present problem. We further propose an evaluation method and illustrate how this method works for different cases.

2 Background

Let t be a piece of text that describes a graphical diagram. Say, g_1 is the correct graphical representation of t. A text-to-graphic conversion system takes t as input and gives a graphical representation g_2 as output. The evaluation task is to determine whether g_1 and g_2 are exactly same and if not, to what extent they are similar. Given this problem, an obvious choice seems to be representing g_1 and g_2 as graphs and then the evaluation task becomes a graph matching problem.

There are many graph matching algorithms [4] but one inherent limitation of these algorithms is that they only check the pattern of connectivity of the edges without considering the geometrical relationship of the edges and nodes. Geometrical relations may not be so significant for comparing chemical structure [5] or floor plan [6] as it is for comparing geometry diagrams. For example, consider the two geometry structures shown in Fig. 1. From the perspective of graph (edge connectivity), these two are identical (isomorphic). But quite clearly they are very different from geometric perspective – one is a parallelogram while the other is a triangle. The standard graph matching algorithms fail to differentiate these two structures. Also, the inexact graph matching algorithms [12] cannot help.

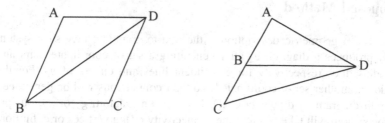

Fig. 1. Different geometry diagrams seen as similar graphs

In the domain of graphic recognition (GR), several objective and quantitative evaluation methods have been proposed [7–9]. All these methods evaluate quality of matches between the entities detected by the GR algorithm and the groundtruth entities based on a pre-defined set of physical matching criteria of elementary graphic entities like line, circle and arc. Though the basic principle of evaluation followed in [7–9] is same, the design of evaluation metrices and algorithmic computation of match scores for a given vectorized output makes [7] apparently more relevant than the other two in the context of the present problem.

As per the method reported in [7], geometry diagrams automatically drawn by the machine (from textual description) can be empirically matched with the groundtruth diagram (drawn in CAD) by comparing physical attributes (of graphic entities) like coordinates, length, angle, projected length, distance, etc. [10]. Accordingly the perfect matches, partial matches and mismatches can be quantified in terms of match score and subsequently the performance metrices can be evaluated. But this approach has a serious limitation for evaluating actual output graphics that can be drawn at any position and in any size or orientation just as a student does on a piece of paper. For example, if a machine-drawn parallelogram and a groundtruth parallelogram are positioned near two different corners of the display screen in different size and orientation, then they will no way match to each other based on physical attributes and the system will reject it as a mismatch. But the machine-drawn parallelogram might be correct geometrically and would therefore deserve full credit. Only if the base figures (parallelogram in this case) are closely positioned (i.e. the vertex coordinates are same or close), the deviations of the connected elements (diagonals etc.) can be physically compared following the matching criterions of [7]. That is why the evaluation techniques described in [7] (and also in [8, 9]), are not practically suitable and hence not applicable for the present problem where physical attributes (i.e. endpoint positions of a line, length of a line or an arc or radius of a circle, etc.) of a groundtruth diagram and corresponding machine-drawn diagram may vary widely compared to GR problems.

The above limitation motivates our work in finding an alternative method that gives an automatic and reasonable quantitative evaluation of geometry diagram drawn by the machine. Just as geometry figures drawn on paper by a student are checked by a teacher for conceptual correctness, the evaluation system should be able to check the geometric properties of the figures rather than relying only on the physical attributes or connectivity of the individual entities.

3 Proposed Method

Input: Given a geometric description t, the text-to-graphic conversion system automatically produces a diagram g_2 after generating a set of coordinate pairs and coordinate-radius duos respectively for constituent lines and circles of g_2. For the same description t, another set of coordinates and their connections will be generated for the groundtruth diagram g_1 drawn in CAD. For a given diagram g_1 or g_2, our proposed evaluation system will take as input the connectivity of the vertices or definition points in the form of adjacency matrix and also the point's coordinate values given in the same order. For example, consider the following geometric diagram (Fig. 2) with vertices A(30,30), B(10,60), C(60,60) and D(80,30). Input to our system for this diagram will be:

30, 30/10, 60/60, 60/80, 30 and

0 1 0 1/1 0 1 1/0 1 0 1/1 1 1 0

  As the coordinate values are entered in the order of A-B-C-D, the adjacency matrix is also entered in the order of A-B-C-D.

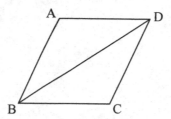

Fig. 2. Edge connectivity and vertices of a diagram

Processing: From the input coordinates and adjacency matrix, the system calculates the length matrix and slope matrix for the edges of a diagram. From the slope matrix it computes the smaller (acute) angle between every pairs of edges connected at any point. A program then searches for the angles of same values and forms different sets of same angles (if more than one). For example, if there are four 90° angles, three 30° angles and one 180° angle between different pairs of edges in a diagram then same-angle sets will be 4 and 3. Similarly, sets are found for same-length edges and these sets are computed for both the diagrams being compared.

  Next, the system evaluates the geometrical similarity of the two diagrams g_1 and g_2 by comparing the following parameters of the diagrams.

  i. Adjacency matrix.
  ii. Total number of vertex or definition points.
  iii. Total number of edges.
  iv. Total number of angles between edges.
  v. Sets of same-length edges.
  vi. Sets of same angle between edges.

  If at first comparison the adjacency matrices (of same order) of g_1 and g_2 do not match element by element then it is checked whether they match if one of the matrices is read in reverse row and/or reverse column direction. For example, consider the two parallelograms with one diagonal each as g_1 and g_2 in Fig. 3. The respective adjacency matrices in the order of points A-B-C-D are shown below the diagrams.

  The matrices are of same order but apparently they do not match. If we read the second matrix in bottom to top and right to left direction and compare with the first matrix read normally in top to bottom and left to right direction, then the matrices match. This implies g_1 and g_2 are geometrically equivalent. Even after this effort if the adjacency matrices (of same order) do not match, then a match score is awarded based on the number of rows completely matched. If only 1 out of 4 rows match, the score is 1/4 out of a maximum possible score of 4/4 or 1. If the orders of adjacency matrices are not same implying unequal number of points, then the score is 0 as no row will match.

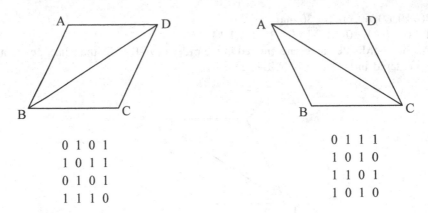

Fig. 3. Geometrically similar diagrams having dissimilar adjacency matrices of same order

With regard to each of parameters (ii) to (vi), the score is simply calculated as the ratio of the parameter value for the machine-drawn diagram g_2 to that of the ground-truth diagram g_1.

If x be a parameter value for g_2 and y be the corresponding value for g_1 then:

$$\text{score} = x/y, \qquad \text{for } x \le y \tag{1}$$

$$= 1 - \{(x - y)/y\}, \qquad \text{for } x > y \tag{2}$$

For $x > y$, penalty is assigned for $(x - y)$ additional elements generated wrongly against expected y elements. It is obvious from the equations above that if g_2 is 100 % correct implying $x = y$, then score = 1.

Frequently, there will be multiple values of x and y against parameter (v) and (vi). Now for each element of set y, the system will try to find a match in set x. For every y:x perfect match, the score is set to 1. Then keeping aside the perfectly matched element (s) of y and x, the nearest match of each of remaining elements of y is searched in the subset of x. The score for each pair of y value and nearest matching x value is calculated following Eqs. (1) or (2). For cases where there is no y value left in set y (implying $y = 0$) to match an unused value in set x, the score cannot be evaluated as per Eq. (2). In such case the score is set to -0.5 to impose a reasonable penalty for undesired value of x that occurs due to incorrect machine drawing. However, if such situation arises for parameter (v) then penalty is not imposed and score is set to 0 because a diagram (g_2) may be correct geometrically with some edges becoming equal which may not be the case in ground-truth diagram (g_1). The maximum possible score for each y:x pair of parameters (ii) to (vi) is 1 except 0 in case of <0, x> match for parameter (v).

For example let the x values against (vi) are <3, 2, 1> and the corresponding y values are <4, 3>. A match is obtained in x for $y = 3$, but $y = 4$ has no match. Now a match for $y = 4$ is searched in x and $x = 2$ is found closest to 4 among rest of the x elements (2 and 1). The unused element $x = 1$ has got no element left in y to match with. The match score calculated for the $<y, x>$ pairs $<3, 3>$, $<4, 2>$ and $<0, 1>$ are $3/3 = 1$ and $2/4 = 0.5$ and -0.5 respectively.

Output: The cumulative score of g_2 considering all the parameters and their multiple values is calculated. Also the sum of the maximum possible scores against each of these parameters is calculated. The maximum possible score corresponds to a 100 % correctly drawn g_2. The final output of evaluation is the percentage of cumulative score of g_2 and this is calculated as:

$$\frac{\sum \text{scores of parameters (i) to (vi)}}{\sum \text{max. scores of parameters (i) to (vi)}} \times 100 \qquad (3)$$

4   Experimental Result

The proposed evaluation method has been tested with 40 geometry diagrams – all of which has been produced by the text-to-diagram conversion system [2, 3]. We present here five representative cases for illustration of the method. In each case the geometric description is cited first followed by the CAD-drawn groundtruth diagram g_1 and then the diagram g_2 drawn by the machine (from the textual description). Subsequently the calculation of scores against individual parameter values and overall score or accuracy percentage (as per Eq. 3) is presented.

Case 1:
Description: PQ is perpendicular to RS such that Q is the midpoint of RS. PT is parallel and equal to RS. Find angle RQT. (See Fig. 4, Table 1) The intermediate output i.e. the

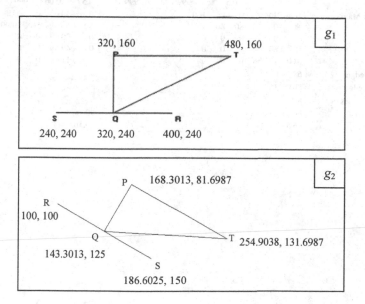

Fig. 4. Correct machine-drawn diagram

Table 1. Score Sheet for Case 1

	Adjacency matrix	Points	Edges	Angle	Same length edge	Same angle
y-values	5 × 5	5	5	8	3	3, 3
x-values	5 × 5	5	5	8	3	3, 3
Score	1	1	1	1	1	1, 1
Max score	1	1	1	1	1	1, 1

$\sum$ score = 7, $\sum$ max score = 7, overall score = 100 %

slope matrix, edge length matrix, same length edge sets and same angle sets given by the evaluation system, are depicted in Table 2. The input adjacency matrix is given in the order of P-Q-R-S-T for both the diagrams.

Table 2. Different Properties for Case 1

	Groundtruth diagram	Machine-drawn diagram
Adjacency matrix	0 1 0 0 1 1 0 1 1 1 0 1 0 0 0 0 1 0 0 0 1 1 0 0 0	0 1 0 0 1 1 0 1 1 1 0 1 0 0 0 0 1 0 0 0 1 1 0 0 0
Total No. of Points	5	5
Edge Slope Matrix	999 $\quad$ −2.29e + 07 $\quad$ 999 $\quad$ 999 $\quad$ 0 −2.29e + 07 $\quad$ 999 $\quad\quad$ 0 $\quad$ 0 $\quad$ −0.5 999 $\quad\quad$ 0 $\quad\quad\quad$ 999 $\quad$ 999 $\quad$ 999 999 $\quad\quad$ 0 $\quad\quad\quad$ 999 $\quad$ 999 $\quad$ 999 0 $\quad\quad$ −0.5 $\quad\quad$ 999 $\quad$ 999 $\quad$ 999	999 $\quad$ −1.73 $\quad$ 999 $\quad$ 999 $\quad$ 0.57 −1.73 $\quad$ 999 $\quad$ 0.57 $\quad$ 0.57 $\quad$ 0.06 999 $\quad$ 0.577 $\quad$ 999 $\quad$ 999 $\quad$ 999 999 $\quad$ 0.577 $\quad$ 999 $\quad$ 999 $\quad$ 999 0.57 $\quad$ 0.06 $\quad$ 999 $\quad$ 999 $\quad$ 999
Edge Length Matrix	0 $\quad$ 80 $\quad$ 0 $\quad$ 0 $\quad$ 160 80 $\quad$ 0 $\quad$ 80 $\quad$ 80 $\quad$ 178.88 0 $\quad$ 80 $\quad$ 0 $\quad$ 0 $\quad$ 0 0 $\quad$ 80 $\quad$ 0 $\quad$ 0 $\quad$ 0 160 $\quad$ 178.88 $\quad$ 0 $\quad$ 0 $\quad$ 0	0 $\quad$ 50 $\quad$ 0 $\quad$ 0 $\quad$ 100 50 $\quad$ 0 $\quad$ 50 $\quad$ 49.99 $\quad$ 111.8 0 $\quad$ 50 $\quad$ 0 $\quad$ 0 $\quad$ 0 0 $\quad$ 49.99 $\quad$ 0 $\quad$ 0 $\quad$ 0 100 $\quad$ 111.8 $\quad$ 0 $\quad$ 0 $\quad$ 0
Total no. of edges	5	5
Same length edge sets	80 -> 3	50 -> 3
Total no. of angles	8	8
Same angle sets	90 -> 3 26.565-> 3	90 -> 3 26.565-> 3

Case 2:

<u>Description</u>: In triangle ABC, angle A = 80 degree, angle CBA = 55 degree, AB and AC are produced to H and K. BE bisects angle CBH, CE bisects angle BCK. Calculate angle BEC. (See Fig. 5, Table 3)

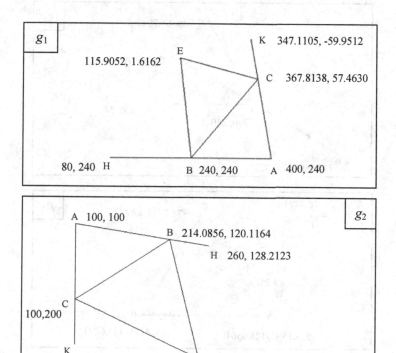

Fig. 5. Almost correct diagram; only instead of <CBA, <ACB is 55°

Table 3. Score Sheet for Case 2

	Adjacency matrix	Points	Edges	Angle	Same length edge	Same angle
y-values	6 × 6	6	7	14	2	3,3,2,2,2
x-values	6 × 6	6	7	14	0	3,3,2,2,2
Score	1	1	1	1	0	1,1,1,1,1
Max score	1	1	1	1	1	1,1,1,1,1

Σ score = 9, Σ max score = 10, overall score = 90 %

Case 3:

Description: BP bisects angle ABC and PB is produced to Q. Prove angle ABQ = angle CBQ. (See Fig. 6, Table 4)

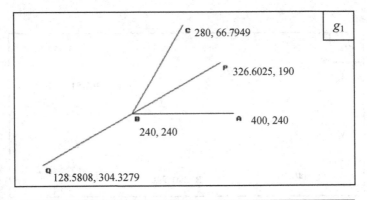

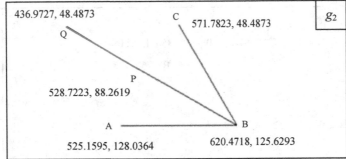

Fig. 6. Incorrect diagram; PB produced in wrong direction

Table 4. Score Sheet for Case 3

	Adjacency matrix	Points	Edges	Angle	Same length edge	Same angle
y-values	5 × 5	5	4	6	0	4
x-values	5 × 5	5	4	4	2	2
Score	2/5 = 0.4	1	1	0.67	–	0.5
Max score	1	1	1	1	–	1

$\sum$ score = 3.57, $\sum$ max score = 5, overall score = 71.4 %

Case 4:

<u>Description</u>: The bisectors of angle B and angle C of an equilateral triangle ABC meet at O. Find angle BOC. (See Fig. 7, Table 5)

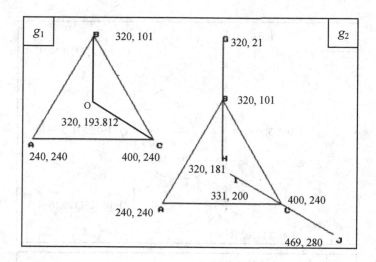

Fig. 7. Incorrect diagram; angle bisectors produced in wrong direction

Table 5. Score Sheet for Case 4

	Adjacency matrix	Points	Edges	Angle	Same length edge	Same angle
y-values	4 × 4	4	5	8	3,2	4,4,0,0,0
x-values	7 × 7	7	7	13	3,2	4,3,2,2,2
Score	0	1 − (3/4) = 0.25	1 − (2/5) = 0.6	1 − (5/8) = 0.38	1,1	1,0.75, − 0.5, −0.5, − 0.5
Max score	1	1	1	1	1,1	1,1,0,0,0

From Table 5, Σ score = 3.48, Σ max score = 8, overall score = 43 %.

Table 6. Score Sheet for Case 5

	Adjacency matrix	Points	Edges	Angle	Same length edge	Same angle	Circle flag
y-values	7 × 7	7	7	13	2	8, 5	1
x-values	5 × 5	5	5	7	2	4, 3	1
Score	0	0.71	0.71	0.54	1	0.5, 0.6	1
Max score	1	1	1	1	1	1, 1	1

Σ score = 5.06, Σ max score = 8, overall score = 63.3 %

Case 5:

<u>Description</u>: PQ is a diameter of a circle centered at O. The tangents drawn at P and Q of the circle are APB and CQD. Prove that AB∥CD. (See Fig. 8, Table 6)

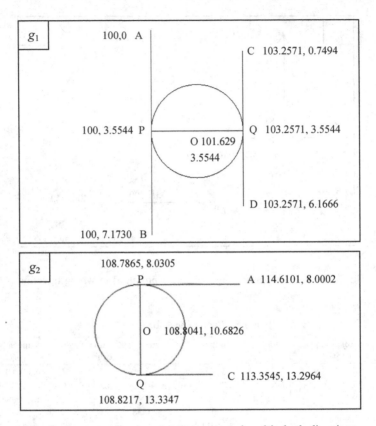

Fig. 8. Incorrect diagram; tangents not produced in both directions

5   Discussion

Quantitative evaluation of five machine-drawn diagrams show reasonably good results from geometric perspective. The intermediate system output is shown for only Case 1 to illustrate the computation of sets of same length edge and same angle. The edge matrix and slope matrix corresponds to the adjacency matrix. A high positive value (999) is assumed in the slope matrix where no edge connection is implied and this value will not be considered as a valid slope while calculating the angle between two edges.

It is evident from Case 1 and Case 2 that the system is able to evaluate correctness of diagrams in-spite of being drawn with different coordinate sets, different order of labeling and at different orientation compared to the groundtruth diagram. Referring to Fig. 1, if we consider the diagram with triangle as the machine-drawn diagram and the one containing parallelogram as the groundtruth diagram then our system gives an evaluation score of 55.6 %. This clearly shows that the diagrams are very different though the number of points, edges, angles and adjacency are same.

Edges or angles that ought to be equal in a correct diagram are actually equal in a machine-drawn diagram may not be always represented by the fact that the scoring against parameter (v) and (vi) is maximum. Different sets of angles or edges may incidentally become same in an incorrect diagram and still the score may be maximum if the number of entities in sets matches. In an experimental set of 40 diagrams drawn by the machine from textual description, 1 such case is found where the evaluation score is 100 % but there is mismatch of same angle sets. Overall, we find that out of 40 diagrams, 31 correctly drawn diagrams (as manually observed) are evaluated correctly yielding a score of 98 %–100 %, 1 incorrect diagram is given 100 % score, and remaining 8 incorrect diagrams score between 43 % and 90 %. 3 incorrect diagrams having circle seems to deserve better score. Though there may be question regarding appropriateness of the scores awarded against incorrect drawings, all correctly drawn diagrams are given high score by the system. Thus we can say that the system near perfectly (if not perfectly) identifies diagrams that are correctly drawn by a text-to-graphic conversion system.

Our system has no provision of counting curved edges, particularly circle. Hence for diagrams with circle, the entire circle or the semicircles on both side of a diameter are not counted as edges. In both the diagrams in Fig. 8, PQ connection is considered only once (as a linear edge) in addition to edges PO and OQ. To compensate this approximation, we introduce a new parameter 'circle flag'. With this flag the total number of parameters against which scores are to be evaluated by the system becomes seven.[1] Whenever the system encounters a coordinate-length pair (center point-radius) as input for a given diagram, the value of the flag will be incremented by 1. If, say, there are 3 circles in g_2 then value of x against 'circle flag' will be 3. For simply point coordinates as input, implying only linear edges, flag value will be 0. The score against this parameter will be calculated as usual using Eqs. (1) & (2) with the following exceptions - if flag values x and y are both 0 then the score will be 0; if y is 0, but x has a positive value, then score (penalty) will be −0.5. The score of the machine-drawn diagram in Case 5 is 58 % without this flag vis-à-vis 63.3 % with the flag. However, the inability to detect connectivity of circular edges with other edges of the diagram cannot be fully compensated by this adhoc measure.

6   Conclusion

Evaluation of text-to-graphic conversion system, which was never attempted before, has been addressed in this paper. It is experienced that the existing techniques are not sufficient to formulate a suitable evaluation method for the present problem. A unique evaluation method has been designed for judging the performance of a text-to-graphic conversion system applied on school-level geometry problems. Evaluation results show

---

[1] Here we have not shown the 7th parameter in the score tables of Case 1–4, though the system actually considers and evaluates all the seven parameters for every Case.

that the proposed method measures the accuracy of the graphical representation of a given text quite reasonably. Yet the method has certain apparent weaknesses which need to be addressed in future. It cannot trace connectivity of curved edges like that of circle which features in many geometry diagrams. It may be possible to consider a set of linear edges connecting the center point and quadrant points of the circle and thereby address the problem of representing a circle in terms of adjacency matrix. Moreover, computation of the sixth parameter considers only the number of same angles between edges but it does not consider which angles are same with respect to the edge connectivity. In most cases, the comparison between g_1 and g_2 on this basis would yield correct evaluation. But in some cases the result will be erroneous. So this approach requires modification.

In the future extension of this study, we are planning to address the above issues. The generic diagram matching problem can be approached from two different viewpoints: (a) involvement of relational graphs [11, 13] where we would try to represent two diagrams as relational graphs and then formulate the evaluation task as matching of two relational graphs, (b) follow reverse engineering process where we want to convert a graphical figure into its corresponding textual description and then evaluation would be done by comparing the two textual descriptions (converted vs. original). In this process, we do not require to use any groundtruth graphical diagram for evaluation.

References

1. Mukherjee, A., Garain, U.: A review of the methods for automatic understanding of natural language mathematical problems. Artif. Intell. Rev. **29**(2), 93–122 (2008)
2. Mukherjee, A., Garain, U.: Understanding of natural language text for diagram drawing. In: IASTED International Conference on Artificial Intelligence and Soft Computing, pp. 138–145, Spain (2009)
3. Mukherjee, A., Sengupta, S., Chakraborty, D., Sen, A., Garain, U.: Text to diagram conversion: a method for formal representation of natural language geometry problems. In: IASTED International Conference on Artificial Intelligence and Applications, pp. 137–144, Austria (2013)
4. Bunke, H.: Recent developments in graph matching. In: Proceedings of 15th International Conference on Pattern Recognition (ICPR 2000), pp. 2117–2124, Barcelona (2000)
5. Raymond, J.W., Willet, P.: Maximum common subgraph isomorphism algorithms for the matching of chemical structures. J. Comput.-Aided Mol. Des. **16**, 521–533 (2002)
6. Dutta, A., Gibert, J., Lladós, J., Bunke, H., Pal, U.: Combination of product graph and random walk kernel for symbol spotting in graphical documents. In: 21st International Conference on Pattern Recognition (ICPR 2012), pp. 1663–1666, Japan (2012)
7. Phillips, I.T., Chhabra, A.K.: Empirical performance evaluation of graphics recognition systems. IEEE Trans. Pattern Anal. Mach. Intell. **21**(9), 849–870 (1999)
8. Hori, O., Doermann, D.: Quantitative measurement of the performance of raster-to-vector conversion algorithms. In: Kasturi, Rangachar, Tombre, Karl (eds.) Graphics Recognition 1995. LNCS, vol. 1072. Springer, Heidelberg (1996)
9. Wenyin, L., Dori, D.: A protocol for performance evaluation of line detection algorithms. Mach. Vis. Appl. **9**(5/6), 240–250 (1997)

10. Mukherjee, A., Garain, U., Biswas, A.: Evaluation of automatic conversion of text to diagram. Int. J. Emerg. Technol. Adv. Eng. (IJETAE) **2**(5), 410–419 (2012)
11. Williams, M.L., Wilson, R.C., Hancock, E.R.: Deterministic search for relational graph matching. Pattern Recogn. **32**(7), 1255–1271 (1999)
12. Armiti, A., Gertz, M.: Efficient geometric graph matching using vertex embedding. In: 21st ACM SIGSPATIAL International Conference on Advances in Geographic Information Systems, pp. 224–233 (2013)
13. Kim, D.H., Yun, I.D., Lee, S.U.: Attributed relational graph matching based on the nested assignment structure. Pattern Recogn. (Elsevier) **43**(3), 914–928 (2010)

Author Index

Printed in the United States
By Bookmasters